"But We See Jesus"

—Hebrews 2:9a

"But We See Jesus"

Messages on
the Life of the Lord Jesus Christ

Stephen Kaung

Christian Fellowship Publishers, Inc.
New York

ISBN: 978-1-937713-12-6

Available from the Publishers at:

11515 Allecingie Parkway
Richmond, Virginia 23235
www.c-f-p.com

Printed in the United States of America

PREFACE

Christianity is Jesus Christ. It is not the teaching, doctrine, system or organization of Christ. Rather, it is Jesus Christ himself. We need to see Him as God sees Him. Yet this can only come about by revelation from above. The Holy Spirit will reveal Jesus to us. And when we do see Him as God sees Him, we will fall down and worship. Such, then, is the intent of this series of messages, whose overarching theme is best summed up in the author's choice of title to the entire series: *"But We See Jesus"* (Hebrews 2:9a).

All nineteen messages were delivered by the author before a Christian audience in Richmond, Virginia over a three-year period, commencing in the year 1992.

May God use this volume to inspire His people to see the Savior and Lord we have so that we may truly worship Him with all our hearts and love Him with all our heart, mind, will and strength. Jesus alone is worthy!

Contents

Unless otherwise indicated,
Scripture quotations are from the
New Translation by J. N. Darby.

Chapter One

EPOCH-MAKING VESSEL: JOHN THE BAPTIST

Mark 1:1-3—Beginning of the glad tidings of Jesus Christ, Son of God; as it is written in Isaiah the prophet, Behold, I send my messenger before thy face, who shall prepare thy way. Voice of one crying in the wilderness, Prepare the way of the Lord, make his paths straight.

Matthew 3:1-4—Now in those days comes John the baptist, preaching in the wilderness of Judaea, and saying, Repent, for the kingdom of the heavens has drawn nigh. For this is he who has been spoken of through Esaias the prophet, saying, Voice of him that crieth in the wilderness: prepare ye the way of the Lord, make straight his paths. And John himself had his garment of camel's hair, and a leathern girdle about his loins, and his nourishment was locusts and wild honey.

Luke 1:76-79—And thou, child, shalt be called the prophet of the Highest; for thou shalt go before the face of the Lord to make ready his ways; to give knowledge of deliverance to his people by the remission of their sins on account of the bowels of mercy of our God; wherein the dayspring from on high has visited us, to shine upon them who were sitting in darkness and in the shadow of death, to guide our feet into the way of peace.

In the Scriptures are to be found some persons mentioned whom we would describe as epoch-making individuals because God raised them up as vessels who were used to change the times. For example, in the Old Testament period God used Noah to change the age of conscience into the age of government: He used Abraham to bring in the age of promise: He used Moses to introduce the age of the law: He used Samuel to end the time of the judges and to bring in that of the kings. We can also say that Daniel was used of God to terminate the time of captivity and to bring in the time of recovery.

At the opening of the New Testament period it is very evident that John the Baptist was likewise an epoch-making vessel of God. We read in the Gospel according to Mark: "Beginning of the glad tidings of Jesus Christ, Son of God." How did the gospel of Jesus Christ, the Son of God, begin? Who brought in the time of grace? It was John the Baptist. The Mosaic law had been given centuries before and the prophets had continually prophesied till John the Baptist (Matthew 11:13, Luke 16:16a). So John was a person used by God to conclude the age of the law and the prophets and to introduce the King, even the Lord Jesus Christ. And, thus, He was an epoch-making vessel.

We know that the last voice heard at the end of the entire Old Testament age was the voice of the prophet Malachi. God had raised up Malachi to reason with His people, to call His people to return to Him, and the message that Malachi brought to the chosen people of God was that of repentance. Unfortunately, it seems as if the people did not hear. So for four hundred long years God was silent. There was no voice from heaven, even though the lives of the people continued on. The remnant had returned from captivity in Babylon to

Jerusalem; the temple had been rebuilt, the priesthood restored; and the sacrifices were once again offered up. Throughout those four hundred silent years, these things continued on. Outwardly the Jews seemed to be a very religious people; nevertheless, God had ceased speaking during this entire four-hundred-year period!

Then, suddenly, God's silence was broken: He began to speak—a voice came forth from the wilderness. What had happened? God raised up a man named John, and he began to preach this: "Repent, for the kingdom of the heavens has drawn nigh." The message of John was one of repentance, but the reason for repentance was most unusual. At that time nobody would ever have thought that the kingdom of the heavens would be the reason for repentance. Nevertheless, John the Baptist was sent to God's chosen people to tell them to repent because the kingdom of the heavens had drawn near. In other words, that which they had presumably been waiting for was now here. Yet the kingdom of the heavens that John was preaching was not the kingdom the children of Israel had been waiting for: they had been waiting for the Messianic kingdom. That is to say, in their state of unrepentance they had been waiting for the Messiah to come and restore the nation of Israel to first prominence among the nations, but God was not at this time intent on doing *that*. The kingdom of the heavens which John preached was a spiritual kingdom because the King was coming; indeed, He was even in their midst.

When this message began to be given, it electrified the whole nation, and people flocked to John to be baptized with the baptism of repentance. Repentance was very real to John: for him, repentance was not simply a change of attitude; for him it was also a change in action and conduct.

What is the meaning of baptism? It means that you go into death, you are buried, and then out of death comes resurrection. It is the death of the whole being. It is not merely a little reform or a little change or a little improvement; rather, it is the death of your whole being. Everything in the past, everything which concerns you—whether you consider it good or evil—has to go down into death and be buried; and then you rise up anew onto resurrection ground (Romans 6:3-5). This is what John the Baptist was preaching and calling the people to experience.

Now who was this John? What was his testimony? And what has this John of long ago to do with us today? These are the things I would like for us to consider together before the Lord.

God Is Gracious

The very name John was given by the angel Gabriel. Before John was born Gabriel was sent by God to his father Zacharias to tell him that his wife would give birth to a child and that he was to be named John. Now this name actually means "God is gracious." The very sending of this child demonstrated the graciousness of God. This child was sent not because the people were ready, nor because the people had changed, nor because they deserved it, but it was solely because of the grace of God. The Jewish nation had remained the same unrepentant people as before, they were no different than they had been four hundred years earlier, but God in His mercy now bestowed grace upon His people by sending this grown-up man John—a Nazarite—into their midst.

A Separated Life

We learn from Luke's Gospel that even when John was in his mother's womb, he was already a Nazarite (cf. Luke 1:15 with Numbers 6:2-4). We know from the Old Testament Scriptures that a Nazarite was a person who separated and devoted himself to God. In Old Testament times some people had separated and devoted themselves to God for a week or perhaps a month or a year; but there were a few who made themselves Nazarites for life, and this was what John was. For even while in his mother's womb, he had been called to be a Nazarite. By implication his mother Elizabeth could therefore not drink any wine herself because a Nazarite would never touch such drink (see again Luke 1:15). So John was separated to the service of God as a Nazarite for life. Moreover, he was filled with the Holy Spirit while yet in his mother's womb (Luke 1:15c) and as a babe had even responded to the greeting of Jesus' mother Mary while in his mother Elizabeth's womb (Luke 1:39-44).

When grown John lived in the wilderness, separated from the world. Following the tradition of the Old Testament prophets, he wore a hairy garment and ate wild honey and locusts. His life was a completely separated one, so that when he was thirty years old, John emerged from the wilderness and began to preach repentance. The day of complacency and the day of waiting were over, because the kingdom of the heavens had drawn near. Or to put it another and simpler way, the King was coming and was so very near. As a matter of fact, the King was already in their midst, and because of this, God's people needed to repent. They needed to repent of their past; they needed to repent of their sins; they needed to repent even of their religiousness; in other words, they needed to go into death completely and prepare themselves for receiving the salvation of the Lord.

Prepare the Way

John's father had prophesied concerning him as follows: "Child, you will grow up to be the prophet of the Highest. You will go before the face of the Lord and prepare His way. You will help the people to know deliverance through the remission of their sins, through repentance and baptism, because the mercy of the Lord has finally visited His people once again. The dayspring from on high has come and will shine upon those who sit in darkness and in the shadow of death, to give them light and to lead them to the way of peace."

This John was raised up by God to be His voice by which to bring His people into the kingdom of the heavens by preparing them to receive the salvation that was coming upon the earth. As Isaiah of old had prophesied concerning the message of the voice, and using vivid imagery from nature: All valleys must be raised up and filled; that is to say, all depravity, corruption, and acts of omission must be eliminated.—All mountains and hills must be brought low and leveled; which is to say, all pride and arrogance must be brought down and repudiated.—All the crooked places, that is, all deceitfulness and lying, must be reproved, rejected, made straight.—All rough places must be smoothed out and made like a plain; which is to say, that all that is of the flesh—of the natural man—must be radically dealt with (see Isaiah 40:3a,4). In other words, a person must bring his or her whole being into a sincere state of repentance—and no matter whether the conduct of that person's being was morally or ethically blameworthy of acts of omission or commission, or whether his or her blameworthy conduct or behavior had been that of pride, arrogance, deceit, lying, gross sin, corruption, or fleshly indulgence of any and every kind: all such must be sincerely repented of. And such was to be the way for the fallen people of God to prepare themselves for the Lord's salvation. Now that was the message of John the Baptist.

Who John the Baptist Was

Who was this John? We will recall Jesus himself asking the crowd on one occasion: "What did you go out to the wilderness to see—a reed plant?" No, said the Lord, John was not a reed, for such a plant is that which is easily swayed by the wind. If the wind blows this way or that, a reed will fall this way or that. John was indeed not a reed: he was neither a diplomat nor a weakling; on the contrary, John was strong, courageous, and faithful to his heavenly-taught message, he not being at all influenced by the world and its faulty standard of morality; for did he not rebuke King Herod in declaring more than once that it was not lawful for him to have married his brother's wife? And for this bold assertion John was imprisoned. Come what may, he had stood firm for the truth (see Matthew 14:3-4).

Yet Jesus further inquired of the Jewish crowd: "If John was not a reed, what, then, did you go into the wilderness to see? A person dressed in fine clothes? Not so, for a person clothed in delicate garments dwells in kings' palaces." John was not a person who was self-indulgent, ever seeking after ease and pleasure; rather, he was a man who pursued a greatly disciplined lifestyle, having lived an extremely simple and separated life.

"Then what *did* you go out to see?" asked Jesus of the crowd one final time. "A prophet? Yes, and more than a prophet, for he was the one about whom it had long ago been written that he would prepare the way of the Lord ahead of Him." Concluded the Lord Jesus concerning this man: "The truth is that among all those born of women there has never risen a person greater than John" (see Matthew 11:7-11a). Now this was John the Baptist.

John's Personal Life Testimony

What was the Baptist's testimony concerning himself? His testimony was as great as his life; and in one highly significant sense, we could say that his testimony was even greater than his life; for though John had been raised up by God to serve as an epoch-making vessel, when people asked him if he were the Christ, he replied with a definite "No." Moreover, when they also inquired—"Are you *the* prophet whom Moses prophesied of, saying: 'One day from among the brethren a prophet will be raised up, and if you do not listen to him, you shall perish'?" (see Deuteronomy 18:15, 17a, 18-19)—John again answered "No," and humbly added: "I am simply a voice in the wilderness" (see John 1:19-23).

What is a voice? A voice is that which is to be heard but is not to be seen. A voice speaks forth something, but it does not attract people to itself. Furthermore, a voice comes and goes and disappears completely. John knew that he was but a voice in the wilderness whose purpose was to introduce Christ. He never sought to draw people to himself; instead, he constantly pointed people to Christ. He was a voice that came, lingered for a while, and then faded away, and John was content to be such and nothing more.

What did this man further testify concerning himself? For people now asked him: "If you are not Christ, if you are not the prophet, why do you baptize?" He said, "I baptize people with water for repentance, but there is One in your midst who is greater and more powerful than I, and I am not even fit or worthy to unloose the thongs of His sandals." In those olden days people did not wear shoes like we do today. They wore sandals, and it was the task of the slaves to untie the thongs of their masters' sandals. John the Baptist, the great prophet that he was, humbly acknowledged and confessed: "I am not in the least worthy to even unloose the thongs of the sandals of the One who is coming after me" (see John 1:24-26, Matthew 3:11a-b, Luke 3:15-16a, b). In other words, he viewed himself as lower in position than even that of a slave. That was his considered estimate of himself.

A further indication of how John viewed himself can be discerned by what he declared on another occasion. It will be recalled that at one time John was baptizing people, and Jesus, too, was baptizing people, but in a nearby area (actually, it was not Jesus himself who was baptizing but it was His disciples who were doing so). And the disciples of the Baptist came to John and said, "Look, the One whom you testified about is baptizing more people than you are and everyone is going to Him." They were very jealous for their master John. But John responded with these words: "It is the Bridegroom who has the bride. I am but the friend of the Bridegroom, and when I hear the

Bridegroom's voice, I rejoice. He must increase, I must decrease" (see John 3:22-30).

Though John was such an epoch-making vessel of God, he knew exactly who he was. Oh, how he effaced himself, ever confessing that he was but a voice, lower in place than a slave, and that he was only the attending friend of the Bridegroom. As such, the friend must now become less and the Bridegroom must become greater.

John's Testimony Concerning the Lord Jesus

John's testimony regarding the Lord Jesus is greater, far greater than his testimony about himself. We believers must certainly know ourselves, but to know the Lord is even greater than knowing ourselves. Let us consider the testimony which John gave concerning Jesus. If we read the Scriptures carefully, we shall find that the testimony of John towards the Lord Jesus is a most full one. I am afraid that many Christians today are not able to bear such testimony regarding the Lord as did John the Baptist. Here is what this man testified.

The Son of God

John testified that Jesus is the Son of God. Here was one particular and very special Man who nonetheless came forth walking in the midst of the multitudes like any ordinary person, and yet John could witness and testify that this was the Son of God. How did he know that? He said that he would not have known Jesus to be God's Son except that the One who had sent him to baptize with water had told him that the Man upon whom he would see the Holy Spirit descend and take up His dwelling place would be the One who would baptize with the Holy Spirit. Added John: I saw this and testify that this is the Son of God (see John 1:32-34).

How can we know that Jesus is the Son of God? The world will never know Him as such; instead, they will only know Him as the son of Joseph—as the son of a carpenter—as Jesus of Nazareth. Even though some people may say He is like Elijah or Jeremiah or John the Baptist raised from the dead or one of the other prophets, none will ever know Him as the Son of God because such knowledge requires revelation. Such knowledge is not simply knowing Him mentally but really knowing Him. Without the Father revealing the Son, as He had done to John, no one in this world would ever come to know Jesus' true identity. John the Baptist was given that revelation, and he accordingly testified that Jesus is the Son of God. What a testimony!

The Lamb of God

John the Baptist had also declared: "Behold, the Lamb of God who takes away the sin of the world" (John 1:29). By still further revelation he came to know and recognize the Lord Jesus as the very Lamb of God. For thousands of years the people of Israel had been offering up sacrificial lambs; even so, they were waiting for *the* Lamb of God who would actually take away the sin of the world. All the countless, numberless lambs which had been offered on Jewish altars throughout the centuries only *covered* sin. They did not take it away; all those sacrificial lambs were just types, figures, or representations of the coming True Lamb. The Israelites were waiting for *the* sacrificial lamb—the Lamb of God—to come and take away the sin of the world. So that when John the Baptist saw Jesus coming towards him, he announced by revelation from heaven: "Look, the Lamb of God!" In other words, John was found testifying here that there can be no remission of sin without the shedding of the blood of the Lamb of God. What a testimony!

The Baptizer with the Holy Spirit

John the Baptist had carefully explained, "I baptize people with water for repentance" (see John 1:11a) as that which will prepare the way for the Lord to come. But he had then gone on to testify and explain concerning the Lord that "the One who comes after me will baptize people with the Holy Spirit" (see John 1:11b, c). Jesus is not only the Lamb of God who takes away the sin of the world but He is also the Baptizer with the Holy Spirit. For shortly after the Lord Jesus was risen and had ascended to heaven, on the Jewish festival day of Pentecost He sent the Holy Spirit and the 120 disciples of His who were assembled in a large upper room of a house in Jerusalem were baptized in one Spirit by the Baptizer—the Lord Jesus—into one body (John 15:26; Acts 1:12-15, 2:1-4). What a tremendous event that was! And what a testimony which John bore here!

Now we are easily fascinated by the report of the sound and the sight of what happened on that memorable Pentecost day. We are attracted by the sound as of a hard breathing, as of a strong wind blowing through that house where Jesus' disciples were gathered together and filling the entire house. We are attracted by the description of tongues as of fire that had separated and then descended upon the heads of each of the 120. But these remarkable manifestations of the Holy Spirit are of secondary significance. Indeed, what is of primary—even essential—significance, and what really happened on that day of Pentecost some 2000 years ago, was that the risen Lord Jesus had baptized His people with the Holy Spirit in order that they might all be one body. Thank God, we are not only saved individually—our sins having been taken away because Jesus is the Lamb of God—but we who have been redeemed have been baptized into one body because this same Jesus is also the Baptizer with the Holy Spirit. And in that one body there is neither Jew nor Gentile, there is neither the circumcised nor uncircumcised, neither barbarian nor Scythian, and neither freeman nor bondman; rather, we are all one in Christ Jesus, and He is all and is in all (Colossians 3:11). Again it needs to be said, What an incredible testimony which John bore here!

The Bridegroom

More than that, John also testified that Jesus is the Bridegroom (see again John 3:28-29). Did the Lord Jesus come into this world in the first place to save sinners? Yes, but to do far more than that. He did not only come to seek and to save the lost; He also came to find His bride, because it is the eternal will of God that—like all other men—it is not good for the God-Man to be alone (cf. Genesis 2:18a). God had wanted His Son to have a counterpart, a helpmeet, a bride (cf. Genesis 2:18b). So the Lord Jesus came not only as the Savior but also as the Bridegroom looking for His bride, but He could not find her anywhere. He therefore had to die in order for that bride to be produced. And we are told in the Scriptures that at the time of Jesus' death on Calvary's cross there flowed forth from out His side when pierced by a soldier's spear both blood and water (John 19:34); and with that God the Father is building for His Son the Bridegroom a fitting, most suitable bride—the church (cf. Genesis 2:21-22). Indeed, Christ the Bridegroom loved the church and gave himself up for her, sanctifying and purifying her by the washing of the water of the word in order that He may one day present to himself that bride—His church—as His radiant counterpart that shall be without stain or wrinkle or any other blemish (Ephesians 5:25b-27). The Lord Jesus is the Bridegroom, as was so beautifully testified to by John the Baptist.

The testimony of John concerning the Lord Jesus is so full: He is the Son of God, the Lamb of God, the Baptizer with the Holy Spirit, and the Bridegroom who is coming for His bride. That is the testimony of John the Baptist; and that was how he—as but a voice in the wilderness—prepared the way of the Lord.

The Gospel of Jesus Christ: Begins with Repentance

Finally to be considered, What has this man John to do with us today? There are two facets to John's essential relevance for us in our day. And the first facet revolves around the matter of repentance. Let us notice again the words with which Mark's Gospel opens: "The beginning of the gospel of Jesus Christ." What is the gospel of Jesus Christ? His gospel is Jesus Christ himself. He is the gospel, He is the glad tidings. And how does that gospel actually begin; indeed, how does Jesus Christ himself begin? Is it not true, is it not accurate, to say that Jesus and His gospel begin with John the Baptist and his message of repentance unto salvation? For according to spiritual principle that is readily made clear in God's word, without repentance there can be no gospel of salvation. In other words, repentance prepares the way for the glad tidings of salvation: in fact, repentance prepares the way for the Lord himself to come into a person's heart and life, for repentance makes straight the pathway on which to meet the King. To therefore sum up on this point, without repentance no one is either fit to receive the King or to enter the kingdom of the heavens.

Today, unfortunately, when preaching the gospel, we seem to make it so cheap. We tell people to just believe and that is all they need to do, as though they do not need to repent at all. That is the reason why, though many who come to the Lord are saved, they are not *soundly* saved; they instead are weak. The spiritual principle is that repentance prepares the way for the Lord. The more thorough the repentance, the more sound is people's salvation. It is because their repentance is not thorough that they are not soundly saved. They may see a little of their sins, but they think they possess much good which can remain to eternity. That is not the meaning of repentance. As was the case in John's day, repentance is symbolized by baptism—a complete going into death, being buried out of sight, and rising anew in Christ Jesus. In other words, people need to repent of the old creation—the old man and all which comes from the natural—and then begin anew their life in Christ Jesus.

This is not only true when we first come to the Lord, it is also true as we ponder the coming of the kingdom of the heavens. In John's time the kingdom of the heavens came in the Person of the Lord Jesus. That kingdom was hidden to the world and only seen by those whose eyes were opened, but we Christians know that one day the kingdom of the heavens shall appear in public for all to see. On that day everyone will see it; and thank God, we are on the verge of beholding its manifestation. Hence, the message today is as it was for God's people in John's time: "Repent, for the kingdom of the heavens is coming." Such is the message today not for the world but for God's people.

As we believers ponder the kingdom of the heavens that is coming—that Christ is returning to establish His kingdom upon this earth—we need to ask ourselves: Are we ready for it? How are we going to prepare to meet the King? God's word tells us that the only way to prepare and make ourselves ready for it is to genuinely and fully repent. As a matter of fact, we need continuous repentance! Let us not think that we are now good enough for the kingdom. If we think we are good enough for the kingdom, most likely we are not.

Jesus' opening word when delivering to His disciples His so-called Sermon on the Mount, that delineates the character of Christ's kingdom, was this very first beatitude: "Blessed are the poor in spirit, for theirs is the kingdom of the heavens" (Matthew 5:3). Are you poor in spirit? Whom will God look to for bringing in the kingdom on earth? He will only look to those who are of a broken and contrite spirit (see Psalm 51:17).

How we who are God's people need to humble ourselves before the Lord! How we need to repent! Oh, we need to see how so unfit we are, how so unworthy and so unready. How we need to give ourselves more fully to Him and let Him do everything which is needful to be done in our lives to prepare us: All the valleys must be filled; all the mountains and hills must be brought low; all the crooked places must be corrected and made straight; all the rough places must be smoothed out. The Spirit of God must do this work in all of us. The cross must work in our lives. Anything that is not of Christ must be dealt with. "Repent"—this is the ongoing message for all God's people today. There is no other message today for the church of God but that of repentance.

A Corporate Epoch-Making Vessel

There is a second facet to John's relevance for us in our day. And this has to do with the fact that John had been raised up by God as an epoch-making vessel for his day and time. For God used him to conclude the Old Testament age and to introduce that of the New Testament. God used him to conclude the prophets and the law and to introduce Christ the King. God used him to conclude the age of law and to bring in the dispensation of grace. He was thus an epoch-making vessel of the first rank.

Whenever God desires to effect a change of time and dispensation, He always raises up a vessel to do that work, and most certainly we in our day are on the very brink of another great change. For two thousand years there has been the age of grace, but we know that this age is coming to an end—that the kingdom age is drawing near, for we know that the King is soon returning. In order for this to happen, however, God is in need of epoch-making vessels whom He can use for this purpose. Yet He is not looking for just one person, as was the case with John the Baptist; rather, He is looking for a corporate epoch-making body as His vessel. God is looking for a people in the collective sense whom He can use as the epoch-making vessel, a people together who can conclude this current age and bring in the age that is soon to come. Who will be such vessels who collectively can be used to effect this transition? I believe that John the Baptist is presented to us in Scripture in order to show us exactly what kind of epoch-making vessel God is looking for today to bring about this grand purpose of His. What follows are a few of the characteristics from John's life and service to God which must mark such a vessel.

Knows the Grace of God Experientially

First of all, if God is to obtain His corporate epoch-making vessel in our day, He will need to have many Johns who know His grace. Do we who are His people know the grace of God and its fullness? What the world of sinners needs is to know the grace of God, to know that He is gracious, to know that His grace is in His Son, and to know that God's grace is sufficient for every need. Even more so, God needs a chosen and prepared people who know the grace of God *experientially*. We believers need to experience the grace of God in our very lives, in our very beings. And then, because we know how gracious He is, we—like John of old—can preach repentance to a needy world. In order for any of us to preach repentance, we need to know in our very life experience that God is gracious; otherwise, we will be *judging* people instead of actually bringing them to Christ.

Is a Nazarite

Second, an epoch-making vessel must be one who, as was John the Baptist, is—spiritually speaking—a Nazarite. Back in the olden days of the Jewish people, a person was not *made* a Nazarite but became one as a result of his having made a special voluntary vow of separation to God for His service. This is made clear in the Old Testament book of

Numbers chapter 6. A Nazarite was thus different from a Levite because the latter was born as such. Whether a Levite liked it or not, he was such by birth and was thus automatically separated to God for His service. In contrast to the Levite was the Nazarite, who voluntarily vowed to devote himself to the service of God. Hence, the Nazarite of old was a totally separated person. Are we in our day separated from the world? Do we voluntarily set ourselves apart for God and His service? God must have such persons today if He is to obtain His corporate epoch-making vessel.

Goes Forth in the Spirit and Power of Elijah

Third, epoch-making vessels must go forth before God, as did John the Baptist, "in the spirit and power of Elias [Elijah]" (Luke 1:17a). We may recall that when Elijah was about to be taken up to heaven by God in a whirlwind, his disciple Elisha asked Elijah for a double portion of his spirit and received it (II Kings 2:1a, 9-15). What exactly was the primary characteristic of Elijah's spirit? We learn the answer from reading I Kings chapter 19 verses 10 and 14. These verses relate what this great prophet's twice-uttered reply of complaint was to the Lord's inquiry of him upon his having fled far away from King Ahab and Queen Jezebel to a cave on Mount Horeb. Elijah's twice-uttered response to God's questioning of why he was there was as follows: "I have been very jealous for Jehovah the God of hosts; for the children of Israel have forsaken thy covenant, thrown down thine altars, and slain thy prophets with the sword; and I am left, I alone, and they seek my life, to take it away." In other words, the essence of Elijah's spirit was a zealousness for God Almighty. Indeed, he was most jealous for the rights of God;

and this jealousy had burned deeply within him. That was Elijah's passion and that was the nature of his spirit.

Now such a spirit was also characteristic of John the Baptist, who went forth in service to God in that selfsame spirit which had marked the earlier prophet of Israel. John continually burned with zeal for the Lord in his day, and in our day God likewise needs those who are jealous for His rights; for His rights on earth are constantly being despised, violated, and contradicted. God needs a people today who are burning within with a zeal for Him and His interests, who are devoured by a jealousy for Jehovah and His rights.

If that was the *spirit* of Elijah, what can we say was the *power* of Elijah? Elijah's power was none other than prayer. The New Testament Epistle of James tells us that Elijah was a man just like us but who earnestly prayed and prayed (see 5:17-18). God needs a people today who truly give themselves to prayer to bring in the kingdom. Through our prayers, judgment may come, just as was true with Elijah; but blessings might also come, again as was the case with Elijah. We need to pray much. Yet let us realize that in our praying we are not wrestling against flesh and blood but against principalities and authorities and the forces of this world's darkness, against even spiritual forces of wickedness in heavenly places (Ephesians 6:12). Where, then, is this source of our power? Our power comes forth in praying earnestly before God. And John the Baptist was one who came forth in his day in both the spirit and power of Elijah. If we be such in our day, God will surely have His corporate epoch-making vessel through whom to accomplish His purpose of bringing in the kingdom of the heavens.

Is a Voice

Fourth, an epoch-making vessel is one who knows who he is and his place in God's purpose. Do we know who we are? Though John was greatly used by God, he knew he was but a voice (see again John 1:23b). He pointed people—even his own disciples—to Christ, not to himself (John 1:35ff.). Do we know ourselves as John knew himself? In spite of all the mercy and grace which God has bestowed upon us, who actually are we? Let us recognize and acknowledge that we are but a voice. We are not to be seen, only to be heard. We are not to draw people to ourselves. We are to be about the business of telling people of the One who alone is worthy, even Christ the Lord. We are willing to be decreased that He may increase (see again John 3:30). We are, as Paul confessed, "less than the least of all saints" and the chief of sinners (see Ephesians 3:8a, I Timothy 1:15b). Do we know ourselves as such? If we do, then God can use us as epoch-making vessels.

Bears a Full Testimony

Fifth and finally, epoch-making vessels are those who—like John the Baptist—are able to bear a full testimony concerning their Lord. Is our testimony of Jesus a full one? How much do we actually know of Him? Do we truly know Christ Jesus as the Son of God? (John 1:34) And do we honor Him as such? Do we really know Him as the Lamb of God who takes away our sins and those of the world? (John 1:29) Do we actually know Him as the Baptizer with the Holy Spirit? (John 1:33b) Do we truly know Jesus as the Bridegroom? (John 3:29) Hence, our testimony of the Lord

Jesus Christ must be based on our ever-expanding experiential knowledge of Him. Are we therefore able to testify of Him in such a full manner? If so, God can and will use such ones as epoch-making vessels.

Consequently, my burden before God these days is that we may all know in experience the gospel—even Jesus Christ himself. Indeed, we must want to know Him experientially and fully. But in order to know Jesus himself as the gospel, we have to know John the Baptist and all he represents, since it is he who—as an epoch-making vessel—prepared the way of the Lord in his day. May we in our day be individually and corporately used of God in similar fashion in preparing the way, and hastening the day, of the Lord's return to the earth.

Chapter Two

THE MYSTERY OF INCARNATION

John 1:1—In the beginning was the Word, and the Word was with God, and the Word was God.

John 1:14—And the Word became flesh, and dwelt among us (and we have contemplated his glory, a glory as of an only-begotten with a father), full of grace and truth.

Philippians 2:5-11—For let this mind be in you which was also in Christ Jesus; who, subsisting in the form of God, did not esteem it an object of rapine to be on an equality with God; but emptied himself, taking a bondman's form, taking his place in the likeness of men; and having been found in figure as a man, humbled himself, becoming obedient even unto death, and that the death of the cross. Wherefore also God highly exalted him, and granted him a name, that which is above every name, that at the name of Jesus every knee should bow, of heavenly and earthly and infernal beings, and every tongue confess that Jesus Christ is Lord to God the Father's glory.

For quite some time God has been exercising my heart concerning but one thing, and that is, the life of the Lord Jesus. The One whom we believe in is the Lord Jesus. The gospel that we have received is none other than God's Son, Jesus Christ the Lord. Our faith is not based on teachings or doctrines or forms or systems or rituals or ceremonies. Our faith is based on one

Person, the living Christ. Our whole Christian life is none other than having a living knowledge of Christ Jesus. Therefore, it is most essential for each one of us to really know Him—not just know Him in our mind but know Him in an experiential way. This was the one passion which was in the apostle Paul. In his Letter to the Philippians he wrote: "To know him, and the power of his resurrection, and the fellowship of his sufferings, being conformed to his death, if [in] any way I arrive at the [out]-resurrection from among the dead" (3:10-11). I do hope this was not only the passion of Paul but it is our passion—to know Him in practical experience. To know Him actually is everything. The genius of Christianity is not to be found in teachings or other things; rather, it is to be found centered upon one Person, the Lord Jesus Christ.

We are living towards the end of this present age. It is coming very quickly to a conclusion, and in our time there are all kinds of strange teachings which are abroad that sway people to and fro. How are we going to stand against all such strange teachings which are around us unless we are rooted and grounded in Christ? And knowing God's ultimate will for our lives should motivate and lead us to be grounded in Christ.

Now what is the supreme will of God? What is His eternal purpose? His will—His purpose—is none other than that His Son may be all and in all (Ephesians 1:22-23). This is God's supreme will, and if this is His will, it ought to be our will too. Hence, how important it is that we know the Lord Jesus, know Him in a real way, know Him in life, know Him in His fullness. This should occupy all our attention.

The device of the enemy, of course, is to distract us from Christ by occupying us with many other things. Sometimes the enemy tries to distract our attention from Christ by occupying us with teachings. Our attention seems to be easily diverted towards teachings—whether true or false—instead of it being focused upon Christ and His Person. On the other hand, he will sometimes try to divert our attention towards certain people to whom we may attach ourselves. Now these people may be spiritual giants who are being greatly used by God, or they may not be so; nevertheless, the enemy tries to attach us to people, and by doing so, he will be detaching us from Christ. Such are the devices of the enemy; and how easily we can be distracted.

In these days, however, our attention must be focused upon just one Person—Christ Jesus. Let us therefore look away from everything and only look to Him, the Author and Finisher of our faith (Hebrews 12:2a).

Christ Jesus is truly inexhaustible. The apostle Paul mentioned in his writings "the unsearchable riches of Christ" (Ephesians 3:8b), and the apostle John told us that if everything our Lord Jesus did while He was on earth were written down, this world would not be able to contain all the books which would be produced (John 21:25). So it is impossible for us to exhaust Christ in our knowledge of Him. It is impossible for us to know Him in such a way that there is no more to know of Him. Throughout our lifetime we have to pursue after Him diligently; yet, even if we pursue after Him diligently, we will only know a little portion of Him. And then, in eternity we shall continue to increase our knowledge of Him. Christ is limitless in every respect and the knowing of Him in all respects is without limit. How thrilling that is! Let us not assume that we have to know all about Him now. Indeed, what we know of Him today is just the beginning of acquiring such knowledge. It should stir our hearts in such a way that as long as we have breath, we will pursue after Christ to know Him in a deeper way. Thank God, in eternity, we will not be at leisure. We will be occupied with Him throughout eternity, and there will therefore always be something new to learn of Him. How inexhaustible is the Lord Jesus!

As we today meditate together on some of the events in the life of Jesus, hopefully, we will learn more of Him. And quite naturally we must begin with His birth. Our own human life, for example, begins with birth, or to be more exact, with conception. When we are conceived in our mother's womb, our life begins at that very moment. Before that, we were non-existent; but this is not true with the Lord Jesus. Yes, in one sense His birth is the beginning of His life on earth, but His birth is different from ours in that it can uniquely be described as incarnation.

What is meant by this term? When used in reference to the Deity incarnation is none other than the manifestation of God come in human form—in this case, in the form of Jesus Christ. In other words, before Jesus was born, He was already there—"In the beginning was the Word" (John 1:1a). The beginning cited in this opening verse of the Gospel according to John is that which goes much further back (we do not know, in fact, how *much* further back) than the beginning we find mentioned in Genesis 1:1. There we read: "In the beginning God created the heavens and the earth." That beginning is what we refer to as Creation—the beginning of the existence of the heavens and the earth; yet even in that beginning, God was already there.

In John's Gospel the phrase, "In the beginning," is none other than God. God is the beginning. We know He was there before there was the Creation because He is the Creator. In short, He was there before time and space ever began. Therefore, God is himself the beginning.

"In the beginning was the Word." In that beginning, there was the Word—that is to say, the Logos, the Speech, the Expression, the Utterance, the Manifestation, the Revelation of the Deity. "In the beginning was the Word, and the Word was with God." This Word has its own personality (John 1:1-2). This Word was with God, co-existing with Him in the beginning, and yet this Word was God (John 1:1c). He was one with God.

The concept of the Trinity shall always remain a mystery to us humans. No matter how we try to explain it, it shall always remain inexplicable. It is the very mystery of the Godhead. "In the beginning was the Word, and the Word was with God, and the Word was God." This Word existed from the *very* beginning. As a matter of fact, it was this Word that created the heavens and the earth, for God created it *by* the instrumentality of His Word. God's Word spoke into existence the Creation and it was done (cf. John 1:1-3, 10b, with Hebrews 1:2c, Colossians 1:16, and Genesis 1:3, 6-7, 9, 11, 14-15, 20-21, 24). But one day, much much later, this Word came into this created world and became flesh. And that was the act of incarnation (John 1:14a). To phrase it another way, God's Word took upon Himself a human form, and the name assigned to this human form—this human being—was simply Jesus.

We read in Luke 1:35 that the angel of God told Mary that the Holy Spirit would overshadow her womb and she would conceive and give birth to a son, and He would be called the Son of God. So in the fullness of time God sent His Son into this world to be born of a flesh-and-blood Jewish woman—the act of incarnation—and would thus be born under law so that He might redeem us out from under the curse of the law in order that whoever believes in Him might receive sonship (Galatians 4:4-5, 3:13)—the ultimate purpose and will of God the Father in this act of incarnation. The Incarnation thus resulted in the birth of the Lord Jesus.

The Concept of Incarnation

We need to realize that the concept of incarnation had been conceived in the mind of God long before the foundation of the world. Let me say again that the Trinity is beyond our full understanding, but we humans nonetheless can try to explain it somewhat using admittedly inadequate language to bring it within a modicum of our understanding. May we therefore say that in the beginning was the triune God. There was nothing else—no worlds, no universes of any kind anywhere—nothing but God. He is the self-existing One. He was always there. He was and is the beginning. There was no time yet, but it came to pass that at some point there was a council held among the members of the Godhead—Father, Son, and Holy Spirit. God the Father loved God the Son so much that He wanted to express His love to Him. Love always seeks out a channel by which to do and give something to the one who is loved. And we well know that God is love (I John 4:8b), and God the Father loved His Son so very much that He wanted to bestow upon His Son that which could express His love for Him.

So God proceeded to create through His Son the heavens, the earth and all things else and give them to His Son as His love gift (Colossians 1:16b, Hebrews 1:2b). And of all the gifts that God would give to His Son there was none more excellent than man (cf. Psalm 8:4-6). He wanted to give man to His Son to be His companion—His helpmate—and who would be together with Him to share in glory as well as in responsibility. God had all this in His mind, and all was therefore according to His good pleasure. No one told Him what to do, it was simply His good pleasure to do so

(Ephesians 1:3-10). He loves His Son, and it pleased Him when He began to conceive of doing all these things.

But being the Omniscient One who knows the very end from the beginning, God knew that after He created man and his universe, man would fall into temptation and rebel against Him; that is to say, man would be deceived into frustrating God the Father's gift to His beloved Son. What, then, should He do? Should He prepare to do nothing? At that moment in the council of the Godhead, it is as though the Son stepped forward and said: "Father, if this is what You want, I want what You want. Go forward, create all things, including man. For I am willing one day to enter this world which You will have created and which, sadly, will become a fallen world, and I will give myself to redeem man and the whole universe so that I may give all back to You as the expression of *My* love for You" (cf. Hebrews 10:5-7). It was decided, then, that all this should be done.

From this we can thus discern that the *concept* of incarnation was not new. It had been there in the mind of God well before the foundation of the world, even though the *fact* of incarnation was not realized until we do not know how long after the idea had entered God's mind.

The Promise of Incarnation

There is not only the concept of incarnation, there is also the *promise* of incarnation. At the very beginning of human history that promise of incarnation had been given and expressed. We will remember the events recorded in the Genesis 2-3 narrative about what occurred in the Garden of Eden: God had created the first man, and had then built the first woman out of man, they being the first couple whom

God then placed in the Edenic garden—a garden of pleasure. God had earlier planted a garden full of beautiful trees producing fruit as food for man, and in the center there was the tree of life. God's desire had been that man should eat of the fruit of the tree of life, receiving His divine life, and by so doing they would be fit to be the life companion of His beloved Son. Unfortunately, the woman was deceived by the serpent and ate the fruit of the tree of the knowledge of good and evil—that forbidden fruit. Man rebelled against God and fell into sin.

But God immediately began to work again: He sought out that first man by coming down into the garden and asking aloud: "Adam, where are you?" Then God began to pronounce His various judgments, and in His judgment upon the deceiving serpent He announced the following: "I will put enmity between you and the woman, and between the seed of the woman and your seed; he shall crush your head, and you shall crush his heel" (see Genesis 3:15). It so happened that in a sense when earlier the woman had been deceived by the serpent, at that moment an alliance had been formed between the two of them; but in His mercy God placed an enmity between the woman and the serpent. In other words, He put a hatred in the woman towards the serpent; for instead of the woman having been thankful to the serpent in his having opened her eyes—though, unfortunately, in having had her eyes opened she realized she was now naked—the woman henceforth began to hate the serpent. This was God's doing in having created a hatred in the woman towards the serpent—even Satan himself. Yet let us not overlook the fact that simultaneously God had placed a hatred in the serpent towards the woman as well. Thus, in His mercy God broke that alliance, and so the enmity which He had mercifully placed between the seed of the woman and the seed of the serpent has continued to exist and will continue so throughout the ages.

Strictly speaking, who is this seed of the woman? In getting at the answer to this question we need first to understand that in Biblical genealogy all generations are delineated according to the male side of humanity. For example, we are told that Adam begat Seth, Abraham begat Isaac, David begat Solomon, and so on. All the genealogies in the Bible follow the male line, and in light of this, we come to understand that when Adam fell, all those who afterwards are born of Adam receive that Adamic life which had been poisoned back at the time of the Fall in the Edenic garden. Sin thus dwells in that life. Consequently, everyone who is born of Adam (and that means each and every one of us) is already a sinner before he or she commits any sin (Psalm 51:5, Romans 5:12). Because we automatically are born sinners, that explains why we sin. None of us needs to go to school to learn how to sin since we all were born sinners. All of us being born of Adam, everyone who comes from the line of Adam is a sinner, under curse, because we inherited his life and the sinful nature which is in that life. But thank God, even under those tragic circumstances, God gave a promise when man first fell into sin: "the seed of the woman." One day there would be a particular Man born into this world in the womb of a woman, yet not by man's effort of the flesh but by the power of the Holy Spirit. That Man is "the Holy Thing," and called the Son of God (Luke 1:35). He was born of a virgin woman by the power of God's Spirit; therefore, He did not inherit the sin of Adam since Adam was *not* His father centuries and millennia removed; on the contrary, God is His Father.

Now we are told in Galatians 3:16a that the promises of God were addressed to Abraham and to his seed. The word seed here is cast in singular number—not seeds plural. Who, then, is that seed of Abraham being brought into view here? That promised seed is none other than Jesus (Galatians 3:16b). He is the seed of the woman, and that seed would crush the head of the serpent; for one day He would come and, on the cross, would deal such a fatal blow to Satan, the enemy of both God and man, that He would destroy his power. But the serpent would nonetheless bruise Christ's heel; that is to say, He would be crucified. Alternatively, some Bible interpreters have surmised that the term heel in God's promise refers to the church—thus meaning that Satan would persecute the church. Regardless which is the correct interpretation, Jesus is the seed of the woman that had been promised by God back in Eden. We therefore learn that immediately after man fell into sin the promise of incarnation came forth from the mouth of Jehovah. It will be through incarnation that redemption can be brought into this world.

Even so, not only at the time of man's fall in the Garden of Eden but also throughout Jewish history there have come forth many other promises concerning incarnation—how God would come into this world in human flesh. Indeed, the Old Testament is full of such promises. For instance, as has already been pointed out, there was God's promise repeatedly reported in Genesis concerning the seed of Abraham: "In thy seed shall all the nations be blessed." And the New Testament book of Galatians, as we saw earlier, confirms that Christ Jesus is that seed of Abraham.

Scripture indicates that Christ is also the seed of David. We are told in II Samuel 7 that God promised David he would have a son who would sit upon King David's throne and that his kingdom would know no end. Who is that son? If we carefully read the history of David's family, we learn that, yes, David's son Solomon sat on the throne and after Solomon, his son too; but for some time thereafter there was no son of Solomon nor son of David sitting on the throne. Even today, we do not find the son of David sitting on his throne in Jerusalem. So who is that son whom God promised David? We will recall that the angel of God came to Mary and, among other things, told her she would give birth to a son who would sit upon his father David's throne. He would rule over the nation of Jacob, and his kingdom would know no end (Luke 1:32b-33). All these were references to Jesus Christ who is indeed *the* son of David—even the Promised One. He is the Incarnate One who has been promised.

The book of Isaiah is likewise full of such promises. For instance, we read in chapter 7 that "a virgin shall conceive and give birth to a son, and his name shall be called Immanuel (God with us men)" (see v.14). Then, in that book's chapter 9 we read this: "Unto us a child is born, a son is given" (see v.6a). The child that is to be born is actually a Son *given.* God gave to this world His Son, who was born into this world as a child. Isaiah chapter 9 also tells us that the government shall be upon this Son's shoulders, and that He shall be called Wonderful, Counselor, Almighty God, Father of Eternity, Prince of Peace. Moreover, His government shall know no end, and the zeal of the Lord shall accomplish all of this (vv. 6b-7). So there are many, many promises concerning incarnation to be found in the Old Testament.

The Fact of Incarnation

Finally, there came the day when the fact of incarnation was realized. Not only was there the concept of incarnation, conceived in the mind of God long before the foundation of the world, and not only was there the promise of incarnation expressed repeatedly throughout Old Testament history, but there was also realized one day the fact of incarnation: Jesus was born. Since we should all be familiar already with the birth of Christ, we are not going to spend much time over that. Instead, what I now desire for us to meditate upon next is the mystery of incarnation.

The Mystery of Incarnation

Incarnation is a mystery. In the context of Biblical history a mystery is that which, being in the heart of God, needs to be revealed; and even after it is revealed, man will probably only comprehend a small portion of its content and/or meaning. When we consider the birth of Christ, for example, do we ever think of it in terms of it being a mystery? We are all so familiar with the story of the birth of Christ who was born in a cow shelter's manger. The angels were singing; the shepherds came to worship; and later the wise men came with their gifts to worship. Because we have become so familiar with this story, we fail to grasp the mystery of incarnation surrounding Jesus' birth. Actually, it is a tremendous event. The mystery of God's incarnation in the world is revealed to us especially through two passages in the Bible.

Here is the first passage: "In the beginning was the Word, and the Word was with God, and the Word was God.

… And the Word became flesh" (John 1:1,14a). That very statement describes the mystery of incarnation. John's Gospel goes on to say that we have contemplated His glory as the glory of the beloved Son with His Father, full of grace and truth (v.14b). Now how can this be? How can God become man? God is infinite; how, then, can the infinite become the finite? How can God, who is the Unknowable, become known? This is explained to us in the second passage, found in Philippians 2: "Let this mind be in you which was also in Christ Jesus, who, subsisting in the form of God, and being equal with God, He nevertheless thought it not something to be grasped after or held on to" (see vv.5-6). Who is this *He*? This *He* is the Word—the Word that became flesh; this *He* is the Son of God whose existence antedates the foundation of the world and who co-exists, and is equal with, God; and yet this was not something He sought to hold on to, though it would have been His right to have done so. This passage further tells us that Christ Jesus subsists in the form of God.

Now this word form in Greek is *morphe*—a word which is only used twice in the entire New Testament. It is used here in Philippians 2:6, and it is again used in Mark 16:12 where we are told that after the resurrection of the Lord Jesus two of His disciples were walking on their way to the village of Emmaus when suddenly out of nowhere there appeared a man walking along with them. The passage says that the Lord Jesus had taken upon himself "another form" and was walking with them, but the two disciples did not recognize Him. Now that Greek term *morphe* translated as form here is the same term used in the Philippians passage cited earlier.

This Greek term *morphe* refers to something far deeper than what we would describe as a form. For when we today think of a form, we have reference in our mind to an appearance—a manifestation. But here, in the case back then of the resurrected Jesus, we learn that the form mentioned is changeable in nature. That is to say, the Lord Jesus had the ability to change His form, and when He did so on the Emmaus road, His disciples did not recognize Him. This term in Greek thus possesses a much deeper meaning than simply conveying the notion of an appearance or a manifestation; it conveys the idea of the essence or the nature of a given being.

Returning to both the Johannine and Philippian passages once again, we learn that long before time—that is, in the very beginning—Christ Jesus subsisted or existed in the form of God. In other words, God the Son has always possessed the nature and the essence of the Divinity; in fact, that is what He is. In existing in eternity past in the form of God, the Son's essence and nature was being manifested in the full expression of deity. In the beginning He subsisted in the form of God, for He is God; He has all the essence and nature of God; indeed, He is co-equal with God. Whatever God is, that is what He is as well. Not only that, this second Person of the Trinity manifested himself in this form of God—a form that is glorious, a form that lives in light impenetrable, a form that is unknowable to human beings, a form that is beyond human comprehension: unlimited in its glory, unlimited in its power, unlimited in its wisdom, unlimited in every respect pertaining to deity. All the fullness of the Godhead dwelt in Him (Colossians 1:19). That is the form in which He subsisted, and in that form was He worshiped by all the angels.

But there came a day in time when God the Son emptied himself and became a man. Yet how could God—the

Infinite, Omnipotent, Omnipresent, Omniscient One—become a man? For by contrast man is so finite, so limited, so restricted. The Bible tells us that "all of the nations are just like a speck of dust in the balance" (cf. Isaiah 40:17). Who, then, are we as individuals? If all the nations are together a mere speck of dust, who and what are we? We are so tiny, so limited, restricted and poor. How could God therefore ever become a man? Impossible! The only way He the Infinite One could become a finite man would be for Him to empty himself. Yet let us forever bear in mind that this is never to be construed as an emptying of His essence and nature as deity. That is impossible, for God the Son is ever and always God. But what He *could* empty himself of is that form of God in which He had continually subsisted from the very beginning—that is to say, God the Son could empty himself of His manifestation of all the unlimited glory, power, wisdom, etc., of the Deity. He could lay all that aside in order that He might take upon himself another form—and that, the form of a slave.

Let me repeat what was said moments ago because it is very, very important for us to be clear about it. When it is said that God the Son emptied himself, let us not conclude that He emptied himself of His divine essence as God. That is impossible because one of the very names of Jesus the God-Man—Immanuel—means *God with us*. Which is to say, that the essence and nature of deity were still there in the man Jesus. God the Son did not, because of incarnation, lay aside His deity. Not so! What He laid aside was the form or manifestation of God—a manifestation that is beyond human comprehension, beyond the finite mind's grasp. He laid down that form in order to take up *another* form, that of a slave; but *with* that form all the essence of deity was still there, yet in a hidden way; it was never manifested unless God the Father so instructed it. Instead, the form of a slave was manifested.

Think of that! From that divine form did God the Son empty himself in order to take to himself the form of a bondslave. To whom was He a slave? To God the Father. That is the form that God the Son took up while He was on earth in the likeness of a man.

Now according to Creation, what should characterize the likeness of a man? The likeness of a man should be in the form of a bondslave to God. When back in Eden man rejected that form, all the problems on earth began. Now there is a great difference between a slave and bondslave. A slave is merely someone who has sold himself, and thus having in the process lost all his rights. A bondslave is quite different; he is one who has become a slave out of love, and hence, he is a love-slave. His slavehood is therefore not by obligation but is because of love. He desires to be a slave forever; he desires to voluntarily give up all his rights, and will thus accept his master as having every right over him all through his life. Actually, in spirit, that is what man was originally created to be in his relationship to God. Man was meant to stand on the ground of a bondslave towards God. In the Edenic garden that should have been his form by choice, but man rejected that choice and that form; he instead wanted to be God himself. Man did not want to obey God; rather, he wanted to have his own rights, and the result is that he fell into sin. But God sent His Son into the world to rescue man from his sin, and the Son of God is therefore *the* Man after God the Father's own heart. For in the Person of Jesus, God the Son took upon himself the form of a loving bondslave to God the Father.

Let me emphasize again that what God the Son emptied himself of was not His deity; rather, He emptied himself of all His glory, all the various attributes attached to or associated with deity. For instance, as God, He the Son is omnipotent, all-powerful; but after being born into this world as the Babe of Bethlehem and having grown into manhood, Jesus often declared: "I can *do* nothing out from myself: only whatever I see My Father doing, that I do; moreover, I can *say* nothing out from myself: only whatever I hear My Father saying, that I say" (see John 5:19-20, 30a; 7:16-17; 8:28b; 12:49-50; 14:10, 24, 31). For instance further, as God, He the Son is omnipresent, able to be present everywhere simultaneously; but on earth as the man Jesus, God the Son was limited: for when Jesus was in Jerusalem He could not at the same moment be in Galilee. For instance still further, as God, He the Son is omniscient, possessing the ability to know everything—even the ability to know everything from beginning to its end; but on earth in the Person of Jesus, God the Son had to confess, for example, the following limitation: "I do not know the timing of my return to the earth and of the end of the age; even the angels do not know, only the Father knows" (see Matthew 24:3, 36; Mark 13:3-4, 32; Acts 1:6-7). Hence, we can see from all this that out of love for the Father and for fallen mankind the second Person of the triune God voluntarily laid aside the form of God within which He had been subsisting from the very beginning and took upon himself the form of a loving bondslave. *That* is incarnation.

What an emptying that was! I do believe that if we see incarnation in this light—what God has indeed done for us in taking upon himself the likeness of a man—there will rise up within us a worship which we have never known or experienced before.

Reading further in Philippians chapter 2, we find these additional dramatic words concerning God the Son: "And having been found in figure as a man, he humbled himself, becoming obedient even unto death, and that the death of the cross." No wonder the Father highly exalted Him and gave Him the name that is above every name, and that at that name every knee should bow and every tongue confess that Jesus is Lord. Such is the mystery of incarnation. Even so, we today have been merely touching the surface of its depths. It is still a profound mystery; and it shall always remain a mystery for us to marvel at, to wonder in amazement that God could—and *would*—humble himself to become a man. What an emptying! And what a mystery!

The Meaning of Incarnation: Its Implication and Application for Us Today

The Love of God

Before concluding our consideration together on this highly significant subject, we must return once more to the meaning of incarnation and give some attention to its implication and practical application for us Christians today as we seek to follow the Lord Jesus in obedience according to God's word. First of all, incarnation shows us the love of God. He so loved the world that He gave His only begotten Son (John 3:16). Why should the triune God love us so? The first man He created was originally quite lovely, but after Adam fell, all the men and women who are born of Adam are automatically sinners. We frustrate the plan of God; we defy Him; we rebel against Him; we stand with the enemy of God instead of being God's instrument for accomplishing His purpose. That is what we human beings are, and yet in so many ways God did not give us up. He extended His love even to the extent of becoming a man in identifying himself with us humans. Think of that! Naturally speaking, because we are so unlovely, He could have simply forgotten about us completely; yet the love of God is so everlasting, so self-giving and so persistent that He is always seeking and pursuing after us. So that eventually He himself became a man. Because we partake of flesh and blood, therefore, He likewise took upon himself flesh and blood in order to be able to identify himself perfectly with us, apart from sin, so that He might deliver us from both sin and death. What love lay behind that act of incarnation! Such love is something for us to deeply ponder upon. God should have distanced himself from us, have kept us far, far away from himself; yet, He drew near to us to become one of us in order to save us. What tremendous love was displayed! This is the kind of love none of us can ever fully fathom or explain. It is beyond our understanding, nevertheless, we mere mortals—and fallen ones at that!—are the recipients of such inexplicable love. Can we who have been redeemed through His love manifested in incarnation fail to love Him in return?

The Mind of Christ

Furthermore, incarnation not only tells us of the love of God, it also tells us of the mind of Christ. What is the mind of Christ? If, prior to becoming Christ, God the Son had decided to hold on to His rights inherent in His being the second Person of the triune God—for instance, the right to sit on the throne with the Father, the right to be worshiped by the angels, the right to rule over the universe, or the right to live in glory and honor—He could have legitimately done so, for those were His rights; but that was not the mind of God the Son who voluntarily became the Christ of God. On the contrary, the mind of Christ was characterized by a decision to do just the opposite: to let go of those rights of His: indeed, to lay aside His glory, lay aside His honor, even lay aside His omniscience and His omnipotence. He as God the Son was willing to lay down everything and humble himself to become the man Jesus and the loving bondslave to God the Father. What humbling that is! Yet without that lowliness of mind, incarnation would have been impossible and we would still be in the grip of our sins.

So God's servant Paul advised us Christians as follows: "Let this mind be in *you* which was also in Christ Jesus." The very act of incarnation should remind us of the humility of the Lord Jesus. Because He as God the Son humbled himself, therefore, let this mind be in you and me which was also in Him. Are we not all naturally high-minded? Yet we are actually nothing; even so, do we not think of ourselves as being something, as being somebody? Here, though, we see the Son of God who is and owns everything; and yet, He considered himself as nothing and having nothing. How we need to learn and live out the lesson of humility. Humility is the mind of Christ. God indeed gives grace to the humble, but He also resists the proud and the high-minded (I Peter 5:5c quoting Proverbs 3:34).

We need, however, to differentiate between humility and humiliation, for they are quite different from each other. Humility is an inward attitude whereas humiliation is an outward act. Humility, or the humbling of oneself, is that which comes from within you voluntarily. Humiliation, on the other hand, is that which is imposed upon you from the outside. It is a truism of life, is it not, that because we are not humble, we are often humiliated; on the other hand, if we are humble, we are beyond humiliation. There is a small book entitled *Beyond Humiliation*; it is a very helpful book whose thesis is that if you are humble, you are beyond being humiliated, and that the corollary to its thesis is, that the reason you feel humiliated is because you are not humble. Let us not blame people who may humiliate us. We need such as a way to develop in us that spirit of humility. Each time we contemplate the Incarnation, let us recall the mind and attitude of Christ.

The Great Power of the Holy Spirit

Further still, incarnation reminds us of the exceeding great power of the Holy Spirit. For how could a woman, who is a virgin but without a husband, ever conceive? The answer is to be found in the power of the Holy Spirit, who overshadowed that womb of hers and enabled her to bring forth the Holy Thing within her—even Jesus Christ, the Son of God. That was the result of the power of the Holy Spirit, which in nature is almighty; and this power that gave birth to Christ is the same power that regenerates us into our spiritual new birth. How can we experience our new birth—that is, of our being born again? It is not by man's natural descent, nor by man's will, nor by the will of man's flesh (John 1:13). We cannot will ourselves to be born again, and nobody else can will for us to be born again; it is only by the power of the Holy Spirit which effects such new birth. Not only that, but we learn from Scripture that this same power was that which raised Jesus from the dead and is likewise the same power that is working in us today. Let us believe that power of the Holy Spirit and let us receive it.

Reconciliation

There is one other application for us of incarnation which I need to mention, which is, that through it God is able to reconcile to himself those in the world who believe in the gift of His Son. Now it is true that the work of redemption was not completed until Jesus was crucified—at which time He declared: "It is finished" (John 19:30a). Yet how could He have been crucified had God the Son not been born as a man? So the work of redemption and reconciliation actually began with the act of incarnation when the Son was willing to empty himself and become flesh. Only by this means was there the possibility of our being reconciled to God. By the blood of Jesus we who believe are reconciled to Him. Not only us believers but whoever else in the world believes, as well as all the created things, are being reconciled to God through the blood of the Lord Jesus (Colossians 1:20). Such is reconciliation.

However, the work of reconciliation also includes that of restoration. Not only that our sins are forgiven and we are received back into the loving embrace of the Father, but reconciliation is in addition restoration. The first man—Adam—fell, and in response God raised up the second Man—even by the birth of the Christ-Child. The first man failed God's purpose, but through incarnation the second Man came into this world and is the Man of God's own heart. Christ Jesus is the Man whom God had had in His mind from the very beginning and is the Man to whom God will give the dominion over all things (Ephesians 1:21-22). Here came Jesus, *the* Man of God, yet He will not be alone; for He came into this world not only to demonstrate to us what kind of Man God desires but also to bring many sons to glory (Hebrews 2:10a): through the Lord Jesus Christ God will recreate a new race by recreating us to be like Him in order that Christ the Son might be the firstborn among many brethren (Romans 8:29b). Reconciliation is therefore so complete that not only do we have our sins forgiven but that we are also, as it were, being reconstructed into that one new man—the church—that God has greatly desired to give to His beloved Son as His helpmate.

All these various facets which we have considered together today are included in the meaning of incarnation and its application to us. Jesus came into this world not just to seek and to save the lost but also to recreate us and conform us to His image (Romans 8:29a) in order that He might receive us as His counterpart so that the will of God concerning man might be fully realized. And such is the purpose which lay behind the incarnation of God in Christ.

Let us indeed meditate on His birth and the historic act of incarnation which brought it about. Yet His birth is more than that which people celebrate once a year; the Incarnation in all its wonderful facets is that on which we need to meditate every day: What love! What mind! What power! And what glorious work of reconciliation and restoration we find in the Incarnation!

Chapter Three

HIS BAR MITZVAH

Luke 2:40-51—And the child grew and waxed strong in spirit, filled with wisdom, and God's grace was upon him. And his parents went yearly to Jerusalem at the feast of the passover. And when he was twelve years old, and they went up to Jerusalem according to the custom of the feast and had completed the days, as they returned, the boy Jesus remained behind in Jerusalem, and his parents knew not of it; but, supposing him to be in the company that journeyed together, they went a day's journey, and sought him among their relations and acquaintances: and not having found him they returned to Jerusalem seeking him. And it came to pass, after three days they found him in the temple, sitting in the midst of the teachers and hearing them and asking them questions. And all who heard him were astonished at his understanding and answers. And when they saw him they were amazed: and his mother said to him, Child, why hast thou dealt thus with us? behold, thy father and I have sought thee distressed. And he said to them, Why is it that ye have sought me? did ye not know that I ought to be occupied in my Father's business? And they understood not the thing that he said to them. And he went down with them and came to Nazareth, and he was in subjection to them. And his mother kept all these things in her heart.

I believe we all agree that God's will is that we behold His Son, the Lord Jesus Christ. Look off to Jesus, the Author and Finisher of our faith (Hebrews 12:2a AV). The more we look at the Lord Jesus, the less we will be distracted. The more we look at Him the more we will love Him. The more we look at Jesus the more we will be like Him. This is the secret of Christian life.

By the grace of God we may be men and women of God; that is, we receive a divine life into us, but that does not make us divine. Rather, we receive the divine life into us, and that delivers us from our fallen humanity. This divine life uplifts us, but it does not make us divine. We are human, and we will remain so forever. We will never be divine, even though we do have that divine life in us.

Yes, it is quite true that God wants to transform us and conform us to the image of His beloved Son (Romans 12:2a, 8:29a); but let us always remember that though we are to be conformed to the image of Christ, there is always something more in Him that is beyond us. He is God; He is the God-Man, and we are but human beings—but thank God, we are human beings with His life in us. This point is very important to emphasize, since we find in Christianity today that there are heretics around who assume that because we receive the divine life in us and our humanity is being delivered from its fallen state, therefore, we become divine, we become gods. Not so; we are and shall remain human beings, and among men only the Lord Jesus is God.

Now from among all the events recorded in Scripture concerning the life of Jesus I would like for us to consider together today His Bar Mitzvah. We know from the Bible that when the Christ-Child was eight days old He was circumcised according to the law and bore the name Jesus that had been given Him by the angel of God (Luke 2:21). We read in Galatians 4:4-5 that in the fullness of time God sent His Son into this world, born of woman and born under the law, in order that He might deliver us from the curse of the law and bring us into sonship. The Lord Jesus was born under the Mosaic law which said that He must be circumcised on the eighth day (Leviticus 12:3). He was submitted to that regulation in order that He might deliver us from the curse of the law.

Scripture also tells us that when the fulfillment of the time of purification came, Jesus was presented in the temple to God. We know from Leviticus 12 that a woman who gave birth to a male child would be unclean for forty days, and after forty days she had to present a sacrifice. If she were poor she would be required to present a turtledove or a pigeon by which to purify herself from uncleanness. According to the custom, this purification should be done at the end of forty days, but sometimes it was done after forty days. Hence, we do not know exactly how long after Jesus was born that He was presented; but after forty days Mary came to the temple in Jerusalem to perform the rite of purification.

At the same time she came to the temple to present to God her firstborn child because under the law all the firstborn sons belonged to God. We know from Exodus 13 that the first male who opened the womb was holy and belonged to the Lord to be sacrificed to Him, and the firstborn son was to be redeemed. Let us recall that on the night God delivered the children of Israel out of Egypt, every firstborn son in Egypt was to be killed, but He prepared a lamb for the children of Israel. When the Israelites put the blood of the lamb upon the doorpost and the lintel, the angel of destruction passed over that house. So all the firstborn sons of the children of Israel were saved, while all those of the children of Egypt were destroyed. Because of what happened on that day of the first Passover, God said that all the firstborn belonged to Him. They all were holy, and they should be presented to God with a sacrificial offering for redeeming the firstborn.

Let us realize that the firstborn actually represents the whole family. Spiritually speaking, therefore, not only the firstborn but all who are born belong to God. We all belong to Him; therefore, we are holy.

The Lord Jesus was dedicated to God in His infancy by His earthly parents. The spiritual significance of this is that every child that is born is holy in the sight of God. As parents you must not overlook the fact that every child that is born to your family is holy in the sight of God; therefore, you must bring them all up in the discipline and admonition of the Lord. It is a holy trust.

Apart from these two incidents—the circumcision and the dedication of Jesus—we do not find anything concerning the childhood of the Lord being mentioned in the Gospel of Luke except for a summary statement (see below). As a matter of fact, Luke does not even mention the Magi who came to worship the child Jesus, which actually did not occur at the time of His birth. At this latter time shepherds had come up from their fields and worshiped Him at the manger; but when the Magi came to worship Jesus, a year or two had already passed because it had taken the Magi that long to travel from the east. Yet Luke does not mention the Magi nor does he mention how the Christ-Child was taken for safety into Egypt. The parents fled down to Egypt because King Herod had wanted to kill all the children in Bethlehem below two years of age. Luke obviously does not mention how long the family spent in Egypt or the return from Egypt or why they then went off to Nazareth. Luke 2:39 simply tells us that after the parents had finished presenting the baby Jesus to God, they left Jerusalem and went to Galilee and lived in Nazareth. Nothing else is mentioned about the childhood of the Lord Jesus except this one sentence: "And the child grew and waxed strong in spirit, filled with wisdom, and God's grace was upon him" (Luke 2:40).

A Normal Childhood

Is childhood unimportant to God? Certainly not! We will recall the attitude of Jesus expressed towards little children: On one occasion He said, "Permit the little children to come to Me, for theirs is the kingdom of heaven" (see Matthew 19:14 ASV); on another, we read that "He took up children into His arms and blessed them" (see Mark 10:16); and on still another occasion He also said this: "Do not despise a little child, because the angel of a child sees My Father's face continually" (see Matthew 18:10). So from these expressions of Jesus we know that a child is very precious to God's heart. Then why is it that in the Scriptures the childhood of the Lord Jesus is not given to us in detail? I think we would all want very much to know about His childhood but, strangely, nothing further is mentioned. I believe the reason is that God wants to show us that the Lord Jesus grew up normally as a child like any other. There is that tendency in us to think that because He is the God-Man, that because He is God become Man and Immanuel, therefore, His childhood must surely have been different. But just as with us He was born as a baby, and just like we do He grew up as a child. In other words, Jesus was a normal child and lived a normal childhood.

Speaking of Jesus the Bible tells us that "the child grew and waxed strong." The first thing we notice in a child is his physical growth. In fact, the way a baby grows physically is the most noticeable part of the growth of a child. And in the case of the Lord Jesus, He grew and waxed physically strong normally.

Speaking further concerning Jesus, we are told in the Bible that "he was filled with wisdom." As a child grows physically, his mind begins to open up; moreover, his intellect begins to grow, too. With Jesus however, we find that He was filled with wisdom—meaning that His mental growth was above normal.

Still further, Scripture adds that "God's grace was upon him." These words signify Jesus' spiritual growth. In childhood Jesus' spiritual growth was supernormal because God's grace was upon Him. He knew and experienced the grace of God. So that we can say that in one sense Jesus was a normal child, but that in another sense His spiritual growth was supernormal.

I have sometimes wondered about Mary and Joseph. She had been told by the angel that the child she was to give birth to would be "the holy thing, and called the Son of God." She witnessed the shepherds come and worship the infant Jesus. She and Joseph later witnessed the Magi come and worship Jesus as the King of kings and the Lord of lords. They thus knew that this child of theirs was different and represented a sacred trust that had been given into their hands. How they must have been before God most intently—asking wisdom from Him for bringing up this unusual Child. Mary kept what she heard and saw in her mind and pondered those things in her heart. I wonder if sometimes she could not restrain herself and would blurt out something to the Child of what she had observed and pondered upon.

Of one thing I am certain, that Joseph and Mary brought up the child Jesus normally and in the admonition and discipline of God (cf. Ephesians 6:4b). In other words, they did not treat him any differently because He was the Holy Child of God; on the contrary, I believe they treated Him just as they would treat their other children later on. They did not show Him any special favor; indeed, from reading the history of this family, we can understand such impartial treatment towards all their children. In fact, they probably did not even tell Jesus as He was growing up that He was different from other children by saying to Him for example: "You are God become Man." I do not believe they ever said anything like that to Him. Rather than spoil Him they brought Him up as He should have been brought up. And I thank God for that.

Now as the Christ-Child grew, growing physically stronger and increasing in wisdom, no doubt a consciousness began to develop within Him to the effect that He sensed there was a relationship between God and himself—a divine Father-and-Son relationship. He may not have come into a full consciousness of this relationship all at once, but I do believe that as Jesus grew, the conscious awareness that He came from the Father began to grow stronger and stronger in Him until He arrived at a crisic moment in His young life, and which came on the day of His Bar Mitzvah.

Jesus' Age-Twelve Temple Experience: This Is My Father's House

According to the law of Moses every man of the Israelites had to travel to the Jerusalem temple three times a year to worship God: on the day of Passover or Unleavened Bread, on the day of Pentecost or the Harvest of First Fruits, and on the day of Tabernacles or Ingathering (see Exodus 23:15-17, Deuteronomy 16:16). It was not required of the women, but later on, the Rabbinical School of Hillel taught that a godly woman of Israel must go to Jerusalem at least once annually on the day of Passover. The children had no legal obligation to observe these feasts until they reached the age of twelve. They then had a legal obligation to keep all the religious statutes and ceremonies, and they would also be held accountable for engaging in these observances.

Now when the boy Jesus was twelve years old, His parents as usual went up to Jerusalem to keep the Passover, but this time Jesus went with them. It is not known whether this was the first time that He knowingly went to Jerusalem. Of course, when as an infant He was presented by His parents, Jesus was in the Jerusalem temple, but He knew nothing about it. Most probably, therefore, this current occasion was the first time of which Jesus was aware. Here, then, was a young Jewish lad who all the years previously had been instructed in his home in the law of God, and now at the age of twelve, He was going up to Jerusalem to receive His Bar Mitzvah—that is to say, to be made a son of the law. Formerly, His parents were responsible for His religious education, but now He was to be responsible himself before God because He was to become a full member of the synagogue and a full member of the commonwealth of

Israel. For the first time He was going to Jerusalem to the holy temple to be made a son of the law: He would now have the right to vote; He would now have the obligation to answer questions and the privilege to ask them; He himself would henceforth be entirely responsible spiritually before God. It was a tremendous crisis for any Jewish boy of that day, but how much greater in its meaning it was for the boy Jesus!

It needs to be understood that though the period of the Passover observance extended over the seven days set aside for the celebration of the Feast of Unleavened Bread, back then many Jews who would travel to Jerusalem to keep Passover ended up not staying for the entire length of the Feast. Instead, after the first few days they would leave and return home. Most likely, therefore, this was what happened with the parents of Jesus: They departed for home after only the initial days of the Passover Feast. It needs to be further understood that according to the custom of that time, when the Jews traveled, they usually did so in groups; the men would be together, the women would be together, and the children would be together. So that during their traveling days together in such fashion, it was only when each evening came and the people would be settling down for the night that each entire family would be together. Quite naturally, therefore, when Mary and Joseph left Jerusalem on their return journey home, they assumed that Jesus had left with them and the other returning families, and that He was traveling with the other boys as would normally be the case. Hence, during their first day's journey out from Jerusalem, Jesus' parents did not bother themselves about Him. But when evening came, they could not find Him with His relations and acquaintances, and thus they were quite worried. So they returned to Jerusalem; and only after searching everywhere for three days did they finally find Jesus—they found Him in the temple!

There this young lad was sitting among the rabbis, the doctors and the teachers of the law. He was listening to them and answering their questions and raising questions of His own. At one's Bar Mitzvah a Jewish boy was supposed to recite by memory certain passages of Scripture, and he would be questioned by the religious leaders and the doctors about what he had learned. Then the boy could also raise some questions which had arisen in his mind during his training time at home. From Luke's description we can readily visualize the boy Jesus sitting among those various grownups and listening to them. Thank God, He was *listening first* and not asking first, as boys would usually do impulsively. There He was, listening to His elders, answering them when called upon to do so, and inquiring of them.

Now when His parents saw and heard all this, they were amazed; but so, too, the other people present who heard His answers were amazed at His understanding. Then, regaining her composure, Mary said to Jesus: "Child, why have You dealt with us this way? In great distress Your father and I sought after you everywhere." But the boy Jesus said in response: "Why did you have to seek after Me anywhere? Did you not know that I must be occupied with My Father's business? Nevertheless, if you had to seek Me, you did not need to do so elsewhere; you should have come straight here to the temple. For did you not know that I must be in the house of God? Why is it that you sought Me everywhere else and only at the very last, after three days, did you come to the temple? Did you not know that I must be in My Father's house and occupied with My Father's business?"

For the first time in his life this Jewish boy was coming to the temple in Jerusalem, but this lad was no ordinary boy. An ordinary boy would be attracted by the ornaments, by the gold, by the beautiful structure, and by all the ceremonies taking place. Any ordinary boy would be stirred to his depths by witnessing such things, but for the boy Jesus, this event meant much more than all that. For there came to Him at this very time a most unusual sense: "This is My Father's house." For Him, to be made a son of the law was more than simply to be brought into relationship with the law of God. There was also, at this very same time, the opening up within His entire consciousness of an awareness that He is the Son of God: God is His Father, and there is an inner relationship which He the Son has with Him. It was not only a relationship He has externally with the law of God, but there was also an inward relationship He has with the One who *gave* the law—His Father. There was now not only the fear or reverence of the Lord, there was also the love of the Lord. For the boy Jesus, the temple was more than merely gold, precious stones, and beautiful architecture; this temple was His Father's house. And since this is where the Father lives, therefore, this is where He the Son must also live.

It was because of this profound awareness which came to the twelve-year old Jesus on this critical occasion in His young life which accounts for this boy's remarkable response to His mother's complaint and inquiry: "Did you not know that I must be in My Father's house? Where else should I be? Why did you go elsewhere in trying to find Me? This here is My place, even the Father's house. Why, then, are you surprised and amazed? Did you not know that I must be about My Father's business?"

At the time of His Bar Mitzvah Jesus awakened to a full consciousness of His relationship with His Father. He now knew with great clarity and certainty that God was His Father. He now knew that He as the Son was sent into this world to do His Father's business, and there and then, He purposed in His heart that He must be occupied with His Father's business. Other people and their boys could go to their homes but, for Him, this temple was His home. Other people could be occupied with many other things but His only occupation was the Father's business. He could not engage in His own or other people's business; He could only be occupied with His Father's business. And at this particular time His Father's business was for Him to sit before those rabbis and teachers in the temple in order to learn more of the law and the will of His Father.

Indeed, at this very time Jesus now purposed in His heart that this was what His life was to be occupied with. And on that His heart was set and fixed; yet He needed to know more of His Father's business: He needed to learn more of the lessons His Father had in store for Him: He needed more preparation in order to fulfill His Father's business. So that at the moment when His parents finally found Him, the Father's will was for Him to know more of the law of God; so there He was seated in the temple among those who knew the law. But being a minor, not fully grown yet, He had a responsibility and duty towards His parents. Hence, after having said what He said to them in the Jerusalem temple, the boy Jesus dutifully returned home with His parents and was in subjection and obedience to them; and *that* was the will of God—even the Father's business—for Him at that moment. Continuing to be in subjection to His parents was the further training which He had to experience. Yes, on the one hand, the young Jesus had sensed in the temple that the Father's business was for Him to learn more of His law from the rabbis; on the other hand, He had also realized that His Father's business was for Him, as still a minor, to return home and be in subjection to His parents. So that when He did return home and submitted himself to His parents, He must have done so with a different attitude—that He was now submitting to His parents as unto God His Father.

Let me pause here and direct a few words to the children and youngsters in our midst. We read in God's word that "children ought to obey their parents in all things, for this pleases the Lord" (see Colossians 3:20). Your business as minors is to do the Father's will, and if it is His will at this moment for you to be in subjection to your parents, and if you obey them, then you are doing your Father's business. Otherwise, you are not.

Most likely the Lord Jesus while growing up was in subjection to His parents for some eighteen years, and Joseph probably had soon afterwards died at an early age, since the Bible does not mention him anymore. Being the firstborn son of the family, Jesus had to take up the family responsibility, and so He now became the carpenter in Joseph's place. And that itself was doing the Father's will. That was part of the Father's business for Jesus at that period in His life. Indeed, that was part of the training and further preparation which His Father had in store for His Son. And hence, it was not a waste of time. Only after He was thirty years old did Jesus step out into His Father's business for His life—which was to save the lost and to build the church.

As Christ Is, So Are We in This World

I John 4 declares: "As he is, so also are we in this world" (see v.17b). This is a basic principle of Christian living. As Christ is, so are we in this world. How? It is not because we can imitate Him, for nobody can do that. It is because the Lord Jesus has given His life to us. The very life with which He lived on this earth is now your life and my life. Let us bear this in mind that when we were saved, not only were our sins forgiven but we also received a new life, and that life is that of the Lord Jesus. It is a divine-human life—a divine life which has come into humanity—and we have this very life in us. And because this life is in us, we must live in this world as He lived. Anything other than that, anything less than that, is not Christian living.

Let me say again that it is not that we by our natural life take Jesus as our example and try to imitate Him. For the more we try the more we find ourselves far, far away from Him because such attempt is an impossible undertaking. But thank God, we have been given the very life of Christ which was once lived out on this earth some two thousand years ago and which is going to be lived out today in you and in me in the exact same manner, since Christ's life cannot live otherwise. If it is otherwise being lived out in us, it is not the Christ-life but is our natural life.

Because you have this Christ-life in you, is it any wonder that you sense growing within you a consciousness that you are different from the people of the world? You are a child of God who has been born of the Spirit and thus God is your Father. Is there thus an ever-growing consciousness within you that you are different and cannot be like the people of the world? Yes, you are a normal human being, but you are a supernaturally normal human being. And because of that, this awareness of your relationship with God as His child must increase to a point when you realize you are not your own; you have been bought with a costly price (I Corinthians 6:19b-20a)—even the spilled blood of God's Son. You have therefore not been saved for yourself but for God. Hence, you have business on this earth which is different from that of the people of the world. Moreover, this business with which you must be occupied is different from any other business on earth. Other people—perhaps even other Christian people—may be occupied with various other things, yet there is but one thing with which you must be occupied, and that is your Father's business. Indeed, that is to be the purpose of your life. And as was true in Jesus' life, that ever-growing consciousness will one day come to a moment of crisis; and when that occurs, it is time for you to present your body to God as a living sacrifice (Romans 12:1a).

What Occupies You?

Has that moment arrived in your Christian walk when you begin to realize you cannot any longer live your own life? The realization has finally dawned upon you that you cannot continue to do things as other people do. You cannot plan to have your own future because you are the Lord's and have been sent into this world for just one thing—to do your Father's business. All people need to be occupied with something. If you and I are not occupied with this thing over here, we will be occupied with that thing over there. I would therefore ask: What occupies you, demands your time, your energy, your life? With what are you occupied today? Has it ever occurred to you, as it did to the Lord Jesus when He was twelve years old, that "I must be occupied with my Father's business"? In other words, have you purposed that purpose in your heart?

Let us recall the teenager Daniel, who had been taken to the Babylonian court and was to be brought up to stand before the greatest monarch in the world of that day; yet he purposed in his heart not to be defiled but to keep himself pure for God (Daniel 1:8).

Because we have within us this awareness that we are God's—that we belong to our Father—is it not time for us to purpose in our hearts, "From now on, we will be occupied with our Father's business"? Do you have such a purpose? If you do not, your life will be a waste. No matter what you otherwise accomplish, your life will end up a waste.

So what occupies your heart? Jesus warned: "Take heed, lest your heart be ensnared by dissipation, drunkenness, anxieties of this life" (see Luke 21:34). In other words, your heart can be occupied with the Father and His business, or your heart can be occupied with something else. What occupies your heart?

What occupies your mind? What are you thinking about day and night? Is it the Father's business or your own business? What consumes all your energy and all your time? What are you here for? Like Jesus, we must be occupied with the Father's business.

The Unfolding of the Father's Business to Jesus—and to Us

As a help to us, let us observe how the Father's business was gradually unfolded to the boy—and later to the maturing—

Jesus. It began to be unfolded to Him when at age twelve He was in the Jerusalem temple. It was unfolded to Him again when He went home and was in subjection to His parents. It was further unfolded to Him when He had to assume responsibility for the family after the death of Joseph. It was unfolded to Him still further when much later He was about thirty years old. Let us see that every unfolding in Jesus' life was not only a period of training and preparation but was also a part of the Father's business. Nothing was a loss but everything was a gain in the accomplishing of the Father's business.

I believe this is to be the same with us. I Corinthians 7:20 instructs us as follows: "Let each abide in that calling in which he has been called." I would take this to mean that when you are called, you are to abide in that calling until God unfolds to you something else. If you are called when you are a student, then purpose in your heart that you are to be occupied with your Father's business, but continue to study. In this connection, when I myself was called, I was in high school. I immediately wanted to quit school and thought it would be a waste of time to continue and then go on to college. Thank God, He overruled. Oftentimes, when a young man or young woman or a teenager is touched by the love of God and called, he or she wishes to leave everything, including one's studies. Their attitude is: What is the use of studying? Since this world is soon passing away, let me go off and be involved totally in God's work. Yet such ones do not even know what God's work is for their life. They need to listen and ask questions. They need to learn more of the ways and the will of God.

Yes, you may be called, but you may still be a minor living with your parents under their roof and care. Nevertheless, purpose in your heart to be occupied with the Father's business. What, though, is the Father's business for you *at that moment*?

It is to be in subjection to your parents. There is sometimes the temptation among Christian young people who are still minors and have purposed in their hearts to be occupied with the Father's business to look down upon their earthly parents. Young people should never do that. In whatever place you are when called, abide in it until the Lord unfolds to you something else. But while you are in that place, do all as to God himself. If, for example, you are a student and are studying with the attitude and purpose of doing so as to the Father, you are in the Father's business. Otherwise, you are studying for your own sake. If you work with the purpose of doing the Father's business, then it is indeed the Father's business; otherwise, it is your business. It may be that in His unfolding His will, God is preparing you at this time for that later life-work in His Father's business; or it may be that this current unfolding is in itself what the Father's business is for you to do for the rest of your lifetime. Yet you may not presently know; nevertheless, one thing is certain: that a priority must be set in your heart of wanting to be occupied with the Father's business.

What Essentially Is the Father's Business?

When the boy Jesus at age twelve was in the Jerusalem temple, His parents departed for home, but He had remained behind in the temple because, as He himself explained, "I must be about My Father's business." The New International Version has translated Jesus' statement as, "I must be in My Father's house." In either case, it is clear that Jesus felt compelled to be engaged in the things of God. Some other Bible versions have Jesus saying, "I must be in the house of God." Strictly speaking, therefore, the Father's business is none other than His house. Is it not that which has continually occupied the heavenly Father from the beginning? In the beginning He had wanted to build a house for himself and for mankind. He has always desired to dwell among man; and hence, that is still His work and His business despite Adam's sin. The Father's mind did not change in the least because of Adam's failure.

God desires to build a home for himself and for us—yet not a physical one but a spiritual one. Let us recall how God met the fleeing Jacob who had fled for his life from his house because there was no place for him anymore in his father Isaac's house. God chased after him, met him in the wilderness, and promised to build Jacob a house; and Jacob in turn promised to build God a house. And we know that God eventually transformed Jacob into Israel (see Genesis 28:20-22).

Then, when God delivered the children of Israel out of Egypt, He led them to Mt. Sinai and confided to them His heart—that He wanted to dwell among them by instructing them to build a tabernacle (see Exodus 25:8). That, of course, was just a type or shadow of what was to come.

Then, Solomon built a temple, but that, too, was only a shadow of what the Father has really been occupied with from the beginning. But then, too, with what was the Son occupied when He was on earth? He announced: "I will build My church, and the gates of hades will not prevail against it" (see Matthew 16:18b).

So what essentially is the Father's business? The Father's business at its core is related to the temple—that is to say, to the Father's house. We ourselves are God's house if we persevere in faith and in the boldness of our confidence in Christ Jesus (see Hebrews 3:6). Hence, the Father's business is that we Christians are all to be occupied—as was

Jesus—in the building of God's house. Each of us is a part of that house, and all of us are to contribute to the building up of that house.

Does it ever occur to you that when you gather to meet with other Christians you are not *going to church* but you are being built up together *as the church*? What a difference! Many people go to church, but in their minds that is a going to a physical building. But if you have the attitude of coming together to be built up together in love as the church—as the house of God—then you are occupied with and doing the Father's business. Whether you are at school, on the street, at home, in the office, or on the mission field, wherever you are and whatever you are doing, remember, you must continually be occupied with the Father's house. Let each of us ask of ourselves: Will what I am doing contribute to the building of God's house? Will whatever I do, say, think, or express attitudinally build up God's house or will it destroy God's house? Is each of us occupied with the Father's business? If so, we will have experienced our own personal Bar Mitzvah. May the Lord help us all.

Chapter Four

His Baptism

Luke 2:52—And Jesus advanced in wisdom and stature, and in favour with God and men.

Matthew 3:13-17—Then comes Jesus from Galilee to the Jordan to John, to be baptised of him; but John urgently forbad him, saying, I have need to be baptised of thee; and comest thou to me? But Jesus answering said to him, Suffer it now; for thus it becometh us to fulfil all righteousness. Then he suffers him. And Jesus, having been baptised, went up straightway from the water, and lo, the heavens were opened to him, and he saw the Spirit of God descending as a dove, and coming upon him: and behold, a voice out of the heavens saying, This is my beloved Son, in whom I have found my delight.

The Formative Years

For the past several weeks we have been fellowshiping together on the life of the Lord Jesus. As we today consider His baptism we shall see that *His* baptism was different from all other baptisms. But before we direct our attention to His baptism, we need to focus in upon that period of Jesus' life from ages thirteen to thirty. Those eighteen years were formative in character. The growth of a child from birth to twelve years of age is more or less the responsibility of his parents, whereas the child's responsibility is to obey his parents; otherwise, all the responsibility for the child's growth will fall upon the shoulders of the parents. The years from age thirteen to age thirty have rightly been described as formative in character because as a child grows further, the responsibility for his growth begins to shift from the parents to himself. Which is to say that the child begins to exercise his own will; he becomes more and more independent. In addition, he is trying to discover his own self, his identity—indeed, who he is; in short, he is eventually to be on his own. That does not mean that his parents are no longer involved in watching, caring, and guiding; nevertheless, the main responsibility for the growing-up child begins to shift away from his parents to himself. These are the adolescent years in any youngster's life, and hence they are very important years. As a matter of fact, the future of that person depends mainly upon what occurs during these formative years and their outcome.

The Lord Jesus, being a perfect man, was born as a babe, grew up as a child, and entered upon His formative years. These thus being very important years for Jesus, it is most surprising, even strange, to learn that the Scriptures are almost entirely silent on this formative period in the life of the maturing Jesus. Indeed, there is but one verse that tells us of what happened during these eighteen years. It is found in Luke 2:52: "And Jesus advanced in wisdom and stature, and in favour with God and men." Is this near silence in Scripture because those years are unimportant? Is that the reason the Bible appears to ignore those years? Or is it because those years were a hidden period in this youth's life and that their history is so sacred that it cannot be recorded? Outwardly, what is visible is that the adolescent Jesus definitely continued to grow, to mature, and to advance in wisdom.

We know, of course, that in God's providence the young Jesus grew up during those important years of His life in the out-of-the-way hilly area of Nazareth. There was a strongly negative proverb bandied about at that time which declared: "Can anything good come out of Nazareth?" (John 1:46a) This particular town of Galilee was such an isolated, out-of-the-way place that it was assumed that nothing good could ever come out of it. However, in God's providence the Lord Jesus was placed by God in that isolated hilly town. Moreover, Jesus was never to attend any rabbinical school so as to be academically trained properly in the Judaic law. In fact, all His learning about Jewish law and about God was acquired from the holy letters of Scripture. In other words, Jesus was not taught by man. In this very regard we are reminded of what Paul wrote to Timothy: that from his childhood Timothy knew only the holy Scriptures that nonetheless made him wise unto salvation (II Timothy 3:15).

The young Jesus certainly advanced in wisdom, yet the wisdom He acquired was not of this world nor taught by this world nor even taught by the religious world—that is, by the rabbis. Rather, He was taught by God (John 7:16-17) and through the sacred letters of Scripture (cf. Luke 24:27, 44; John 5:39b). To put it another way, it was the wisdom that is from above and which in its nature is first pure, then peaceful, gentle, yielding, full of mercy and good fruits, impartial and sincere (James 3:17). Such was the wisdom which the Lord Jesus acquired when growing up; and He grew in *that* wisdom day after day.

People could see that Jesus not only advanced in wisdom but also advanced in stature; which is to say that He continued to grow physically. I believe that the Lord Jesus had a well-built physical body, about which He was not negligent. Although He did not live a life of luxury, I believe that His parents provided Him with sufficient food to fulfill all the needs for His body. So Jesus advanced in stature, and this the people could readily observe.

The Lord Jesus advanced as well "in favour with God and men." Jesus found favor with God many times over because He was a God-pleaser, not a man-pleaser. He was constantly intent on pleasing God the Father in His daily life (John 5:30c, 8:29b). Indeed, it was quite evident to the people that He was in favor with God and with man because during those formative years a godly character was being developed in Him, and people could not help but notice it.

Yet let us take note that all these positive traits in Jesus were visible things, but what was not visible in Him is not recorded; nevertheless, it is a truism of life that the *in*visible is that which makes the visible. Hence, the secret behind the visible lies in the invisible. It could therefore be said that the manifestation of a godly character outwardly in the youthful Jesus meant that godliness had first been developed inwardly in Him.

Evidently further, during these same formative years in Jesus' life He was being trained by His earthly father Joseph to be a carpenter. In fact, He was described in the Scriptures as being the son of a carpenter (Matthew 13:55); and later on He was even called *the* carpenter (Mark 6:3a), most likely after Joseph had passed away. We can thus imagine that in the process of learning carpentry Jesus did so with all His heart; and because of that, He became the master carpenter of Nazareth. Everything He set His hands to do, in fact, was qualitatively the best.

But besides His daily hours of labor, what did Jesus do with the remaining time each day? I am of the opinion that after He had finished His hours of heavy labor, He most probably climbed one of the surrounding hills and there He would have daily communion with His heavenly Father. And during these times of communion, Jesus the Son learned to know the will of His Father more and more. He also learned to deny himself, even that holy self of His. In addition, He learned the discipline of the heavenly Father in His daily life—unknown to man but certainly known to God His Father.

Furthermore, during these hidden hours, days, and years the maturing Jesus—ever observant of nature all around Him—learned to see the loving care of the Father for the birds of the air and learned to see the beauty of God's creativity in the lilies of the field (Matthew 6:26, 28-29). Moreover, the various Gospel accounts of His life are replete with evidence of the fact that nothing, it seems, escaped Jesus' observation concerning all aspects of Jewish life, culture and manners of His day. As a matter of fact, His awareness and understanding of all these matters are readily reflected in what the Lord Jesus would much later share in His public and private teaching as a result of what He continually observed and learned during all these formative but hidden years at Nazareth. Unknown to man because He was hidden away in the backwater community of Nazareth, the world neither knew Him nor took any notice of Him, and yet the maturing Jesus was well known by His heavenly Father. These hidden years constituted a very significant period in Jesus' life which the Father used to build Him up so as to arrive at what he was to be and do in ministering to both God and man during His later years.

I well recall our dear brother Watchman Nee telling us on one occasion that all our principal spiritual lessons are learned by the time we are thirty. In other words, after we turn thirty in age we have no more *new* lessons to learn; for the lessons we will have learned before age thirty will later simply be *deepened*, with no new lessons to be learned. All lessons must be learned during those highly important formative years before we reach age thirty.

As was indicated earlier, physically speaking, the years from thirteen to thirty are quite formative in nature. What you become afterwards depends very much upon these critical years. Outward developments of yours are obviously visible to others: you are physically growing up, you are also trying to absorb all the knowledge that you can, you additionally are beginning to exert your independence, and you are associating with various other people much of the time; but your inward development for the most part is invisible to others; in fact, you find yourself very much alone. You probably even have the feeling that nobody really knows you: perhaps even your parents do not know you anymore. In short, there is a secret part of your life developing during this formative period, and if early on you have become a Christian and that secret life of yours has its proper relationship with God, there will definitely be inward spiritual growth.

On the one hand, therefore, there will be outward growth and many activities, achievements, and other events happening all around you; you may even be involved in so-called Christian activities. And so, people can see and know what is going on on your outside. On the other hand, they cannot know what is occurring on your inside. You may sometimes even wonder if you yourself know: you are often very much alone, and possibly even feeling lonely. So these are important years in your life, even dangerous years—in that, what occurs during this period could well determine whether your future path will be good or bad for you. If you have a real living relationship with God, you will begin to discern that during these hidden years there has been a godly character gradually being built up in you that will set a good, positive course for your future, just as was the case with the young man Jesus who advanced in wisdom and stature and in favor with God and men. But if you do *not* have a living relationship with God, you will be adversely influenced and molded by the world; indeed, you will become a victim of your circumstances—many, perhaps, of even your own making—and all of which will determine your future course negatively. Hence, it cannot be over-emphasized that these formative years are very, very significant for any person who is in the process of growing up and maturing.

Before proceeding further, however, let me pause briefly in order that we may apply all the foregoing observations to ourselves in a more direct way spiritually. When we are first born again, we are babes in Christ (cf. I Corinthians 3:1b). We go through a period of babyhood, and we have to be fed with the milk of God's word (cf. I Corinthians 3:2). Other Christian brothers and sisters have to nurture and take care of us, and if they do not do as we wish, we may cry, we may even shout and kick (cf. Hebrews 12:11a). Now we are allowed to behave this way when we are babes in the faith; for such behavior is willingly tolerated by others. But we cannot remain a babe in Christ forever: we must grow, and as we begin to do so we realize we must take up spiritual responsibility: we cannot depend upon our Christian brethren all the time. It is quite true that those brethren in Christ who are more advanced than we are are to still keep a caring eye on us; they are to still try to help us; but, gradually, we discover that we will need to be responsible for our spiritual life ourselves.

Moreover, during this same formative period you will probably be active outwardly. Yet it needs to be asked: Do you have a hidden life with God? That is the most critical factor here. If you are without a hidden life with Him and you try to be an active Christian just to be outwardly visible, sooner or later you will be found out. You will not be able to stand, and when life's circumstances change, you will change accordingly. But if during this adolescent period you do in fact cultivate a secret life with God, then you will grow into spiritual maturity. To sum up, therefore, these formative years are very, very critical, for they make you what you will be later on.

The life of the Lord Jesus from age thirteen to age thirty was completely hidden from the world, but it was known to the heavenly Father. Throughout those years He learned all the lessons He had to learn before He stepped out into the public arena. But after the Lord did step forth into public ministry, He was equipped to use the many illustrations gleaned from both nature and human life that He had observed all around Him, and these illustrations were the very lessons He had learned during all those hidden years of His.

At one point in Jesus' public life He was heard to say twice: "My time has not yet come" (John 7:6a, 8b). When and how did He learn God the Father's timing for His life? It was during those formative years, for let us recall that when He was twelve years old, this young lad had purposed in His heart to be occupied with His Father's business and so He stayed behind in the temple to learn more of the law of God (Luke 2:46, 49b). Yet, He soon afterwards had to return home and be obedient to His parents (Luke 2:51) because God's timing had not yet come for Him to fulfill in His life the Father's business. He had to spend eighteen long years more waiting for God's timing.

If we sense that God has called us, we too often want to plunge right away into so-called ministry. We cannot wait; our flesh is impatient. But the Lord Jesus learned the timing of His Father during those formative years of His. Besides the aforementioned "timing" statement He also said this: "I cannot do anything of Myself" (see John 5:19a, 30a). When did Jesus learn such a lesson? It was certainly not after he started to work; rather, it was during those days, months and years of preparation that He learned He could not do anything on His own, but that only what He saw the Father doing did He ever undertake to do anything (John 5:19b). He further said this: "I cannot say anything on my own accord" (see John 12:49a, 14:10b, 24b). When did Jesus learn that lesson? Surely, it was not when He began to talk, preach or teach, but it was when He was experiencing those hidden preparatory years of His. He learned not to say anything except first to hear what the Father had to say, and then He spoke it forth (John 8:28b; 12:49b, 50b; 14:10b, 24b). Hence, whether it was some aspect of Jesus' life or ministry, all the preparations for much later manifesting these behaviors, attitudes and undertakings were made during the time of those hidden years of spiritual maturation. These formative hidden years were very important ones for the Lord Jesus, and I would therefore hasten to impress upon all young brothers and sisters who currently find themselves in their formative years to cultivate a hidden life with the Father. That is the key. Without it the Christian's life will be a spiritual failure, no matter how successful it may be in the eyes of the world. But *with* such a hidden experience one's life will be a success in the eyes of God.

Jesus spent eighteen hidden years as preparation, and when He arrived at the age of thirty, He stepped out into the public sphere at last. Yet it is thought by Bible scholars that well prior to that moment His earthly father Joseph had died early, and from the human standpoint Jesus, being the eldest son, had to take up the responsibility of now being the new family head. Consequently, He could not enter upon the ministry which God had called Him to before He was thirty. He had to take care of the family until His half-blood siblings had grown up, and only then was He thus freed from His family duty.

Let us note that during Old Testament times a priest, when he reached the age of thirty, became a full-fledged servant of God (see Numbers 4:3). So that is most likely another reason why Jesus was thirty when he began His public ministry. We Chinese have a proverb which says that upon reaching thirty years of age you are firmly established. In other words, before you arrive at age thirty, you are not fully settled in life yet; therefore, you are not really ready to enter upon your life's work or career; but once you are thirty, then you are completely established and prepared to do so.

The Call to Repent

Now when Jesus was about thirty years old (Luke 3:23a), the time had come for Him to be manifested and to appear before the public; and He commenced His public manifestation by being baptized. But as was noted in the very first message in this series on the life of the Lord Jesus, His ministry was immediately preceded by that of John the Baptist, which was a ministry of repentance. It would be well, therefore, to pause briefly here and review in summary fashion what in part was shared earlier concerning John's call to the Jewish nation to repent and which thus would pave the way for the soon-coming of the kingdom of the heavens.

At the outset it is quite interesting to note that John would commence his own ministry to which God had called him to undertake when he, like Jesus, was thirty years old; for he was only six months older than the Lord when he became the forerunner of Christ. We will recall that John emerged from the wilderness as a voice urgently crying, "Repent, for the kingdom of the heavens has drawn nigh" (Matthew 3:2). That voice electrified the whole nation, and people began flocking to the wilderness to hear him. And many received his baptism of repentance (Matthew 3:5-6).

In the economy or administration of God He had ordained that at this particular time the nation of Israel should repent. Outwardly speaking, the remnant of the children of Israel had returned from Babylonian captivity and had rebuilt the city and temple; they had restored the priesthood; and everything seemed to be able to continue on as usual for hundreds of years—in fact, for the four centuries from the end of the Old Testament period to the beginning of the New. And during those centuries the Israelites were considered a very religious people, with the world looking upon Judaism as one of the purest religions on earth. As a consequence, even a number of Gentiles became proselytes or half-proselytes because they admired the purity of the Jewish religion.

The Jews themselves, of course, took great pride in their religion, as well as in the beautiful temple they had, in the elaborate priestly ceremonies and rituals they performed; and, not least, they also had the word of the one true God with them. It was but natural, therefore, that they, too, considered themselves to be a highly religious people. In God's eyes, however, they were just as sinful as the rest of the world. Hence it was that before Messiah Jesus came forth, God sent John as the forerunner to turn the people back to himself—that is to say, to call them to repent. Yet, they were not just to repent of their evil deeds but also to repent of their self-righteousness. They were not only to repent of their sins of commission but also to repent of their sins of omission: that is, those things they should have done but had not done. They were not only to repent over what was wrong but likewise over what was missing.

To sum up, the people of Israel were not to repent just because of having sinned but also because the kingdom of the heavens was soon coming. In other words, they could not play at religion anymore. Their faith in God had to be real. They had to repent for the kingdom's sake, for when the King of the kingdom comes into their midst, they would have to confront Reality (see Luke 3:3-14).

Even the rabbi of Israel, Nicodemus—that noble, intelligent, moral, elderly man and a model of the truly spiritual man in the eyes of the Jews—thought that he was almost within the kingdom's gates. So, being somewhat confused by Jesus' ministry, he came to the Lord Jesus in the night. He was humble enough to come to Jesus and inquire as follows: "What must I do? Is there anything more that I must do in order that I may enter the kingdom of God?" And the Lord had answered: "Truly, truly, I say to you, except you are born from above, you cannot even see, much less enter, the kingdom of God. Currently you are unqualified" (see John 3:1ff.). Thus implying that no one in the whole nation of Israel was fit for the kingdom of God. They had to repent of their religion, their self-righteousness, and all else that was wrong with them; but in order to do that, they had to receive the baptism of John.

The Baptism of John

Why was baptism necessary? Simply because baptism—symbolizing as it does the death, burial, and resurrection of a person—is most thorough in its meaning. In other words, repentance is to be so thorough that the entire being goes into death. There is to be nothing good in the person that remains, nothing good in oneself to hold on to. In short, everything must be repented of—one's goodness as well as one's badness. The whole being must go into death, be buried out of sight, and then come out onto resurrection ground in newness of life. Baptism is as drastic as *that* (cf. Romans 6). And such was the baptism of John.

Many Pharisees came to John, wanting to be baptized (cf. Matthew 3:7 with Luke 3:7), yet not because they repented but because they merely wished to exhibit before men their righteousness. So John the Baptist warned them: "You need to repent and demonstrate its reality by exhibiting fruits of true repentance; otherwise, your coming to me for baptism will not help you in the least." Many publicans and other sinners, however, really did repent and gladly received the baptism of John, but the Pharisees and the scribes in the end rejected his baptism; they thought they were too good for that (see Matthew 3:4-10, Luke 3:3-9).

Eventually, and according to His Father's timing, the Lord Jesus himself came to John the Baptist to be baptized, but when John saw Him coming to him, his reaction was one of amazement and perplexity; for he said to Jesus: "I need to be baptized by You. How is it, then, that You are coming to me to be baptized?" (see Matthew 3:13) Humanly speaking, these two were cousins, but probably they had seldom, if ever, seen each other because John the Baptist had grown up in the wilderness whereas Jesus had grown up in distant Galilee in the hilly area of Nazareth. So it is not known whether or not they had ever met, and even had they met, such interaction had probably been at most casual in nature. Hence, it would appear that they really did not know each other, or if they did, their knowledge of each other was not that great, even though they may have heard of each other.

Nevertheless, when Jesus came to John the Baptist, John became conscious that here was a man who was perfect, a man who did not need to repent; therefore, there was no need for Jesus to be baptized. On the contrary, in standing before that Man, John immediately realized that he himself needed to be baptized—and to be baptized by Jesus. John had had no such reaction when baptizing other people, but when he stood before *this* Man, he realized *he* needed to repent and be baptized. The very presence and holy character of the Lord Jesus immediately touched John the Baptist because he—John—was a person who from his birth had been filled with the Holy Spirit (Luke 1:15c); so he quite naturally responded to God's presence in the Person of God's Son (cf. John 1:34). Yet, the Lord Jesus in response was moved to say: "Permit it to be done for you and me for righteousness' sake" (Matthew 3:15).

What is the meaning of Jesus' phrase, "for righteousness' sake"? To put it most simply, it means to be right with God. At different times God brings into view what is called in Scripture "present truth" (II Peter 1:12). The truth of God is eternal, but at certain periods in man's history one particular truth is especially required or demanded by God of all people. And at this specific time period the truth which God especially required of the Jewish people was that of repentance—and the receiving of the baptism of repentance. That was now being required by God of every Israelite, and if and when they accepted that truth in practical experience, they were immediately reckoned as righteous before God. But if they did not accept that truth and experience it, then they were still deemed to be unrighteous and condemned before God.

Now John had come forth in the righteousness of God to perform upon those responsive Israelites the baptism of repentance, and the Lord Jesus came to John and asked to be baptized in order to fulfill all righteousness. He himself had no need to repent; He was sinless—the only one among all of mankind who knew no sin. He therefore did not need to be baptized for himself; nevertheless, He came to John to be baptized in order to fulfill all righteousness. In other words, when he stepped forth to be baptized, He was offering himself as a sacrifice for the sin of the world. He came forward to be baptized not because of himself but because He offered himself as a substitute for the sin of the entire world—not just for the nation of Israel but for the rest of the world as well. In anticipation of Calvary's Cross Jesus took all the sin of the world upon himself, and then and there He repented for us and was baptized in our stead. This was fulfilling all righteousness because this that was done between these two men was the right thing in the sight of God—for John to baptize the Lord and for the Lord to be baptized by John. And because of this truth and this understanding, John agreed to baptize Jesus (Matthew 3:15b).

The Baptism of Jesus

Now we are told in Luke's and Matthew's Gospel accounts that when Jesus was being baptized and came up out of the water, and as He was praying, the heavens opened and the Holy Spirit descended as a dove upon Him and remained on Him. Then a voice came forth from the heavens which declared: "Thou art my beloved Son, in whom I have found my delight" (Luke 3:21-22, Matthew 3:16-17).

And John's Gospel reveals that John the Baptist testified as follows: "There is One among you who is greater than I am, but I did not know Him. But I was told by Him who sent me to baptize with water that when I see the Holy Spirit descending upon that Person and abiding upon Him, that is the One who will baptize with the Holy Spirit; and, furthermore, that One is the Son of God" (see John 1:32-34). And sometime after Jesus' baptism, John the Baptist saw Jesus coming towards him and testified: "Behold the Lamb of God, who takes away the sin of the world!" (John 1:29) It can therefore be said that when the Lord Jesus was baptized, He committed himself to the work of redemption as the Lamb of God.

Why did the Holy Spirit come down *as a dove*? This is because during the Old Testament period a dove was the sacrifice of a poor sinner: the sinner needed to offer a sacrifice to die in his stead and thus atone for his sin: and if the sinner was very poor and could not afford a bullock or even a lamb, he could offer up a pigeon or a dove (Leviticus 5:7). Hence, the Holy Spirit came upon the Lord as a dove because by the eternal Spirit He who was "poor in spirit" (Matthew 5:3) had offered himself to God as a sacrifice for the sin of the world. The heavens which prior to this moment had been closed to mankind were now torn open and God was so pleased that He was moved to announce: "This is My beloved Son, in whom I have found My delight" (see Mark 1:10-11). Such was the baptism of the Lord Jesus. His baptism commenced His ministry, and His crucifixion at Calvary concluded His ministry. Yet, even from before the foundation of the world, we are told in Scripture, Jesus was the Lamb slain (Revelation 13:8b AV, NIV); so in anticipation of actually being slain at Calvary, He was baptized, offering himself in type as the Lamb of God; and on Calvary's cross He actually died—and died as the Lamb of God that is able to take away the world's sin.

Let us be clear, however, that Jesus' baptism was different from all other baptisms. All the baptisms of the Jewish people at that time were of John. They received John's baptism because of their own sin and thus were baptized for their own sake. By contrast, the Lord Jesus received the baptism of John not for his own sake but for the sake of the Jewish nation and for that of the rest of the world. Let us also be clear that Jesus' baptism was different from the Christians' baptism, for the latter is not the baptism of John but is the believer's baptism that was commanded by the Lord Jesus himself: "Go to the world, preach the gospel, disciple all nations, baptizing them into the name of the Father, the Son, and the Holy Spirit; teaching them all things that I have enjoined you, and I will be with you to the end of the age" (see Matthew 28:19-20).

Accordingly, the baptism we Christians receive is the believer's baptism and not the baptism of John, which is the baptism of repentance. First, we do repent, but then we believe in the Lord Jesus, and then we are baptized as believers who are now identified with Jesus in His death, burial, and resurrection. Hence, our baptism is different from the Lord's. His baptism was actually redemptive in nature, in that He was baptized in our stead. In contrast to His baptism ours is testimonial in nature: a testifying that we have truly repented, have believed in the Lord Jesus, are no longer ours but who now belong to Him, and that because of such faith, we are being baptized unto Jesus as those who have died with Him, been buried with Him, and are now raised up with Him in newness of life (Romans 6:3-4). Such is our testimony, and this is the reason believers must be baptized.

From the above description, therefore, we realize that though our baptism as Christians is different from that of the Lord Jesus, there is nonetheless a basic truth which is common to both. For what is the meaning of baptism at its core? Baptism is nothing less than that which symbolizes one's death, burial, and resurrection. So that when a person goes down into the water, he as it were goes down into death; and when a person is covered over by the water, he as it were is buried out of sight;

and when a person comes up out of the water, he as it were is raised up from the dead to live again in the newness of Christ's life. That at its core is what baptism typifies. Hence, what goes down into death is a person's old self (Romans 6:6a); what is buried out of sight is that very person himself; and what comes up out of the water is the resurrected-ascended Christ in the person, for it is no longer I myself but it is Christ who lives in me (cf. Galatians 2:20). That is the basic meaning of baptism.

Ministry Begins with Baptism

Let us please note again that the Lord Jesus began His ministry with baptism. This is most important for us to understand. No one can begin to minister to God without that person having first gone through death, burial, and resurrection. Thus one's ministry begins with that most essential personal spiritual experience. Anyone who has not gone through death, burial, and resurrection will not have his ministry accepted by God. This is true not only today but was likewise true during the period of the Old Testament. Let us recall that famous occasion when a number of Reubenites and Levites had begun to murmur against God's servant Aaron (as well as against Moses) by saying: "Are we not also holy? Can we not minister to the Lord as does Aaron? Why should he be allowed to do all these services but we are not permitted?"

In response, Jehovah God said, "All right, I want you to get twelve rods, one for each tribe of Israel." Let us understand that rods are taken out of trees, so that whereas a tree is that which is living, a rod is something dead. God then instructed that the name of the leader of each tribe was to be written on each of the twelve rods, with Aaron's name having been written on the Levite rod, and that all the rods were to be placed within the veil before the ark—the presence of God—overnight in total darkness. Let us recall that on the next day it was discovered that overnight the rod of Aarron had not only sprouted and budded but had also blossomed forth and had even produced fruit. Such was the proof that Aaron's ministry had been accepted by God, for only his rod had become alive; the rest were therefore rejected (Numbers 16-17). Here we see that back then the same principle had been in operation—the principle of death, burial, and resurrection. Those dead rods had to go through death's darkness, be hidden away out of sight, and only that which was resurrected into new life could minister to God. And Jesus commenced His ministry to God the Father on the same basis: He first underwent baptism.

As was noted earlier, the Lord Jesus did not minister to God on the basis of His own wisdom, strength, experience, or power. Rather, He was willing to go into death, to let go of everything and be buried out of sight completely, and then He ministered in the resurrection power of God. And that is why His ministry was effective.

The same experience must be true with us. After we believe in the Lord Jesus we need to be baptized. And after being baptized we need to function in the house of God. But do we proceed in our functioning on the basis of the principle of baptism? Do we continually acknowledge that we are dead? If we still try to serve God with our old flesh, if we still want ourselves to be displayed instead of being buried out of sight, if we still attempt to function in our own power and not by the resurrection life of Christ, then in the sight of God such ministry will be deemed to be a disservice and not a service. Such so-called ministry will only corrupt the church and not build her up. We must therefore always bear in mind that our ministry to the Lord must always be undertaken on the foundation of our baptism. We must continually stand on the ground of death to ourselves, of our burial out of sight, and of our being raised up from death to walk in newness of life by the power of the Holy Spirit. It is on that ground alone that we can serve God.

May viewing the baptism of the Lord Jesus afresh today teach us a very important lesson in our service to God.

Chapter Five

THE TEMPTATION

Matthew 4:1-11—Then Jesus was carried up into the wilderness by the Spirit to be tempted of the devil: and having fasted forty days and forty nights, afterwards he hungered. And the tempter coming up to him said, If thou be Son of God, speak, that these stones may become loaves of bread. But he answering said, It is written, Man shall not live by bread alone, but by every word which goes out through God's mouth.

Then the devil takes him to the holy city, and sets him upon the edge of the temple, and says to him, If thou be Son of God cast thyself down; for it is written, He shall give charge to his angels concerning thee, and on their hands shall they bear thee, lest in anywise thou strike thy foot against a stone. Jesus said to him, It is again written, Thou shalt not tempt the Lord thy God.

Again the devil takes him to a very high mountain, and shews him all the kingdoms of the world, and their glory, and says to him, All these things will I give thee if, falling down, thou wilt do me homage. Then says Jesus to him, Get thee away, Satan, for it is written, Thou shalt do homage to the Lord thy God, and him alone shalt thou serve.

Then the devil leaves him, and behold, angels came and ministered to him.

We have been considering together these days the life of the Lord Jesus. There are many voices being sounded and many visions being projected in our day. It is therefore very important that we not be distracted from *the* voice and *the* vision which God desires us to hear and to see. And the Bible's response to such a challenge is for us to "look off to Jesus, the author and finisher of our faith" (see Hebrews 12:2a AV). So it is our prayer in these last days that our eyes be focused upon, and our ears be attuned to, but one Person, the Lord Jesus Christ; for seeing and hearing Him is to be transformed (Romans 12:2b) and conformed to His image (Romans 8:29a) and makes us ready to be welcomed as the bride of the Lamb (see Revelation 21:9b, 27).

Tempted As the Son of Man

Now as we today consider together the matter of Jesus' temptation, we shall come to realize that His being tempted in life was very different from what happens to us. As the Son of God Jesus, being God, could not be tempted by evil things nor, incidentally, does He ever tempt anyone (James 1:13). So, not being able to be tempted by evil things, the Lord Jesus was tempted in His humanity as the Son of man.

Let us be clear here that Jesus, being a perfect man, possessed in himself everything that is in our human nature. That is to say, He had all the desires, instincts and urges which every descendant of Adam is created with but with one very distinctive exception: there was no lust in Him. There are instincts in mankind which are God-created and which are legitimate, but when these instincts or natural desires cross their boundaries, then they become lusts. The Bible teaches us that when we are tempted, we are drawn away and enticed by our lust, and when lust is conceived, it gives birth to sin, and sin when fully grown ends in death (James 1:14-15). Yet, though Jesus is truly man, with all the human desires in Him, His humanity was nonetheless in union with His divinity as He experienced temptation while on earth; for He is the God-Man. All His human desires were under the perfect control of His divine nature. That explains why even though Jesus was tempted in all things, He was without sin, knew no sin, and had no desire to sin: He was sinless perfect. Though tempted as a man, His natural desire never got out of control nor, consequently, ever developed into lust; and because of this, it could truly be said that He was sinless perfect.

Why Temptation Is Allowed

Matthew's Gospel informs us that Jesus was carried into the wilderness by the Holy Spirit "to be tempted of the devil." Why did He as the Son of man need to be tempted? There were two reasons. One is that before the Lord Jesus could begin His ministry He had to be brought to the wilderness to confront mankind's archenemy—he who was holding humanity under the bondage of sin; for it must not be forgotten that at His baptism Jesus had already offered himself up as the Lamb of God to be the world's Deliverer. Hence, immediately following His baptism it was necessary for the Holy Spirit to drive or carry Jesus out to the wilderness for this purpose. Moreover, let us take note of the fact that it was not the devil who sought out Jesus; rather, it was Jesus, as led by the Spirit, who sought out the devil for the purpose of confronting and defeating him so that as Conqueror, Jesus could commence His ministry of deliverance of mankind from the enemy's bondage. In this connection, we will recall that Jesus once said: "Unless you first bind the strong man, you are not able to spoil and plunder his house" (see Matthew 12:29). So there in the wilderness Jesus defeated the enemy, and on that basis He is able to rescue from the bondage of the enemy whoever of mankind responds to Jesus in a positive way.

There is a second reason Jesus was tempted as the Son of man. We learn from Scripture (see Romans 5:12-21, I Corinthians 15:45, 47) that the Son of man is the federal head of a *new* mankind; whereas the *first* man, Adam, became the federal head of the old mankind, for since Adam, having been tempted, had yielded to the devil's temptation, all who are in Adam have automatically fallen under the control of mankind's archenemy. So God's Son, having come to this earth as the *second* Man, became the federal head of a new mankind; and consequently, Jesus had to face the enemy and defeat him. His victory therefore becomes the victory of all those who are in Christ. He was tempted for our sake, not for His own sake; therefore, His victory is our victory.

Now we are told in Hebrews 4:15 that Jesus was tempted in every way that we are—yet without sin—so that He as our faithful high priest would be able to sympathize with our weaknesses. Thank God that we are saved and are thus His people; but He has not promised us that we will never be tempted. Nevertheless, He does promise us that we will not be tempted beyond what we are able to bear, for at the time of temptation God will open up for us a living way so that we are able to endure it (I Corinthians 10:13).

God allows us to be tempted in order that we may realize two basic truths. One is that temptation enables us to recognize the true nature of our flesh that it is weak. But secondly, when God allows us to be tempted, it also enables us to realize and experience His grace which He has already deposited in us.

Hence, when we are tempted by the devil, there is no reason why we must yield to his temptation. On the contrary, there is a very good reason we should be able to endure or outlast every temptation. Yes, the enemy is busy tempting us; and it is quite true that there is that within us—our flesh—which can be tempted. And through the enemy's temptation we begin to realize just how weak our flesh truly is: that there is no good whatsoever in it (Romans 7:18); even so, we can thank God that He has already deposited enough grace in us to endure and outlast the devil's temptation. Let us recall what James 1:12 declares: "Blessed is the man who endures temptation; for, having been proved, he shall receive the crown of life." We do thank God that though in our lifetime we shall indeed be tempted, such temptation if successfully endured demonstrates the power of God's grace which He had already deposited in us; and having thus been strengthened to outlast temptation, we shall receive the crown of life—that is to say, the privilege of reigning with the Lord Jesus in His kingdom.

Jesus' Three-fold Temptation Illustrates Three Basic Principles of the Christian Life

.Jesus was led by the Spirit into the wilderness to be tempted of the devil. There He fasted forty days and forty nights, after which the devil came personally to Him. Yet this particular information from Scripture does not mean that at this moment was the first time the devil had tempted the Lord (cf. Luke 4:13). As a matter of fact, during His many hidden formative years He must have been tempted all the time by the devil; and now during these forty days and nights of fasting, He was tempted continuously by the devil (Luke 4:2a). But the Bible record tells us that at the end of this lengthy period of fasting, Jesus was tempted by the devil along three particular lines of temptation that in summary fashion typify all temptations with which mankind will ever be tempted. Or to put it another way, these three specific temptations illustrate three basic principles of the Christian life. The first temptation illustrates the principle of living; the second reflects the principle of believing; and the third illustrates the principle of worship. Let us consider each one of these temptations separately.

The Principle of Living

Jesus was quite naturally hungry after forty days and nights of fasting, He having eaten nothing (Luke 4:2b). During His period of fasting He may not have sensed any hunger because in His total being He was concentrated and focused solely towards God. Only at the conclusion of His fasting did He become hungry. It is natural for mankind to be hungry and it is legitimate to take food. Let us never forget, however, that this matter of eating had constituted the first problem of life for mankind back in the Garden of Eden. God had actually provided for mankind in advance as a food source all the fruit trees in the Garden of Eden, and their fruits were indeed good for food (Genesis 1:11-12, 29). Having given Adam an appetite for eating, God had created all those trees by which to fulfill that physical appetite. Yet, in the very center of this garden, God had also planted the tree of life. By this means God was specifically wishing to tell man the following truth: "Human life is not only physical in nature, and hence the satisfaction of one's bodily need is not the primary purpose of human life. There is something more, much more, for mankind—a spiritual life." Had Adam, before the Fall, also eaten the fruit of the tree of life he would have received God's life into him and thus his spiritual life would have begun, and that would have completed his manhood.

Unfortunately, instead of Adam and Eve having chosen to be spiritually satisfied by eating of the tree of life, they ate of the tree of the knowledge of good and evil. Instead of receiving into themselves the life of God and thereby developing a spiritual life by which to fulfill the purpose of God in man, Adam and Eve chose to eat the forbidden fruit of the tree of the knowledge of good and evil in order that they might satisfy the desires of their soulish life and, now being independent of God, they could develop themselves. Thus, they fell into sin and reaped death as a consequence.

There in the wilderness the enemy came to tempt Jesus with regard to how mankind should truly live: "You are hungry, but God has made no provision for You. If You are the Son of God, You can turn these stones into loaves of bread to satisfy Your physical hunger. It is but right for You to do that, since, if You are God's Son, You have the power to do that. Why not therefore do it?" That was the temptation. Jesus' answer, as recorded in Matthew 4:4, is His quoting from Deuteronomy 8:3: "Man shall not live by bread alone, but by every word which goes out through God's mouth"—which declaration brings into view this most fundamental truth of how we should live.

What, then, is the principle of living for the Christian? Do we live by bread alone? Or do we also live by every word which comes from God's mouth? Do we live only for our physical well-being? Do we live merely for ourselves so as to develop ourselves? Do we live so independently that we do not need God anymore and become as God ourselves—even as the tempter in deception had said to Eve? (Genesis 3:5) Or do we in our physical bodies pursue a spiritual life and live for God and His glory?

The people in this world basically live by bread alone because within themselves they have no spiritual life by which to live differently. So in this world people are continually asking, "What shall we eat? What shall we drink? With what shall we be clothed?" (cf. Matthew 6:25) That, in fact, is what the nations are seeking after for satisfaction, because that is all they have. But we who are the Lord's, we who have the life of God in us, have a spiritual life to live out. We cannot live like the people of the world who live only for themselves; rather, we live not for ourselves but for God. If that is indeed the case with us, then we do not live by bread alone.

Now it is true, we, too, need bread because we certainly do have a physical body; but we do not live solely by bread but live in addition by every word that comes from the mouth of God. Significantly, the Greek term for "word" in the phrase, "every word," is not *logos* but *rhema*; which is to say that we Christians are to live by every living word, every personal word, every word of God recorded in Scripture that is quickened by the Holy Spirit to us as we read and/or meditate upon it; and if we do live by such word, then we unmistakably realize that we have a spiritual life and we live for God.

So this temptation—whether to live by God's life and for God or to live by and for ourselves—was the first one with which Jesus was confronted and which we all who are His followers are faced with as well on a continuing basis.

What is the principle of our living today? In the so-called Sermon on the Mount the Lord Jesus counseled His disciples as follows: "Do not ask what you shall eat and what you shall drink or with what you shall be clothed. Instead, look at the birds and observe the lilies: Your heavenly Father will take care of you far better than He has done for them. The satisfaction of these various physical concerns are what the nations pursue after, but as for you disciples of Mine, seek first the kingdom of God and His righteousness and all these things shall be added to you" (see Matthew 6:25-33).

The world does not have the heavenly Father and hence, they must try to take care of themselves as best they can. But we are not orphans; we have our heavenly Father, a Father who cares (see John 14:18, 23). So let us not live by bread alone but let us live preeminently by every word which comes from the mouth of God: Let us listen to Him; let us commune with Him; let us hear from Him; let us obey Him; and if we seek first the kingdom of God and His righteousness, then all these physical concerns—what we shall eat, what we shall drink, with what we shall be clothed—shall be added to us. In this very connection, the Lord Jesus later warned His disciples: "Take heed lest, when the day of the Son of man's return shall come, you be so weighed down with dissipation and drunkenness and cares of this life that it will catch you unawares" (see Luke 21:34). Are we being tempted in this matter? What in fact is the principle of living to which we are adhering today?—living by bread only or by every *rhema* word of God as well? Let us settle this issue in favor of God's glory as early as possible in our Christian walk, for it will spare us many unnecessary troubles thereafter.

The Principle of Believing

For his second temptation of Jesus the devil took the Lord up to the edge of the Jerusalem temple, that location of which was most likely the highest point within the temple area. Though some Bible commentators say this highest point could have been situated in the temple porch, others believe that it was probably located in the southeastern corner of the temple area where every morning a priest would be stationed at this highest pinnacle. And from that vantage point he would look out over the hills and observe the sun beginning to rise—and at which moment he would sound the call for launching the day's temple activities: for example, the temple gate would be opened and the morning sacrifice would be offered up. That area's highest point was in fact so elevated that it had a drop of some 450 feet.

So Satan took Jesus up to that temple pinnacle and said to Him, "If You are God's Son, throw yourself down." The tempter even quoted a passage of Scripture. Let us acknowledge that the devil knows the Scriptures fairly well, and that at times we are put to shame for not knowing them as well as he does. If we do not know the Scriptures as well as the devil does, then we certainly will be tempted. Here Satan quoted from Psalm 91: "God will send His angels to lift you up and thus protect your feet from harm or hurt" (see vv.11-12). And if that be the case, implied the tempter, why not do it?

But let us note here that Satan, in quoting this passage of Scripture, has taken it out of context. Let us therefore consider several of this Psalm's verses which surely contradict Satan's incorrect use of the passage quoted by him.

Verse 1 of Psalm 91, for example, states this: "He that dwelleth in the secret place of the Most High shall abide under the shadow of the Almighty." So who are the ones who will abide under the shadow of the Almighty? Only those who dwell in the secret place of the Most High. Furthermore, verses 9 and 10a declare this: "Because thou hast made Jehovah, [who is] my refuge, [who is also] the Most High, [as] thy dwelling-place, there shall no evil befall thee." Upon whom, therefore, will no evil fall? Only those who make Jehovah their dwelling place.

And finally, speaking in the first person, God says this, as recorded in verse 14a: "Because he hath set his love upon me, therefore will I deliver him."

Hence, we can readily conclude from these *other* verses in Psalm 91 that the promises of God's protection stated therein are conditional in nature: only to those who dwell in the secret place of the Most High, who make Jehovah their refuge, and who love God with all their heart are such promises made. On the other hand, should people step outside the will of God and still claim these promises for themselves, such conduct is not faith but is the sin of presumption. Essentially, therefore, the devil was here tempting Jesus by telling Him in so many words that if He had faith, He could cast himself down without fear of incurring injury or death because God's word says so. But the Lord knew that if, outside the Father's will, He took such action without the Father ordering Him to do so, it would be the sin of presumption and not faith. Indeed, it would be tempting and testing God the Father and not acting according to the principle of believing. So, for the second time Jesus is seen giving answer to the tempter with Scripture, and once more it was from Deuteronomy: "Thou shall not tempt (or, test) the Lord thy God" (see 6:16a).

Many times the children of Israel tempted the Lord God. We are told in the book of Numbers, for instance, that they tempted Him ten times during their wilderness journey to the Promised Land (14:22b). Their hearts had become so hardened that they no longer believed; instead, they tested, they doubted, they wondered: "Can God provide a table in the wilderness? Is He able to lead us into the Promised Land? Is He even here with us anymore?"

We in our day are confronted with the same issue. How often we are tempted in this area of faith. Are we living out our

Christian walk according to the principle of believing? Do we maintain a daily, intimate life of faith with the Lord? Are we walking in the will of God? Or do we tempt and test Him by acting outside the bounds of His will to see if He is faithful in His response or to see whether or not He will do this or do that for us? We would do well to pray frequently the prayer of the psalmist: "Keep back thy servant also from presumptuous sins; … and I will be innocent from great transgression" (Psalm 19:13). We too often misunderstand and mistake presumption for an act of faith. Faith, as we learn in Scripture, comes from "the word of God," and the Greek term for "word" there is once again *rhema* and not *logos* (Romans 10:17); which signifies that it is the living word of God which produces faith. When we have His living word, then faith rises up and responds, and that is believing. But if we lack that living word and step outside God's will by doing something on our own, such action constitutes the sin of presumption; it is definitely not an act of faith.

But was there not a second reason which motivated Satan to take God's Son into the Holy City and set Him atop the highest pinnacle of the temple and tempt Him to throw himself down that 450-foot drop? Why *did* the tempter tempt Jesus in this manner? By way of explanation it is thought that had the Son of God obeyed the enemy and cast himself down from that elevated height, then all those Jews who came to the temple to worship God that day would have witnessed the dramatic descent of Jesus as though out of heaven and would have immediately acclaimed Him as indeed the Messiah! And thus there would have been no need for Jesus to experience the cross in order to obtain the kingdom.

In other words, the enemy tempted Jesus to go about acquiring the kingdom by bypassing Calvary. Yet the will of

His Father was that He, God's Son, must go *through* the cross. Ever in opposition to God's will, however, Satan's strategy had always been to keep Jesus off the cross. But the Savior of the world successfully resisted Satan's temptation by responding to the enemy in accordance with the quickened, living *rhema* word of God: You shall not tempt the Lord your God, and which produced in Jesus at that very moment the faith to believe and trust in God the Father and His will concerning the cross.

Now if this was true of our Master, should not this also be true of us His followers today? Yet we too often succumb to the enemy's temptation to avoid the cross. For the tempter is always tempting us with thoughts like the following: "You do not need to suffer. You do not need to bear the cross. You can obtain entrance into the kingdom without the cross." And how frequently we take up the devil's word, act upon it outside God's will, and in the process we become presumptuous by tempting the Lord; but let us always bear in mind that the way to the kingdom is *through* the cross. This is the will of the Father, and that requires of us to walk continually according to the principle of believing.

So in applying to ourselves this second area of the tempter's temptation of Jesus, we must ever be on the alert that we are being tested all of our lives concerning this issue of faith. Do we believe and trust God in all things? If we believe and trust Him, then we can patiently wait, accepting and embracing the will of God in all matters, always willing to follow the way of the cross and not attempt to bypass it by taking short cuts; for our God is *worth* trusting.

The Principle of Worship

For his third and final temptation of Jesus the enemy took Him to a very high mountain and showed Him all the kingdoms of the world and their riches and declared: "If You bow down and worship me, all these I will give to You." Actually, is that not the crux of all temptations? And Satan spoke forth these words in such a straightforward manner because he could not hold this thought in himself any longer, for worship is what he had been seeking to gain for himself throughout the centuries. Worship is *the* issue in the universe: who is to be worshiped? God is the only One to be worshiped because He is the only One who is *worthy* of it.

What is worship? Simply put, worship is placing God in His proper place and placing ourselves in our proper place. And Satan, not wanting to do this any longer, had rebelled against God; and ever since then he has sought to steal away worship from God for himself. Yes, it is true that he is presently the ruler of this world; and it is also true that all the kingdoms and their wealth are currently in his hands; nevertheless, Satan had acquired it all through craftiness and subtlety. God had originally given man dominion over the world back in the Garden of Eden, but Satan tempted man and, when he fell, Satan "inherited" from man, as it were, all the kingdoms and their wealth. Yet none of it is really Satan's, for he has been nothing but a usurper; and so, by means of deceptive bribery he uses all this acquisition to obtain worship.

Satan said to Jesus: "I will give You all these if You will but worship me." He wants worship more than anything else. Indeed, it would appear that he is willing to give up all the kingdoms and all their wealth in order to gain worship of himself; but let us recognize Satan's subtlety for what it is: If he gains your worship, he gets you; but along with you there is returned to him all which had been given you of this world. That has been the craftiness of the enemy ever since man's fall. Jesus, however, saw right through the tempter, for immediately upon hearing these words of the tempter He dismissed him by saying: "Satan go away," quoting as He did so from the book of Deuteronomy one final time: "You shall worship the Lord your God, and Him alone shall you serve" (see 6:13).

Let us never forget that Satan is always using the world he currently rules to gain worship of himself from mankind. But I John 2 tells us this: "Love not the world, nor the things of the world. If you love the world, the love of the Father is not in you. The things of the world—the lust of the flesh, the lust of the eyes, and the pride of life—all these are passing away" (see vv.15-17a).

Whom do you love? Or what do you love? If you love the world, then the love of the Father is not in you. Worship springs forth from love. Hence, if you love the world, then you will worship mammon and only mammon, for the Lord Jesus had made it clear that you cannot worship and serve mammon and God at the same time (Matthew 6:24). It is an either-or proposition. If your heart is set on mammon, then you worship mammon; if your heart is fixed on God, then you worship God. Do not assume that loving the world is not that serious a matter. It is *most* serious because when you love the world, the love of the Father is not in you, and the result is that you worship mammon instead of God. Here again, as in the other two areas of temptation, we must settle yet another fundamental issue, which in this case is: Who or what is to be worshiped by us? If we love the Lord our God with all our heart, all our mind, all our soul, and all our strength, we shall be delivered from the temptation of worshiping the wrong object.

Satan, having exhausted all his temptations in his personal confrontation with God's Son, departed—but only temporarily: he would continue to tempt the Lord Jesus on this or that occasion thereafter (Luke 4:13), but Jesus never succumbed to any of the enemy's attempts to cause Him to fall.

So I trust that from this entire discussion today we have come to understand that in these three fundamental areas of temptation all the basic principles of the Christian life are challenged; moreover, all three need to be settled in each one of us; for the earlier we settle these basic issues, the better. Furthermore, we all can take solace and be encouraged by the Son of man's experience, for Jesus was tempted in all respects as we are and yet He overcame them all (Hebrews 4:15). His victory is therefore ours and hence we today need not fear being tempted. In addition, we have the assurance that we *can* endure and outlast every temptation of the enemy (I Corinthians 10:13), but only if we look to the Lord Jesus (Hebrews 12:2a) and let His victory be ours.

Chapter Six

HIS WALK

John 1:35-41—Again, on the morrow, there stood John and two of his disciples. And, looking at Jesus as he walked, he says, Behold the Lamb of God. And the two disciples heard him speaking, and followed Jesus. But Jesus having turned, and seeing them following, says to them, What seek ye? And they said to him, Rabbi (which, being interpreted, signifies Teacher), where abidest thou? [Where do you live?] He says to them, Come and see. They went therefore, and saw where he abode; and they abode with him that day. It was about the tenth hour. Andrew, the brother of Simon Peter, was one of the two who heard this from John and followed him. He first finds his own brother Simon, and says to him, We have found the Messiah (which being interpreted is Christ).

John 1:14—And the Word became flesh, and dwelt among us (and we have contemplated his glory, a glory as of an only-begotten [Son] with a father), full of grace and truth.

After Jesus was tempted and overcame the enemy, He came back from the wilderness to John the Baptist. It was but natural that He should come back to John again. In John 1:29 we read: "On the morrow, he [John the Baptist] sees Jesus coming to him, and says, Behold the Lamb of God, who takes away the sin of the world." That happened after Jesus came back from the wilderness temptation.

"Again, on the morrow" (that is, the next day), John and two of his disciples were standing there, and Jesus walked by. When He walked by, John looked at Him, and the look was not a casual glance; it was an intense looking at Him as He walked by. In a sense, John beheld the glory of God in Jesus (cf. John 1:14). So once again he declared, "Behold the Lamb of God" (John 1:35). Upon his saying this, the two disciples who were standing with him left him and followed Jesus. What a tremendous testimony John must have given that impelled these two disciples of his to leave him and follow Jesus! Jesus turned back and asked them, "What are you seeking?" The answer of these two disciples was most unusual, for they said, "Where do You live?" Jesus replied: "Come and see." So they went with Jesus and dwelt with Him that day. Andrew, one of the two, then went to find his brother Simon and said, "We have found the Messiah." We notice here the sequence of events: first, Jesus walked by; then two of John's disciples followed Him, and finally they dwelt with Him.

Knowing the Life of Jesus

We are aware, of course, that the four Gospels provide us with the life narrative of the Lord Jesus. Yet, when we read them, what are the things which really impress us? What do we actually see? Do we see the teachings of Jesus? Do we see His doings? These four Gospels record many of His teachings, and, oh, how He taught! They also document for us many of His works, and, oh, what wonders and miracles He had done! But is that all we are concerned with? What do we truly see in these four Gospel accounts of Jesus' life and work?

At the time Jesus was on earth some of the Jewish people heard Him teach, and after He taught they declared that His teaching was different from the scribes and Pharisees because He taught with *authority* (Matthew 7:29). They were impressed by His teaching; nevertheless, very soon thereafter they found that His teaching was too difficult to adhere to it. It was hard on their flesh, and in time they could no longer follow it. We may recall the outcome from John 6, in that, many, even of Jesus' disciples, left Him. Furthermore, Jesus while on earth also healed the sick and did wonders and miracles; and though at that time the people were amazed at all these wondrous works of His, they nonetheless, upon discovering that He would not do what they expected Him to do, grew tired of Him.

Indeed, these very same people who had heard Jesus' teachings and were impressed, who had witnessed His works and were amazed, eventually rejected Him and ultimately crucified Him because in reality they did not know Him. And why? They had not seen how He walked and how He lived; they had neither followed Him nor had dwelt with Him. In other words, they lacked a seeing of who He really was in terms of His person and His life. Yes, these people were impressed with Jesus' teachings and His works, but they had no impression of His person and His life.

If all we know about the Lord Jesus is His teachings or His doings, we do not know Him. We have to know His life—how He lived, how He walked on the earth, what kind of person He was, and why He was so different from everybody else. Unless we know this, we shall soon tire of His teachings and grow weary of His doings.

Here I would like to quote the words of J. G. Bellet, who wrote a book entitled, *The Moral Glory of Our Lord Jesus Christ*: "What a picture! Who can conceive such an object? He was a perfect Man. He walked here on this earth in the fulness of moral glory, and His reflections have been left by the Holy

Spirit on the pages of the [four] Evangelist[s]." So these four Evangelists' Gospel accounts do give us Jesus' teachings and do show us His works; but above all they present to us a Man, a very special Person, a God-Man, a perfect Man, a Man whom God has been looking for ever since the creation of mankind.

When God created man, he created him in His image, after His likeness. He had in His heart a man who would satisfy His every desire. Unfortunately, countless numbers of men and women have come and gone through all the centuries since, but none of them turned out to be the person whom God had had in His heart when He first created man. However, the four Gospels provide a record of the life of such a man.

Throughout His entire time on earth Jesus was the perfect Man. We must acknowledge, of course, that Jesus was and is God; nevertheless, the emphasis I wish to place here is upon His life and walk during His years on earth. He was a man totally after God's heart. Perhaps those words will remind us of David, for the prophet Samuel declared that God had sought out "a man after His own heart"—David (I Samuel 13:14), and Paul could say in one of his sermons that God had testified, "I have found David, a man after My own heart who will do all My will" (see Acts 13:22). But let us understand that though in fact David was a man after God's heart; even so, he only serves as a type of Christ; and hence, though David may have been perfect in heart, he certainly was not perfect in walk. Jesus, however, was not only perfect in heart but was also perfect in walk.

Jesus lived on this earth some thirty-three years. During the first thirty of those years, He was hidden from the public, and only during the remainder of those years was He in the public eye. As a matter of fact, those many hidden years prepared Him for those few years of public life. Or to describe the matter another way, His public life was actually simply an outward demonstration or reflection of His inward private life. There was no difference. Whether Jesus was out in public or was hidden away alone, He was the same. Indeed, He was not like most of us, who live a double life most of the time. Before man we are one way; behind man's back we may be or act another way; but not the Lord Jesus. His thirty-three years on earth manifested the same kind of life that He lived before God. When He was publicly in the eyes of the multitude, He lived before God. And when He was all by himself, unseen by other people, He likewise lived before God. Therefore, it could be said that Jesus' life was but one life. And what a beautiful and wonderful life He indeed lived!

Jesus once said the following: "He that has sent me is with me; he has not left me alone, because I do always the things that are pleasing to him" (John 8:29). Several times during His life heaven opened and there came forth a voice out from heaven declaring: "This is My beloved Son in whom is My delight" (see Matthew 3:17, 17:5; II Peter 1:17). Such was the earthly life of the Lord Jesus: how He both lived and walked on the earth.

His Early Life—a Meal Offering

In the book of Leviticus there are five different kinds of sacrifices and offerings described, all of which serve as types of Christ. In chapter 2, for instance, there is mentioned a sacrificial offering called the oblation—a meal or grain offering. When a meal offering was offered up, it consisted of fine flour—that is to say, it was the finest part of ground wheat; oil was then poured on it, and finally frankincense was added to it (vv. 1-2). So we can say that the meal offering is a type or figure of the earthly life of the Lord Jesus. His earthly life of some thirty-three years was like the burnt fine-flour grain offering offered up by fire to God. Let us pause and consider this meal offering in greater detail and observe how the threefold process by which it was produced readily typifies the kind of life Jesus lived while on earth.

John 12:24 presents Jesus as announcing: "Verily, verily, I say unto you, Except the grain of wheat falling into the ground die, it abides alone; but if it die, it bears much fruit." This He spoke concerning His forthcoming death. Is it not true that in this world only tares can be found? There is no wheat—only all weeds—which is to say, the sons of the devil. Jesus was the very first grain of wheat that fell into the ground and died. He came to this earth and He died. Flour, of course, is produced through the process of grinding the wheat. In other words, we learn from the four Gospels that throughout Jesus' life He was continually being tested, proven, and ground; yet, every aspect of His life came forth as flour-like: pure and fine. And such constituted the first step in producing the meal or food offering for God.

Oil was then poured upon the flour. In Scripture oil is representative of the Holy Spirit (cf., e.g., Psalm 133 with I John 2:20, 27). The whole life of Jesus was mingled with the Holy Spirit. The Holy Spirit had overshadowed the womb of a virgin, and thus Jesus was born of the Spirit (Luke 1:34-35). At His baptism the Holy Spirit came upon Him and took up His abode in Him (cf. Matthew 3:16). He was then led by the Spirit to the wilderness to be tempted of the devil (Matthew 4:1), and after He overcame, He came back in the power of the Holy Spirit (Luke 4:14a). And when He began to preach, which occurred in Galilee, He opened the book of Isaiah in the synagogue of Nazareth and quoted from it, saying: "The anointing of the Lord is upon Me" (see Luke 4:18a). He did everything in the power of the Holy Spirit. And, finally, when He offered himself as a sacrifice for the world's sins, it was by the eternal Spirit (Hebrews 9:14b). Thus, Jesus' entire life had been mingled with the Holy Spirit.

And lastly frankincense was added to the flour mingled with oil. Frankincense means "frank incense." It was a frank and open fragrance which constantly exuded from the life of Jesus. Wherever He went there came forth from Him a sweet savor pleasing to both God and man. His walk on earth not only meant life unto life but also meant death unto death (2 Corinthians 2:16a). Such was the earthly life of the Lord Jesus.

It was Bellet who also said: "Aside from that personal love that our Lord Jesus has for us, the one thing that really draws us to Him is the discovering of Himself. If we discover Him [in terms of] what a Man He is, what a Person He is, what a Life He is, we will be drawn to Him; we will desire Him with all our hearts. [And in the end] we will know Him, and we will be transformed according to His image, because as He lives, so shall we live."

There is a Christian song which is entitled, "I Stand in Awe." I like that song, but I must confess that I believe there is something not quite right in it, for after expressing its true lyrical sentiment—"You are beautiful beyond description, too marvelous for words"—the song states this: "And I stand in awe of You." Yes, it is quite true that Jesus' beauty is so marvelous that it is indescribable. But instead of it saying "I stand in awe of You" it should say, "I fall in love with You." There is, of course, an awesomeness there; but the sentiment of the entire song is actually an expression of love. When a person beholds Jesus' beauty, which is beyond description, that causes the person to fall in love with Him.

The Kind of Life Jesus Lived

He Lived a Holy Life

What a life Jesus lived! First of all, He lived a holy life. Now sometimes, when we mention the word holy, we are fearful and even afraid of that word. That is because the holiness which we see in people today is not a true holiness. Holiness means "set apart for God." We are being separated from everything in order that we may be fully devoted to God. That is holiness. Unfortunately, in this world there is a false holiness—that which the Pharisees practiced back in their day and which many today are practicing. In the days of the Lord Jesus the Pharisees broadened their phylacteries and widened the borders of their garments in order to show that they were holy. They also stood on the street corners and prayed long prayers as well as offered the tithe of their costly spices: mint, anise and cumin. In short, they had presented themselves to people as those who were very holy; but Jesus had declared that within them there was nothing but dead men's bones, everything unclean, and wickedness to the full (see Matthew 23). In other words, their holiness was external and man-made; their holiness was nothing more than an appearance of being holy before people. And in order to show that they were so holy, they separated themselves from the sinners: they would not eat with them because their attitude concerning the sinners and themselves was, "Stand by thyself, come not near to me; for I am holier than thou" (Isaiah 65:5a). To put it most succinctly: their holiness was not real.

The kind of holiness as displayed by the Pharisees is frightening. It is no wonder that at the mention of the word holy, we immediately grow afraid. But let us look at the life of the

Lord Jesus. He lived a normal life. He ate; He drank. He was not a hermit or a recluse; He lived among the people and was a friend of sinners and tax-collectors (Matthew 11:19). Yet through it all there was a great difference: though Jesus was tempted in all things, He was without sin (Hebrews 4:15b). Yes, He may have been outwardly with sinners but inwardly, He was far apart from them, for He was in the world but not of the world. His holiness was an inward character and was separated from sin. No matter how varied and intense the devil tempted Jesus, He did not sin. Moreover, He was completely separated from the world; the world could not in the least defile Him. He made no compromise with the world even though He loved and mingled among the people of the world.

In fact, Jesus was even separated from His sinless self. By contrast our self is sinful, contaminated by sin. Therefore, whatever comes from our self has the element within it of sin. But the self of the Lord Jesus was sinless. Had He in fact wanted to do something out from His self on his own there would have been no sin involved. What has just been said concerning Jesus and *His* self is difficult for us to understand because if we do anything on our own, sin is always involved. But the Lord Jesus was separated even from His sinless self. He as God's Son-become-man even denied His sinless self—"Not My will, O Father, but Thine be done" (Luke 22:42). Jesus was a human being who was completely set apart for only one purpose: devotion to the Father and His will. For did He not confess when but twelve years old, "I [must] be occupied in My Father's business" (see Luke 2:49). His whole life was devoted to God His Father. And that alone is the character of holiness.

Holiness is not just carrying out holy acts. Yes, you may do some so-called holy acts, but that is not the meaning of holiness in its totality. A life of holiness is one that is completely separated and fully devoted to God and His will: indeed, not unlike Jesus (see again Matthew 11:19) you may eat and still be holy, you may drink and still be holy, you may even be a friend of sinners and publicans and still be holy. True holiness in a person draws people; it does not drive them away. No wonder children loved to come to Jesus. True holiness in someone draws others to God, whereas false holiness attempts to draw others to one's self: "Look how holy I am."

The entire life of Jesus is nothing less than a demonstration to us of perfect holiness. And hence, Jesus could legitimately say: "Be ye holy for I am holy" (see I Peter 1:15-16). We all are supposed to live a holy life that is separated and devoted to God. How, then, can we live such a life? If we try to do so in and of ourselves we shall be accomplishing only as much as the Pharisees had achieved. We must realize that our holiness is a Person, and that Person is Someone other than ourself; which is to say, that the Lord is himself my holiness just as the Bible has declared: God has made him our very holiness (I Corinthians 1:30). We need to see that the life Jesus lived on this earth is for us. He lived that life in order that He could give that life to us, and by that life of His in us, we could be made holy as He is holy.

He Lived a Heavenly Life

Jesus also lived a heavenly life. In referring to Jesus Scripture has informed us that "no one has gone up into heaven, save he who came down out of heaven" (John 3:13a). While He was on earth He lived an entirely heavenly life. Wherever Jesus went He brought with Him a heavenly atmosphere. Let us recall what He told Nicodemus: "If I tell you earthly things, and you do not believe, how, if I tell you heavenly things, will you believe?" (see John 3:12) The Lord Jesus teaches us not only earthly but also heavenly things. Yet He came to do something even more wonderful than to teach us heavenly things: He brought heaven itself to earth! He brings heaven to you and me. So we do not need to wait until we enter heaven to live a heavenly life; instead, we need to live a heavenly life right here on earth in preparation for when we enter heaven. For if we do not live a heavenly life on earth, we will find ourselves very uncomfortable when we do go to heaven.

In this connection, I remember reading a story about an eagle and a cat. The eagle said to the cat: "How good it is to fly in the sky and see the wide horizon and all the wonderful things from above. Why are you always staying here and moving about upon the earth?" And the cat replied, "I would not go to the sky unless there were rats there." Hence, if you do not live a heavenly life on earth, when you go to heaven and all the earthly things which you today hanker after are not to be found there, you may want to depart heaven!

Jesus continually lived on earth as though in heaven. This was because He constantly placed himself under the heavenly jurisdiction. He did not live according to the opinions of this world, nor did He live trying to please the world; rather, He lived under the rule of heaven. His life was a complete reflection of the kingdom of heaven, and this is what the Lord Jesus is calling us to be today.

Do we realize we have a heavenly calling? (Hebrews 3:1a) We are called to live on earth a heavenly life. We are therefore instructed in God's word to not seek the things below but seek the things which are above (Colossians 3:1-2). What are the things that attract us? What are the things which we set our mind and heart upon? What kind of life do we actually live on this earth? Thank God, the life of Christ that has been given to us is a heavenly one. When we seek after earthly things and set our mind upon them, do we find any pleasure, joy, peace, and satisfaction within us? No; because that heavenly life within us cries out against those worldly things. It is wounded; it is hurt. We must therefore learn to hear and obey the voice within us. If we listen to the teaching of the anointing of the Spirit within us, then we will abide in Christ (I John 2:27), and by abiding in Him we will live in the heavenly realm—which places us above the earth and thus enables us to overcome our unseen enemies in the heavenlies.

He Lived a Spiritual Life

Jesus lived on earth a spiritual life as well. He was not a spirit or a ghost but was a perfect man—spirit, soul, and body. Let us not imagine that He was merely a spirit while He was on earth, therefore, He could live a spiritual life. Not so! Scripture informs us that the Word became flesh and dwelt among men. He had a body just like we have, and that body of His had its needs and desires. He likewise had a soul just as we have, with a will, thoughts, and feelings. Having a soul, Jesus, too, had soulical needs needing to be satisfied. Yet His soul was sinless, whereas ours is contaminated. He also had a human spirit, but His human spirit was so indwelt by the Holy Spirit that they were at one with each other. In other words, Jesus' human spirit was never divorced from the Holy Spirit. Or to put it another way, His human spirit was always in subjection to, in obedience to, in cooperation with, and in one with, the Holy Spirit.

God's will and desire in the creation of man has always been that his spirit in the innermost part of his being should lead because God's Spirit is able to dwell in man's spirit. And with our quickened spirit we Christians are thus able to commune with God, to know His will, and to love Him. So God's divine order in and for redeemed man is that his spirit should be in leadership. Then after our spirit has communed with God and the Holy Spirit has revealed God's mind to us, our spirit will order our soul to carry out God's will; that is to say, our will shall will the will of God, our mind shall think the will of God, and our feelings shall be in agreement with the will of God. And finally, our soul will command our body to live and work out God's will. Now that is the divine order for the walk and work of man; unfortunately, the passion and the lust of the flesh are so strong in us that, oftentimes, we are swayed by them to walk in the opposite direction. We are dominated by our mind's sentiment or our stubborn will or our wavering emotion, instead of learning to walk in the spirit by the Holy Spirit.

What is spiritual life? Spiritual life is a life that is living in a person's spirit by the Holy Spirit of God. The earthly life of Jesus was a spiritual life. He fasted forty days and nights and, naturally, He became hungry. He needed food; but when He was tempted to turn stones into loaves of bread, His response to the devil was that "man does not live by bread alone, but by every word that proceeds from the mouth of God" (Matthew 4:4). And so He put His body under the control of His spirit. In other words, Jesus did not let His body dictate to Him and master Him. The apostle Paul explained the matter this way: "I discipline my body, and make it my slave, so that, after I have preached to others I myself should not be disqualified [for the prize]" (I Corinthians 9:27 NASB).

The tempter came at Jesus again and tried to stir up the pride of His soul: "If You are God's Son, jump down from this high place; let the people see You do this, and they will accept You as the Messiah." But the Lord replied with this Scripture: "No, you shall not tempt the Lord your God" (Matthew 4:5-7).

By His conduct here Jesus was indicating that He was willing to forego any and every shortcut in gaining His kingdom but instead to go the way of the cross because this was the Father's will. He lived both in the spirit and by His spirit. Because He lived in the spirit and, since a spiritual man discerns all things (I Corinthians 2:15), therefore, Jesus could see through everything and any person. People could come to Him and pretend, but He could see through them because He was spiritual. Oftentimes we are deceived by others because we cannot see through people. We are deceived by what people say or by what people appear to be because that is the way we ourselves live. But if we are truly spiritual, someone can come to us and try to *say* something in pretense or pretend to *be* something else, and we will know just as the Lord Jesus was able to know. Because He lived in the spirit and pursued a spiritual life of always being in contact with the Spirit of God, He was always in subjection to God His Father. Such is the kind of life which He demonstrated to us while on earth, and this is the kind of life that God desires of man.

He Lived a Beautiful Life

In addition to all the above descriptions of His life Jesus lived a beautiful life. What is beauty? One brief definition of beauty is to be found in this one word: harmony. When you see a picture or a painting harmonized in color, design, and form, there is beauty there. What, then, is a beautiful life? Such is a life that has no jarring notes about it. Instead, there is unity and there is oneness; in short, there is harmony. Jesus' life was in perfect harmony with God. There was no clash or controversy between God the Father and Him because He was always in subjection to His Father, never questioning His Father but always thanking Him for whatever happened to Him. There was perfect harmony between God the Father in heaven and the Son of man on earth. That is indeed something beautiful to behold.

Yet Jesus was also in harmony with himself. There was no conflict within himself. On the other hand, our inner life is torn, riven by dissension. We are in a state of civil war all the time. In the case of Jesus, however, His spirit, soul, and body were united in harmonious oneness. Therefore, one finds such peace and rest there.

Let us take note as well that Jesus was in harmony with all the creation of God. He could see God in all things—whether that have been the loving care of God for the birds or for the lilies or for whatever else (Matthew 6:25-30). Not only was Jesus not afraid of the storm, He could even sleep soundly while it was raging. We will recall that some of the disciples were fishermen who were used to storms on Lake Galilee where they fished. On one occasion, though, they were so afraid of a severe storm which had arisen that they thought they were going to drown. Not so with Jesus, who was aboard the disciples' boat and was sleeping through it all. How much He was in harmony with creation—so much so that He could stand up and calm the storm (Matthew 8:23-27). He had power over all God's creation; and thus we can see beauty there.

Another definition of beauty is to be found in the word: well-balanced. If everything is well-balanced, people can observe the beauty that is there. In Greek classical times men were very careful about their bodies; which impelled them to establish the institution of the gymnasium, which thus became famous in developing a perfect well-balanced body in Greek youth and men. So whenever you behold a body that is well-balanced, there is beauty there.

Similarly, it could be said that Jesus lived a beautiful life because it was so balanced—for instance, love and righteousness were well-balanced in Him. We must acknowledge that too often if we love, we cannot be just; with Jesus, though, love and righteousness balanced each other in perfect harmony. There was also compassion and yet severity in the God-Man Jesus. He was compassionate with sinners and publicans, but He could be severe in His judgment of the rank hypocrites of His day: the scribes and the Pharisees (Matthew 23:1-33). He was soft and tender with people, nevertheless, He was not weak in the least, for let us recall that He cleansed the temple by driving out the oxen and the sheep which were there and overturning the table of the numerous money changers (John 2:14-15). We cannot find a more balanced life than that of the Lord Jesus. He is genuinely holy, and yet He is accessible and most approachable; whereas in our pretended holiness we become most *un*approachable. He was the meekest of all, and yet He was most powerful.

The four New Testament Gospels present to us a perfectly balanced and beautiful life. He knew exactly what to speak, when to speak, and when not to speak anything. How beautiful! May the beauty of the Lord Jesus become ours.

He Lived a Glorious Life

In conclusion, it can be said as well that Jesus lived a glorious life. What exactly is glory? To put it simply, it is the appearance of God when He is satisfied. God appears whenever and because He is satisfied. Scripture tells us that the glory of God was manifested in the face of Jesus Christ (II Corinthians 4:6). We can see the glory of God in Jesus' earthly life because He never sought man's glory; He sought only His Father's glory. If in our Christian walk we seek only the glory of God, then that glory will be upon us even as His glory was continually manifested and expressed on Jesus' face.

We could go on and on and on because Jesus' beauty is beyond description, too marvelous for words; but this is the life we have before us. When we come in touch with *that* life, it stirs within us a desire to know Him more. We will want to follow Him and be with Him. "Oh, that I may be with Him" will be the cry of our heart.

Those two disciples of John the Baptist saw Jesus walking by, and they immediately left John and followed Him. And why? They were attracted by Him and simply wanted to be with Him. Do we have such a desire? Are we only attracted by His teachings or by His doings? Or are we attracted by Him himself? Do we meditate on Him? As we read the four Gospels about Jesus, we should try to see Him *through* His teachings and His doings, and then we will desire Him and long to be with Him. We will want to know Him and to be like Him.

Then you will see that this life that is presented to you on the pages of each of the four Evangelists in each of their Gospels is for you. It is not merely to display and show forth a beautiful life and that be the end of it. God has but that one Man, and that Man came not only to demonstrate the kind of man whom God desires, but He came to give that Man—even Jesus himself—to you and me in order to make you and me like unto that very Man. In other words, Jesus came to give you and me His life that He might live that life of His in and through us.

Do we realize that the life we have in us today is this life that has been described above? It is a holy, heavenly, spiritual, beautiful, and glorious life. Do we know that such a life is the very life that is in us? If we want to live out *that* kind of life, then we should simply let Jesus live in us.

The apostle Paul wrote in Philippians 1:21 this seemingly radical assertion: "For me, to live is Christ." Is that not it? We shall find that everything about the Lord Jesus which has been shared during these past few weeks is for us: His incarnation, His Bar Mitzvah, His temptation, His baptism, His earthly walk—all of it is for us in order that we may live as He had lived on the earth. May we open our hearts and let the Lord Jesus live in and through us to the glory of God.

Chapter Seven

His Teachings

Matthew 4:12-17—But having heard that John was delivered up, he [Jesus] departed into Galilee: and having left Nazareth, he went and dwelt at Capernaum, which is on the sea-side in the borders of Zabulon and Nepthalim, that that might be fulfilled which was spoken through Esaias the prophet, saying, Land of Zabulon and land of Nepthalim, way of the sea beyond the Jordan, Galilee of the nations:—the people sitting in darkness has seen a great light, and to those sitting in the country and shadow of death, to them has light sprung up. From that time began Jesus to preach and to say, Repent, for the kingdom of the heavens has drawn nigh. [Notice the word nigh.]

Matthew 11:12—But from the days of John the baptist until now, the kingdom of the heavens is taken by violence, and the violent seize on it. [Notice the word now.]

Matthew 24:37-42—But as the days of Noe, so also shall be the coming of the Son of man. For as they were in the days which were before the flood, eating and drinking, marrying and giving in marriage, until the day on which Noe entered into the ark, and they knew not till the flood came and took all away; thus also shall be the coming of the Son of man. Then two shall be in the field, one is taken and one is left; two women grinding at the mill, one is taken and one is left. Watch therefore, for ye know not in what hour your Lord comes. [Notice the word Then.]

I would like to share today concerning the teachings of Jesus in order that we may know the Lord through His teachings. In the New Testament we have four Gospels which record the life and work of Jesus, and each one has its emphasis. The Gospel of Matthew emphasizes the teachings of Jesus, the Gospel of Mark stresses His work, Luke's Gospel focuses upon His life or walk, and the Gospel of John lays emphasis upon the heart of Jesus; even though, of course, in every Gospel there is space given over to the Lord's teachings, work, life, and heart. But because today we shall be considering together the teachings of the Lord Jesus, we will want to pay special attention to what is revealed to us in the Gospel according to Matthew.

When God's Son was on earth, He taught much and taught in a manner which all others had never before taught because He taught things that the world had heretofore never known, for He taught with authority (Matthew 7:29). We will remember what Jesus had said on one occasion: "I speak the things I have heard my Father say" (see John 8:28). Moreover, He had also said this: "It is not I who is speaking, it is the Father who speaks in Me" (see John 12:49-50, 14:10). His words of teaching were life and spirit (John 6:63b). As we therefore consider the teachings of Jesus this morning, let us bear in mind that these words of the Lord shall be life or death to all of us who hear.

The Kingdom of God

As was noted already, Jesus taught a great deal, touching as He did so upon many matters; but I believe that all the things He taught were centered upon only one theme: the kingdom of

God or the kingdom of heaven. Now we have heard much about Jesus' teachings but, strange to say, the subject of the kingdom is that which is very much missing when people give instruction on the teachings of the Lord. Yet, it is the very focus of His teachings. We must acknowledge, however, that the kingdom is such a large subject that it cannot be covered adequately within an hour; and hence, only a broad outline will be given as a way of helping us to remember.

I would like to present this kingdom teaching along the lines of three timings indicated in Matthew's Gospel: the kingdom "near," the kingdom "now," and the kingdom "then." Early on in Matthew we read that Jesus announced: "the kingdom of the heavens has drawn nigh"—that is to say, the kingdom is approaching; it is near. Further on in this Gospel Jesus is recorded as declaring in so many words that "the kingdom of the heavens is now here and is taken by violence, and the violent seize on it." And much later on in Matthew Jesus is quoted as explaining that one day the King of the kingdom shall come and then, two people will be grinding at the mill in the morning, with one of them being taken and the other being left; two will also be working at noontime in the field, with one being taken and the other being left; and Luke 17 tells us that two will be sleeping in bed, with one of them again being taken and the other being left (v.34)—all of which is to say that the kingdom will arrive in the future with the coming of the Son of man.

As an aid to your remembrance, whenever you think of the kingdom *near*, remember this one word: *repentance*, because repentance is related to the kingdom near. Whenever you think of the kingdom *now*, recall the word *holiness*, because the very nature of the kingdom is a holy one. And whenever you think of the kingdom *then*—that is, at some point in the future, bring to your remembrance the word *glory*, because that will be the time when God's glory will fill the earth.

The remainder of our time together today will be spent in considering each of these three timings related to the kingdom and what is expected of us who are Jesus' followers in qualifying for entrance into the kingdom.

The Kingdom Near

For four hundred years God was silent towards His chosen people. A remnant of the Jews had returned from Babylonian captivity. They had rebuilt the temple and restarted the temple service. Even so, we are informed in the book of Malachi—the record of the last voice of God in the Old Testament—that He had a controversy with His people: they had unrestrainedly argued with Him, they having become extremely hard-hearted and stiff-necked over time. And because of this, for four hundred long years thereafter God remained totally silent towards His people. Yes, outwardly, they continued to be a highly religious people: the priests were serving in the temple; the temple service went on day after day; the people traveled to Jerusalem and worshiped the Lord three times every year, and there they offered up sacrifices and offerings. They were indeed a very religious people, but they were not spiritual; therefore, God could not speak to them. That does not mean, however, that God had given up on His people. As a matter of fact, the less they loved God, the more He loved them.

We know, of course, that after those four hundred silent years, suddenly and unexpectedly, a voice sounded forth from the wilderness. It was a voice from God through the mouth of John the Baptist crying out and saying, "Repent, for the kingdom of the heavens has drawn nigh." After four centuries of silence God was now offering the best gift He could give to His stiff-necked people—even the kingdom. In fact, the kingdom had been in God's mind long before He created this world. Or to phrase it differently, when He created this world and man, He had already had the kingdom in view. Regrettably, the world's concept of the kingdom—and even the children of Israel's concept of the kingdom—was quite different from God's.

The Bible places a very different emphasis on the word kingdom from what we have in our minds concerning the concept of a kingdom. Whenever we think of a kingdom our concept mainly centers upon the notion of a territory, a domain, a sphere; in other words, we think in geopolitical terms. It is quite true, of course, that a kingdom does have a territory: there is a domain with boundary demarcations; but a kingdom in God's concept is much more than that. The word kingdom in the Bible is best translated as "sovereign rule," or as brother T. Austin-Sparks has put it, "kingship." Hence, in thinking of God's kingdom we need to do so in terms of the *King* of that kingdom first. Succinctly put, God's emphasis has always been placed on the King and His Kingship; and that should be our emphasis, too. And hence, it can be said that the kingdom of God is where God's character is being impressed upon, and incorporated or constituted within, the *people*—indeed, the citizens—of that kingdom. What is therefore primarily in view is that the character of the kingly-rule of the King is that which characterizes the entire kingdom, and such is the concept of the kingdom in the Scriptures.

Now John the Baptist came forth and declared, "Repent, for the kingdom of the heavens has drawn nigh" (Matthew 3:1-2). And even Jesus himself, following the conclusion of John's preaching ministry, went forth and began His own ministry by preaching the very same message: "Repent, for the kingdom of the heavens has drawn nigh" (Matthew 4:17).

Well before this moment in their history, of course, the children of Israel had already lost their kingdom. And even though they had returned home from their captivity in Babylon, their land continued to be under the rule of Gentile kings. And by the time of John the Baptist and Jesus, the Israelites were under the rule of the Roman Empire. They were looking forward very much to having their kingdom restored, but their concept of the kingdom to which they were eagerly looking forward was still an earthly one. They hoped that when the Messiah came He would restore them to first place among all the nations instead of remaining in last place among the nations of the world. But the message which God was now delivering to them was: "Repent, for the kingdom of the heavens has drawn nigh." Which is to say that when Messiah Jesus came, He was actually offering them something far more than an earthly kingdom; He was offering them the kingdom of the heavens. That is the reason the kingdom of the heavens is called the glad tidings, the gospel, the good news (Mark 1:14-15). God had good news for His people. He was offering them a heavenly kingdom, a real kingdom, a kingdom God had had in His mind for all these many centuries past. Sadly, however, the children of Israel did not understand.

Yes, their Messiah had come, but He came as the Lamb of God. They were looking for the Lion of Judah, but by sending His son as the Lamb, God was indicating that it was not yet time for His Son to come as the Lion of Judah. God's people needed to understand that before there could be any *physical* manifestation of God's kingdom there must be its *spiritual reality*. Is that not the way God always works? Man tries to obtain something physical because that is all he can see and all he desires. But we who have believed in Jesus Messiah know that that which is merely physical and material is transient in nature because it shall soon pass away (see I John 2:15-17). On the other hand, what God does and what God gives is always eternal; and that is the reason, so far as the kingdom is concerned, God wants one that lasts forever. So there must first be manifested the spiritual reality of God's kingdom, and then what is physical can remain. Otherwise, a merely physical kingdom will soon pass away. Such, therefore, is the way God always works.

So in view of God's working principle—first the spiritual, and then the physical—it should not be surprising to us who know God that when Jesus came, He did not come at the beginning as the Lion of Judah to establish an earthly physical kingdom that would be above all the other earthly kingdoms: that *will* come most certainly; but at His first coming to the earth Jesus came as the Lamb. Nevertheless, because He at His coming did not restore Israel to being the first nation of the world, the Jews were disappointed in Him and rejected him and even had Him crucified. But the wonder of it all is that as the Lamb of God Jesus took away the sin of the world. Yes, the Lord Jesus came as the King of the Jews (John 19:19b), for He was born to be King (John 18:37) and came at His first coming to bring not a man's but *God's* kingdom upon this earth; and hence, He came as the Lamb of God.

That was and still is the only way to bring God's kingdom upon this earth. It is quite true that Jesus came to take away the sin of the world, but He came to accomplish more than that: He came to demonstrate to the world in His Person the very nature of God's kingdom. His kingdom's nature is that of a lamb; His kingdom's nature is one of sacrificial love—the giving up of Jesus' life as a ransom for all; in sum, the nature of God's kingdom is to serve and not to be served (cf. Mark 10:45). So in coming to the earth as a lamb Jesus set before the world what the kingdom of God really and truly is.

Repentance—the Condition for the Kingdom

Yet there is one condition which must be met if one is to gain entrance into that kingdom, and that is—repentance: "Repent, for the kingdom of the heavens has drawn nigh." We realize that the word repentance is a very strong one. It does not mean to improve, repair, or change somewhat; rather, its meaning conveys the idea of a very drastic alteration in one's thought and conduct; in fact, it means a radical change of mind, a complete change in one's behavior, even a total about-face. To put it another way, repentance implies that a person is going in the wrong direction and needs to turn completely around and go in the right direction, which is the opposite direction.

Now at the time of Jesus the Jews had assumed that they were walking in the right direction towards the kingdom. We may remember the incident of Nicodemus coming to Jesus at night; and before he could ask the question that was really on his heart, the Lord said the following to him: "Verily, verily, I say unto you, unless you are born from above, you cannot see the kingdom of God" (see John 3:3). This prominent rabbi of all Israel, who represented the best among the Israelites, had assumed that he was very near to the kingdom of God. Nicodemus had probably thought that all he needed was a little more instruction, but Jesus explained further: "You are far from the kingdom of heaven. In fact you cannot even see it because you are walking in the wrong direction."

The children of Israel were not perfect, but they were religious. Their thought was that all they needed was a little improvement and they would automatically become the kingdom of God, but the Lord's word to them was, "Repent." To be fit for the kingdom of heaven, there needs to be a one-hundred-percent repentance. In other words, they needed to repent of themselves—to repent of their good as well as repent of their evil; repent of their irreligious, immoral deeds as well as of their religiousness. They must totally repent of everything pertaining to themselves, and that was best symbolized by undergoing the rite of baptism.

Physical baptism is not experiencing a few sprinklings, a washing of the hands; physical baptism is a total immersion: one's whole being is immersed beneath the water, which speaks of death: one's entire self—the entire old man with both its good and evil, with both everything religious and irreligious—all needs to go down into death, to be buried out of sight, and then the person will come up out of the water with heart set on walking in a new and living way. Now that is the description of physical baptism; which is a perfect representation of repentance.

It needs to be repeated that repentance is not a *little* change of direction; rather, it is a *complete* change of direction. It is a stripping away of everything so that a person is able to enter the kingdom as though going through a needle's eye (cf. Matthew 19:24). Only those sinners and publicans in John the Baptist's day knew there was nothing good in them, and hence they readily repented. They came to him and received the baptism of repentance. But the scribes and Pharisees thought they were so much better and they therefore did not need to repent. They may have acknowledged that they needed to improve, but not to repent. So they refused to accept John and his baptism. In their own eyes they considered themselves as being too good for baptism.

The Lord Jesus was now in their midst, offering His kingdom to them, but they rejected Him and would not repent. Why did John declare: "Repent, for the kingdom of the heavens is approaching and has drawn near"? It is because the King was already in their midst, and they did not know Him. And when finally Jesus himself came forth, He preached the very same message to them: "Repent, for the kingdom of the heavens has drawn near." In other words, the kingdom of the heavens had come to them in a person, even in the Person of the Lord Jesus. He as King was already there, but He still announced that "the kingdom is near." And why? It is because He needed a people who would listen to Him, who would repent and thus qualify to become His kingdom. Let us understand that historically speaking—and not prophetically—the kingdom of the heavens is now here in the Person of the King; but, spiritually speaking, the kingdom of the heavens has remained just "near" for many of God's people today rather than that the kingdom has become a reality in their lives "now."

The Kingdom Now

To really experience the kingdom *now*, we need to be disciples of the Lord Jesus. If we are not being discipled to Him, then we are no different in attitude and conduct from many of the children of Israel who were present during the time of Jesus' first coming. If that be our situation, then the kingdom for us is only near and not now. If we are still living our own lives, if we are still living according to the flesh, if we do not accept the discipline of the Lord, if we have not been buried out of sight—which is to say that even though we have been baptized, we are not in the good of baptism—then we are not in the kingdom.

Let us ask ourselves: Is it true that we see in us, that is, in our flesh, that there is no good? Are we rejecting not only our bad flesh but also our good flesh? Or are we living today according to our carnal mind? If the latter is still our condition, then for us the kingdom is only near—for us it is not now. It has been offered to us, but we are not yet in it. We therefore need to repent, for it is only through repentance that we can enter the kingdom of the heavens.

Spiritually speaking, we need to be before the Lord to see whether we are living today in the kingdom or whether the kingdom is only near but not now. For us to be able to experience the kingdom *now* we need continuous repentance. The act of repentance is not simply to bc undertaken once; instead, we need to be in a continuous spirit of repentance, and only in that spirit will we experience the kingdom today.

Thank God that when Jesus came and preached the kingdom of the heavens, there were people who listened to Him and repented, and those who believed in Him became disciples. Jesus began to surround himself with disciples, and it was at that time that He uttered these words: "From the time of John the Baptist until now, the kingdom of the heavens is taken by violence, and the violent seize upon it." He uttered those words in the presence of His disciples who were around Him. It was as though He were saying to them: "The kingdom is now here; how are you going to seize it? How are you going to live in the reality of it? You need to be violent, and the violent seize upon it."

In those early days back then all the believers in Jesus were called disciples; this you find throughout the four Gospels. Today, however, we tend to distinguish "believers" from "disciples." By this is meant that a person can be a believer in the Lord Jesus but he or she may not be a disciple. But in those early days all those who believed in the Lord Jesus were considered to be disciples of His. It was not the case back then that a person could believe in Him but not be discipled to Him: Back then it was unthinkable that people could receive Jesus as their Savior but not surrender their lives to Him as their Lord: these two actions simply went together. And later on in the book of Acts those disciples of Jesus were called Christians (11:26c).

Now what is the meaning of that word Christian? It simply means a Christ-one. Which is to say, that in the days of Acts, whenever the world looked at the Lord Jesus' disciples, they discovered that all of them were like their Lord. So they remarked: "They are Christians; they are Christ-ones." The very character of Christ had characterized these disciples. That, in fact, constitutes the finished work of Christian discipleship—a being conformed to the image of Christ (Romans 8:29a).

Disciples are apprentices and not merely students in the modern academic sense. You are an apprentice to a master, which means that you leave your home, stay with your master, and constantly serve him. You not only learn his skill or his trade, but you observe and learn all about his life: his living, his conversation, his behavior; you are under your master completely. You learn of him until, one day, at the conclusion of your apprenticeship, you not only have learned his skills but you also have learned and assimilated his way of life. That is a disciple. And in like manner, Christian discipleship is for a person to partake of Christ's very nature.

Holiness—the Nature of the Kingdom

What is the nature of God? What is the nature of the kingdom of the heavens? What is the nature of Jesus the King? The answer is to be found in the one word—*holiness*. We are told in Isaiah 6 that the heavenly seraphim were crying out, "Holy, holy, holy is Jehovah of hosts; the whole earth is full of His glory!" (see v.3) Revelation 4 tells us that the four living creatures were before the throne of God crying out, "Holy, holy, holy, Lord God Almighty, who was, who is, and who is to come" (see v.8b). From these Scriptures we can conclude that the very nature of God is that of holiness; the very nature of the kingdom of God is therefore holiness as well. And we read in Leviticus that the Israelites were instructed by God as follows: "Ye shall be holy unto me; for I Jehovah am holy, and have separated you from the [other] peoples to be mine" (20:26). In other words, Jehovah God was saying to *His* people: "I am holy; therefore, you shall be holy." Hence, holiness is the law of the people and house of God.

What is the meaning of being holy? The word holy means "uncommon, separated, set apart for God." In reading Matthew 5:47 we take note of Jesus using an unusual word in His teaching—it is the word: extraordinary. "If, for example, you greet only your brothers," taught Jesus, "what is at all extraordinary about that in you more than what the people in the world do? But to be holy, now *that* is something extraordinary—something out of the ordinary." Moreover, Jesus continued in His teaching, saying: "Be ye perfect as your heavenly Father is perfect" (5:48). To be holy is to be perfect. So we may truly say that everything about our God is extraordinary: everything about Him is holy, is perfect, different, unique, uncommon, special, the only one of its kind. Indeed, He cannot be compared with anything or anyone else. That is our God. In a word, God is holy.

But let us now look at God's Son and His life while on earth. In one sense He was no different from any of us humans; He lived a normal life just like we do. But in quite another sense

Jesus was altogether different. For instance, His love is different, even extraordinary: whereas we love the ones who belong to us, He taught that we are to, "love [our] enemies" (Matthew 5:44a). His grace, too, is different: whereas we bestow grace upon those who are worthy, He grants grace to those who are undeserving. Then, also, He is light, the world is darkness; He is pure, the world is polluted. Everything about the Lord Jesus is holy, unique, extraordinary, perfect. Such is the nature of the King and His kingdom, and that is the reason why He and the Father each counseled us on this wise: "Be ye holy as I am holy."

Why is it that we need to be discipled to Christ? It is in order that we may be partakers of His holiness (Hebrews 12:10b). Thank God, He has redeemed us and given us a new life, and that life is a holy life. And if we live by that life, we are not only holy but we are *happy*. Indeed, that is the unusual thing about Christians. For do we not have recorded in Matthew 5:3 the very first beatitude uttered by King Jesus in describing those who are qualified to be citizens of His kingdom: "Blessed [Happy, in the original Greek] are the poor in spirit, for theirs is the kingdom of the heavens"? Furthermore, it does *not* say "shall be" but it says, "theirs *is* the kingdom of the heavens." So, it is the kingdom now. To whom is the kingdom now? "Blessed are the poor in spirit." If you are poor in spirit, the kingdom is now for you.

We have the holy life in us, and therefore we have the kingdom life in us. If we allow this life to live itself out through us, we are happy. But if we do not let this life live itself out through us, we are not happy. You and I as Christians are unusual beings. Should people treat us badly and we pay them back, we are happy if we are *not* Christians. But if we *are* Christians and people ill-treat us and we ill-treat them in response, we are not happy. On the other hand, if we forgive them and love them, we are happy. Even so, it is not you and me; rather, it is the holy life in us that is being expressed. It is in that sense, therefore, that we are a peculiar, unusual people, and thus we are a peculiar treasure to the Lord, as the Old Testament prophet Malachi has written (3:17a).

It is unfortunate today, however, that Christians have lost their "extra-ordinariness." It is because too many of us today wish to be like the world and actually decide to live like it that our spiritual peculiarity and unusualness have vanished; and thus it is no wonder that we are not happy. If we Christians want to be happy, we must live by the life of Christ that is in us; and the consequence shall be that we become partakers of God's holiness and shall be most happy.

Regrettably, the lives of many Christians today are not that simple. If it be true, of course, that if only that new life were in us, then our lives would be very simple, indeed—we could simply let that life live itself out through us. Unfortunately, that old Adamic life lingers on in too many of us. And hence, that is the reason the Lord Jesus felt compelled to declare: "From the time of John the Baptist until now the kingdom of the heavens is taken by violence, and the violent seize upon it." We do not like the word violence; to us it is a bad-sounding word. However, that word is actually a neutral term. Its character depends solely upon the connotation within which it is employed. Some Bible versions avoid translating the Greek word into English as *violence* and instead translate it as *force*—"the kingdom… is taken by force." Nevertheless, whether one uses the word force or violence, it matters not since both words have the same meaning. For if anyone wishes to seize hold of the kingdom, that one must be violent and take it by force.

Yet Jesus' words here were not to be understood as meaning that His followers were to be violent to others; on the contrary, His disciples were given to understand that they must be violent to themselves. In fact, that is the very meaning of Jesus' other words to His disciples: "Deny yourself, take up your cross, and follow Me" (see Matthew 16:24). Who among us wants to deny himself/herself? Rather, we want to gratify ourselves; we want to please ourselves; we love ourselves overly much. But Jesus said, "No, you have to deny yourself." Tell your self-life: "I do not know you. I have nothing to do with you; I put you to death. I deny you. I ignore your feeling. I let you be hurt." In short, do violence to yourself by putting your self under strict discipline; and if you do that, that holy life in you is given the opportunity to live itself out through you. In other words, the cross has to work in our lives to remove what hinders that holy life from coming forth. Yes, during the time of discipline, of chastening, of bearing the cross, you will feel sorry for yourself for a time but, afterwards, it will be happiness and joy because you are now living in the kingdom of the heavens.

Jesus' so-called Sermon on the Mount is actually a picture of the kingdom *now* because whenever *spiritual* things are talked about, there is no time factor involved. So, wherever there is kingdom reality, the kingdom is there. Indeed, if you live in the nature of that kingdom, the kingdom is in you and you are in the kingdom. That is the essence of Matthew chapters 5, 6, and 7—Jesus' Sermon on the Mount. This, in fact, is what Christian living is meant to be. That was the way Christ lived on earth, and that is the way He expects us to live. Even so, that is not all which the Scriptures have had to say about the kingdom. For there was one other "timing" related to the kingdom which Matthew's Gospel records Jesus as having mentioned and described to His disciples.

The Kingdom Then

We have considered together the first "timing"—the kingdom has drawn nigh—and also the second "timing"—the kingdom is now here; but Jesus has additionally told us that in one future day the kingdom of the heavens shall be manifested publicly upon this earth—that is to say, the kingdom *then*. Do we realize that when Christ came into this world, it was the first invasion of heaven upon earth? Heaven invaded the earth in the Person of the Lord Jesus Christ. He came to establish a foundation for the eventual coming of His kingdom. By His very own life He defeated the king and ruler of this world (John 14:30b). And by His death on the cross He spoiled the principalities and authorities and made a public show of them for our sake (Colossians 2:15). Jesus then ascended back to heaven where, now seated at the right hand of the Father, He is waiting for the time when He can return and claim His kingdom upon the earth. But let us take note of the fact that when Jesus ascended back to heaven, He was not altogether gone. He left behind upon this earth some people—even His church. There in Jerusalem was a heavenly colony. He himself was gone, but He left behind 120 people on earth, a heavenly colony, as it were, in the enemy's territory. And on the day of Pentecost, His people—His church—increased to 3,120 (Acts 1:15, 2:41).

Now back in the days of the Roman Empire its citizens were quite familiar concerning colonies because that was the way Rome ruled and administered much of the world of that day. For after Rome had conquered her territories, the Roman Caesar left colonies all over his occupied areas of the world.

Retired veteran soldiers would be relocated to such places as Philippi and Tarsus where they would form a colony or community of officials and, through these administrative colonies, Rome was able to rule that part of the known world that was under her jurisdiction. And hence, these colonies developed into communities of people which were simply little Romes. All the people there dressed like the Romans, and Roman law held sway over the colonies; and so the inhabitants either became, or already were, Roman citizens: they stood for Rome; they lived for Rome. To put it briefly, everyone in, and everything about, these colonies was Roman, whether located in Asia, Europe, Africa, or wherever. They were not ruled by other laws of government or by local governments but were ruled by the central government of Rome and in accordance with Roman law. Such was the nature of a colony back in Roman times.

In like manner, the Lord Jesus left a colony of 120 people on earth before ascending back to heaven. These people were governed by heaven, not by earth. They lived for heaven and not for earth. They were there in Jerusalem to witness to the kingdom of God in the midst of the kingdom of darkness. And over time this Jerusalem colony propagated other colonies which began springing up not only in the cities of Judea but even in half Jew-half Samaritan Samaria, and from Samaria, even to the uttermost parts of the earth, including even here in Richmond, Virginia, USA. This, I believe, is the strategy of the Lord Jesus: He has been planting His colonies all over the world throughout these twenty centuries, and these colonies are established to stand for, and witness to, the kingdom of the heavens. The spiritual power being released by these colonies is in the process of destroying the kingdom of darkness and, one day, that power and that witness will bring back the King to the earth. And that is what the church of Christ—comprising all His colonies—is about the business of accomplishing.

Now the verses from Matthew 24 which were read at the beginning of our time together today is only a part, but a very important part, of what is called the Olivet Discourse that appears in Matthew chapters 24 and 25. This lengthy discourse consists of the words of Jesus which He imparted to His disciples as He prophetically taught them while He and they sat together on the Mount of Olives shortly before He went to Calvary. Jesus' discourse can be divided into three sections, each of which more or less addresses one of three different groups of people: the Jews, the church, and the Gentiles. And though there is some overlapping among Jesus' three sets of words directed towards these groups, the discourse can nonetheless be divided roughly as follows: 24:4-31 are His prophetic words concerning the Jews, 24:32-25:30 are His words for the church, and 25:31-46 are those intended for the Gentiles.

One day the Lord will come as the Lion of Judah. He will come to judge the world, but judgment must begin with the house of God (I Peter 4:17a), then the Jews, and then the Gentile nations. Jesus has told us that at His coming, two women will be grinding at the mill. People generally do not grind their grain at the mill except in the morning when they are preparing the food for the day. Two will also be working out in the field, and that certainly occurs during the daytime. And as is indicated from the parallel passage in Luke 17, two will be sleeping in bed (v.34), and that, of course, occurs at night. Suddenly, in each case, one is taken and one is left, all because the kingdom of the heavens in the Person of the Son of man is coming. So far as the people of the church are concerned—and to which these words of Jesus are addressed—when the Lord comes, that is what will happen. Two is the number of witness (cf. Revelation 11:3ff.). These three sets of two people grinding, working, and sleeping represent Christians who are living at the soon coming of the Son of man. And we today are living at this very time.

Outwardly, we find everything going on as usual, as it was in the days of Noah and, incidentally, as it was in the days of Lot. Let us note that in each of these three situations both of these two people are engaged in the same activity together—if it is grinding, both are grinding; if the activity is working out in the field, both are working; and if the activity engaged in is that of sleeping, both are found to be sleeping. Let none of us be fearful of going to sleep and let none of us cease grinding or working because of the fact of the Lord's soon coming. Let us all continue to do our duty and/or to rest, for it is the Lord Jesus who knows the hearts of the two people representing all the living Christians. These Christians will be of two kinds, in terms of attitude and/or conduct. One is watching and waiting, ready for Jesus' return (Matthew 24:42-44). The other one believes that He delays His coming and so he beats his fellow servants (Matthew 24:48-49) and buries his talent in the earth—in other words, he is a lazy, wicked servant (Matthew 25:24-26a). Thank God that it is the Lord who knows the hearts of all. For outwardly, nobody but the Lord knows. Let us therefore not try to figure out the spiritual condition of our brother or sister. None of us will ever be able to, and it will be a great surprise to many at the coming of the Lord; for those whom many think will be taken will be left and those whom many think will be left will be taken.

Reigning with Christ in Glory

The Lord Jesus knows the heart of each of us and if today we truly endure with Him, then at His coming we will reign with Him. Those who are ready will be taken, those who are *not* ready will be left. One day we all will be judged at the judgment seat of Christ and by the grace of God some will reign with Christ in glory.

Jesus is coming again and He will come in glory. He will reign over the whole earth. His kingdom in righteousness shall reign upon this earth (Isaiah 9:7). Moreover, there will be peace throughout the world because the Prince of Peace will have come (Isaiah 9:6b-7a). That is the day that we are looking forward to. When Jesus and His kingdom shall come, many—but not all—will be sharing in His glory. In fact, He wants to share His glory with *all* of us. If, however, we are not willing today to suffer for His and His kingdom's sake, then it will surely not be the case that He does not want us to share in His glory but that we disqualify ourselves. So may the Lord really encourage us. As long as there is still time—and indeed, the time is short, nonetheless, there is still time—then let us repent, let us pursue holiness, and let us watch and pray, for Jesus is coming again.

Chapter Eight

His Doings As Servant

Isaiah 42:1-4—Behold my servant whom I uphold, mine elect in whom my soul delighteth! I will put my Spirit upon him; he shall bring forth judgment to the nations. He shall not cry, nor lift up, nor cause his voice to be heard in the street. A bruised reed shall he not break, and smoking flax shall he not quench: he shall bring forth judgment according to truth. He shall not faint nor be in haste, till he have set justice in the earth: and the isles shall wait for his law.

Acts 10:38—Jesus who was of Nazareth: how God anointed him with the Holy Spirit and with power; who went through all quarters doing good, and healing all that were under the power of the devil, because God was with him.

John 5:17—But Jesus answered them, My Father worketh hitherto and I work.

John 21:25—And there are also many other things which Jesus did, the which if they were written one by one, I suppose that not even the world itself would contain the books written.

The Servant of God

So far as Jesus' relationship with God the Father in life is concerned, He is His only begotten Son in whom the Father is well-pleased (Matthew 3:17). But so far as His relationship with

God in work is concerned, He is the Servant of God. So we find that in terms of life, He is God's only Son, but in terms of work, He is *the* servant of God. In the passage from the book of Isaiah which today we read at the beginning, it commences with these words of God: "Behold my servant." God wants us to look upon Jesus as His Servant. God's words continue: "My servant whom I uphold, mine elect in whom my soul delighteth." He is *the* servant of God, and God gave Him the Holy Spirit without measure. While He was on earth He fulfilled God's further words by not crying or lifting up His voice or causing himself to be heard on the street; nor did He break a bruised reed nor quench a smoking flax. Moreover, God's Servant never fainted or was ever in haste, but worked steadily in bringing judgment upon the nations and establishing justice in the earth.

As quoted in Isaiah 52:13, God also declared this: "Behold, my servant shall deal prudently; he shall be exalted and be lifted up, and be very high." Here again, God is telling us once more to behold Jesus as His Servant. "My servant shall deal prudently." While He was on earth everything He did was done prudently, wisely, and in just the right manner; and consequently, He would be exalted and lifted up and assume a very high place. And we now know, of course, that Jesus is at the right hand of His Father, high above all (Acts 1:33a, Romans 8:34, Ephesians 1:20), He having been given the name which is above every name, and that to that name every knee shall bow and every tongue confess that Jesus is Lord of all (see Philippians 2:9-10).

Furthermore, the prophet Isaiah informs us that "many were astonished at [God's Servant]—his visage was so marred more than any man and his form more than the children of men" (52:14). In other words, while Jesus was on earth, people were amazed and astonished at the fact that His visage was marred above that of any man and His form above that of any of the children of men. This verse obviously has reference to Calvary. We know that before Jesus was brought to the cross He was whipped, scourged, and crowned with a stinging, prickly thorny crown (John 19:1-5). And then at the place of the cross He was cruelly nailed to that tree of undeserved punishment. Such treatment astonished many nations: as Isaiah further informs us, "so shall he astonish many nations; kings shall shut their mouths at him: for what had not been told them shall they see, and what they had not heard shall they consider" (52:15). On the cross Jesus as Servant finished the work of redemption. It was something which the world had never seen or heard about, and yet it was accomplished. This was the work of Jesus, the Servant of God.

Not only did the Old Testament book of Isaiah announce that Jesus would be the Servant of God when He came to the earth; the New Testament has also declared the same thought. For instance, when Peter and John were used of God to heal a man born lame and that man began jumping and leaping and praising God, a crowd had gathered around them, causing Peter to say the following: "Do not look at us; it is not because of our piety that this man was healed; it is because the God of Abraham, Isaac, and Jacob, the God of our fathers, has glorified His own servant Jesus" (see Acts 3:12-13). Again, when these same two disciples of Jesus returned to their company of believers after being threatened by the Jewish authorities, the whole company began to pray, saying: "God, how true it is that all the nations, according to Thy word, were raised up against Thy servant Jesus" (see Acts 4:27).

I believe God wants us to know Jesus as the Servant of God. As God's servant He was fully obedient—even unto death, and that the death of a cross (Philippians 2:8). When He came into this world, He is prophetically revealed as saying: "Behold, sacrifices and burnt offerings are not what You want, O God, but You have prepared Me a body to do Thy will, and Thy law is in My heart" (see Psalm 40:6-8).

As the Servant of God Jesus was faithful to Him to the very end. Revelation 1:5 tells us that one of His names is the Faithful Witness. Again, Revelation 19:11 tells us that His name is Faithful and True. How faithful the Servant Jesus was to God in doing everything that God had commanded His Servant to do!

The Work of God

Jesus lived on earth only a little more than thirty-three years; yet during that period, thirty of these years were hidden. He was exposed to the public for some three years only, but during those few years He traveled through all parts of Israel doing good, teaching people, preaching the kingdom of God, healing the sick, and casting out demons—and all because God was with Him. He did many wonders and miracles and many other things, and these are all recorded in the four New Testament Gospels. So if we want to know what Jesus did, we need to go to these four books—Matthew, Mark, Luke and John—because these four accounts record His doings, which were many. But what was recorded is but a very small part of what He did, even as John, in closing his Gospel, indicated with these words: "And there are also many other things which Jesus did, the which if they were written one by one, I suppose that not even the world itself would contain the books written" (21:25).

The average public library has many books. In the nation's capital of Washington, D.C. is the Library of Congress in which there are millions of volumes. Nevertheless, if you were to write down everything which God's servant Jesus did during those three some odd years, the whole world as a library could not contain the books produced. Within such a short time period Jesus did so much—yet not only in the sense of quantity but especially in the sense of quality. What He did no other man has ever done and will never do.

Let us take special notice of what Jesus said immediately after healing a paralyzed person: "My Father worketh hitherto and I work" (John 5:17); which is to say that all the work He did on this occasion was only what His Father had been doing. In other words, His work was simply a continuation of the work of His Father—nothing less and nothing more.

Let us recall that day on which Jesus had performed a mighty miracle with five loaves and two fishes. And let us bear in mind that these loaves and fishes were given to Him by a little boy, they constituting that boy's one meal; so we can imagine how small those few loaves and fishes must have been—five little loaves and two small fishes. Nevertheless, Jesus used those meager food items to feed five thousand men besides the women and children also present, and still there were twelve sizable basketsful of broken fragments of both bread and fish leftover (Mark 6:43). People were truly amazed, so much so that they wanted to force Jesus to become their king (John 6:15a) because He had solved a major food problem before their very eyes. Jesus, however, sent them away (Matthew 14:22b); and He even sent His disciples away (Matthew 14:22a) because they, too, had probably wanted to make Him king.

Jesus' disciples and the crowd of people found Him the next day on the other side of Lake Galilee, at which moment He was moved to say: "Do not work for the food that perishes, but work for the food that is for eternity" (see John 6:27). Then the people asked this of Him: "What must we do to do the works God requires?" (see John 6:28) Jesus responded by saying: "This is the work of God, that you believe on Him whom [the Father] has sent" (see v.29). Now if you read verse 28 very carefully you will notice that the people had asked: "What must we do that we may do the *works* God demands?" They had used the plural and not the singular number in their question. In other words, in their mind (as well as ours!) it is a matter of works—many, many works; and in our minds some works are secular in nature while others are sacred in character—they being the works of God. So what, the crowd had asked Jesus, must they do?

In His response Jesus had made it quite clear: "This is the *work* of God"—singular number—which is to say that to God there is but one work which He requires. So if you wish to do that work of God, it is simply this: Believe on the One whom He has sent.

It is true that when Jesus was on earth He did many things, so many they could not be recorded. They were beyond counting, and yet He did only one work because God does only one work. Yes, God created the heavens and the earth and man; in fact, He created all things. Throughout human history God has done so many works, and He is still doing many works; however, from His perspective He is doing but one work. All of God's many works are indeed included; yet they are all for the sake of that one work: "My Father works until now" (see John 5:17). From the creation of the world and of man until the time that Jesus spoke those words God had been doing His one work, and Jesus added these words of personal testimony: "and I am continuing in that work" (see John 5:17b).

In Psalm 103 we are told: "God made known to the children of Israel His acts, but to Moses, His ways" (see v.7). The Israelites only witnessed the acts of God; for example, they saw manna coming down from heaven, and they were glad; they beheld water coming out of the smitten rock, and their thirst was quenched. Yes, they saw the various acts of God—this, that, and the other act—and when God acted, they were happy; but they soon forgot. But to Moses were made known the ways of God. He knew that God always does things according to certain principles, and if a person keeps to this or that principle, he or she will be in the will of God, which is far better than merely knowing His acts. Even so, the Lord Jesus showed us an even greater thing: God's purpose—not only His acts and His ways, but His grand purpose. Essentially, God has only one work to accomplish. Let us here make clear what that work is.

We will recall from the book of Genesis that after our original ancestors, Adam and Eve, had sinned, God came down into the Edenic garden seeking man: "Adam—Man—where are you?" (see 3:9) The man whom God had created and greatly desired after in his heart had fallen, and now the Creator had come down to the earth to seek, to recall, to recover, and to restore that man. Such has ever been the work of God since man's fall.

Throughout human history God has been steadily working with that one objective in view—to recover man; to find and to save lost human souls; to bring mankind back, not only to that Edenic sinless state he had possessed prior to his fall but even to the superior state of holiness. So we may accurately declare that God's work has been centered upon just one purpose: to bring man back into God's original design for man. And what exactly is that original design of God for man? It is that man may be joined to Him in life. His original design and purpose has always been to give man as a life companion to His only begotten Son. Or to put it another way, God wants man to be His Son's bride and helpmeet—yet not merely one individual but man as a corporate being. That has been God's purpose all along the way of human history; and it is towards the achievement of that purpose that God has been steadily working, and Jesus while on earth continued to do that work and He still continues to do so up to this very day.

We mentioned before that the Gospel according to Mark is a book which deals especially with the works and doings of Jesus. As a matter of fact, all three Synoptic Gospels—Matthew, Mark and Luke—record the doings of Jesus, but it is the Gospel of John which interprets His doings. So when John set about interpreting His doings, he did not employ the word miracles or the word wonders but employed the term *signs*. The same doings were recorded in all four Gospel accounts, yet whereas in the Synoptics they were called wonders or miracles, in John's Gospel they were termed signs because John was interpreting—not simply recording—the doings of Jesus. Everything the Lord Jesus did had a meaning behind it, and so John referred to each of them as a sign. Each such doing of Jesus recorded in John's Gospel serves as a signpost because each one points the reader of his Gospel to something else.

Throughout the Gospel of John can be found eight different signs, and all these signs are pointing to but one issue: at very near the conclusion of his Gospel John declared this: "I write these signs that you may believe that Jesus is the Christ, the Son of God, and in believing Him, you have eternal life" (see John 20:31). This in essence is the one work of God—that each of us believe Him whom God has sent, and in believing Him, we shall have eternal life. Speaking in terms of the individual, the Lord Jesus came to this earth to fulfill one purpose—to seek and to save the lost; but speaking in terms of the corporate vessel known as the church of Christ, Jesus came into this world to again fulfill but one purpose—to prepare His bride. When He came to this earth He could not find His bride anywhere, so He had to seek and to save the lost and bring them into life union with himself, and by so doing bring them into the place and position whereby they would begin to take upon themselves His very own holy and righteous character and thus become like Him; and by this means they would one day become His like—His bride, His helpmeet. Such, then, has been, and continues to be, the one work of the Lord Jesus.

Oftentimes we are attracted by Jesus' many remarkable doings. We are naturally amazed that He used five loaves and two fishes to feed well over five thousand people, but God wants us to see behind all these doings so as to perceive and understand the purpose of His work. If we are able to see the one purpose which lay behind the one work of God's sent Son, then we, too, can do the work of God.

So far as Jesus himself is concerned, when He was on earth He was *the* servant of God, but so far as our relationship with Jesus is concerned, He is our Master and we are His servants; indeed, we are called to be His servants. Do we know that it is He who teaches us servanthood? If we want to serve Him, if we want to be His servants, we need to learn from Him what servanthood really is. Otherwise, we will be like the Jews at that time who asked Jesus: "What shall we do that we may do the works of God?" (see again John 6:28) We will be thinking of, and mounting, many works—this good work, that good work, this is God's work, that is also God's work—and we will be occupied with all these various works. But we need to realize what is *the* work of God, and after we understand what that is, then all these other works will find their proper place within that one work of God. They will not be scattered, isolated, unrelated acts: "You are doing this for God, and I am doing that for God." No; whatever we are doing, there is only one work, and it is to bring man to God and for him corporately to be perfected in Christ Jesus. It is for the purpose of preparing us to be the bride of the Lamb (cf. Revelation 19:7-9). Now *that* is the one work of God.

In the secular world a disciple is never higher than his master and the bondman or slave was never higher than his lord. On the other hand, it is sufficient and quite proper if a disciple becomes like his master and quite proper if the bondman becomes like his lord. So we who are spiritual need to know the Lord Jesus as *the* servant of God because it is He who teaches us true and godly servanthood. Let us consider this matter of servanthood more closely.

Yoked with Jesus

First of all, let us recall these instructive words of God's Servant-Son: "Be yoked with Me and learn of Me, for I am meek and lowly in heart, and you shall find rest for your souls" (see Matthew 11:28-30). Whenever a yoke is mentioned, do we not immediately think of *work*? For the purpose of yoking oxen together is in order to till the ground. Now there is a work to be done called the work of God, and Jesus is *the* Servant-Worker of God. He voluntarily placed His neck under the yoke of God's work and proceeded to plow the field of God's purpose, He remaining obedient and faithful to the very end during His time on earth.

You and I must acknowledge that we are wild oxen: we have never been broken nor are we trained; nevertheless, we have been called into the one work of God. Each and every believer in Jesus has been summoned to *the* work of God. Moreover, we have been called to work together with God's servant, the Lord Jesus, by voluntarily placing our neck under the same yoke as His and not work alone. Like most farmers' yokes, this yoke of God's Servant has two harnesses—one for Jesus on one side and one for you and me on the other side. We are yoked together with Him, and that is the only way for any of us to learn. For as we are plowing the field and we see something good on the other side, being untrained and undisciplined, we will want to go there. We easily forget that we are under the yoke of our Master and there is a work to be done. But the Lord Jesus, being strong and steady, will pull us back to the work of God, and thus we begin to learn. To be obedient and faithful servants of Jesus, we need to see Him as *the* servant of God, and from whom we must learn everything necessary in accomplishing God's work. Otherwise, we are merely doing our own work for God and not doing God's *one* work.

Hence, first of all, we must realize that God has only one work. And Christ Jesus is continuing to do that one work and is calling every one of us to participate with Him in that work. On the individual level we are to present every man perfect in Christ, for the apostle Paul wrote in Colossians 1:28-29 that he labored and toiled endlessly to present every man perfect in Christ. And collectively speaking, Paul also declared that all of us together—corporately and not just individually—are to grow up into maturity, into that full-grown man, into the fullness of Christ (Ephesians 4:12-13): so that we may become the life companion, even the bride, of God's beloved Sent-Son. That has always been God's one work, and we are all to be involved in *that* work only.

Do Nothing Out from Oneself

A second facet to Jesus' servanthood which we, His would-be servants, must learn is this: that He never did anything out from himself. While on earth Jesus did many kind and helpful acts and performed many wonders and miracles; nevertheless, He said *this* about all of *that*: "I cannot do anything of myself. What I do is what I have seen My Father doing; and what My Father does, I do also" (see John 5:19). Whenever Jesus was doing something, He never did it out from himself. Jesus was and is the only sinless, perfect man. For even had He *wanted* to do something out from himself, it would not have been wrong for Him to have done so. In contrast to Jesus, whenever *we* do something out from ourselves, it is *always* wrong; with Jesus the perfect man, however, it would never be wrong but would always be right were He to do anything out from himself. Even so, Jesus refused to do such a thing; He refused to do anything by and for His own self; instead, whatever he did do was the will of His Father only. Nevertheless, let us not assume that because He *is* the perfect man, therefore, He could do anything He wanted; let us not assume that because He is the Son of God, therefore, He could do anything He wished. Not so!

Recall how He was tempted by Satan out in the wilderness. Having fasted for forty days and nights there, Jesus was naturally hungry, and it was then that Satan came forth and personally and directly tempted Him, saying: "You are the Son of God, aren't You? Then turn these desert stones here into bread. Satisfy Yourself and Your hunger. You can do it." But Jesus replied, "Man does not live by bread alone, but by every word that proceeds from the mouth of God" (see Matthew 4:1-4). Jesus would not do anything for himself and He would not do anything out from himself; rather, He waited for His Father's will to be indicated. If the Father wanted Him to remain hungry, He was content to remain so. And that was precisely how Jesus continually did the work of God while He was on earth: "Not My will, but Thine be done."

Such is true spiritual servanthood. Today the Lord Jesus is teaching us how to do the work of God. Ofttimes, we initiate a work for God out of our good intention, perhaps out of our cleverness. We assume such works ought surely to be pleasing to God, we not realizing that anything which comes out from ourselves, however good it may be, may not be God's will at all. Good will is not necessarily God's will. If we truly want to serve God, we need to learn of Jesus as *the* Servant of God. Let us do nothing out from ourselves, let us do nothing for ourselves, but always wait to know the will of God and then faithfully do it.

Do Nothing by Oneself

A third facet to Jesus' servanthood is manifested in the fact that he not only did nothing out from himself but that He never did anything by himself—that is, by His own wisdom, intelligence, or cleverness. Do we think we are clever? even more clever than God? The Bible says that the foolishness of God is more clever than the cleverness of man (I Corinthians 1:25a). Sometimes we may think God is foolish, that in *our* eyes He at times does something very foolish; but let us never forget that His foolishness is more clever than our cleverness.

The Bible tells us that as Jesus grew up, He increased in wisdom (Luke 2:52a). He became the most clever and wise person in the entire world. Even Solomon—for all time the world's symbol of wisdom—was not His equal. Though Solomon was indeed a very, very wise man, Jesus, the

Scriptures inform us, is greater than Solomon (Matthew 12:42 ASV). Yet, Jesus never initiated anything for God out of His own mind. He constantly denied himself and obeyed His Father—even to the point of submitting himself to Calvary's cross.

There is nothing considered to be more foolish to the world than the cross. Can you think of anything more foolish than that? To the Gentile nations the cross is deemed to be foolishness (I Corinthians 1:23). Why should God himself come down to the earth as a man and then be crucified on a cross? What, indeed, is the sense of it all? Yet, did God's Servant question God's wisdom? No, He was totally obedient even to the extent of death for himself, and that the "foolish" death of the cross (Philippians 2:8). Today, however, we who believe know that the cross is God's wisdom (cf. I Corinthians 1:21).

Do Nothing Out from One's Natural Power

While on earth Jesus never did anything out from His own power—that being a fourth facet to His servanthood. He had power to feed more than five thousand people with five loaves and two fishes, but when tempted of the devil He would not use His power to turn the desert stones into bread to feed himself. Jesus had power to summon twelve legions of angels to come and rescue Him (Matthew 26:53), but instead, He allowed himself to be crucified on the cross by man. He never did anything out from His own power. In fact, whenever power *was* manifested in Jesus' ministry, it was the power of God.

Let us take note that when Jesus began His earthly ministry, He first opened the book of Isaiah to chapter 61 and read from it as follows: "The Lord has anointed Me and sent Me forth to preach the gospel to the poor" (see Luke 4:18). This betokens the fact that everything He did was under the anointing power of God's Holy Spirit. He never did anything out from His own power. This should be a very important lesson for each one of us to learn. As we are serving the Lord, do we do so out from *our* strength, or do we serve under God's anointing power?

Do Not Seek Glory for Oneself

A still further facet to Jesus' servanthood can be seen in the fact that when He was doing the countless works of service, He sought no glory for himself. Did not Jesus say on one occasion: "He who seeks the glory of the one who sent Him is true; unrighteousness is not in Him"? (see John 7:18) Unfortunately, we are too often seeking our own glory, whether we are engaged in Christian service or not: concerning whatever we do, there is a secret thought within us: we want to be recognized and thus glorified. That, in fact, is one of the reasons why we want to do some kind of service which can be seen by everybody. Too many of God's servants like to preach because they will be seen of men. By the same token, people do not like to pray in their closets because nobody can see them and thus praise them (cf. Matthew 6:6). Sad to say, in too much of our service to God we seek our own glory rather than His; but when Jesus was on earth, He never sought His own glory for a single moment. Throughout His entire life His one aim was to glorify His Father. Is that not a good lesson for us to learn, too? Whenever we serve our Master, the Lord Jesus, let us not seek any glory for ourselves but let all glory be to Him, because He is the only one who is worthy.

Serve God Diligently

A sixth and final facet to Jesus' servanthood which I wish to mention can be observed in *how* He served God. The Gospel according to Mark especially tells us all about the many works of service God's servant Jesus did; and in doing so, Mark expressed one thought many times over in describing how Jesus performed all these works of service. For this same thought is repeatedly expressed by this Evangelist throughout his Gospel narrative by employing several different words over and over again to describe the way Jesus did the work of God: diligently, straightway, immediately, right away. That is the right attitude of a true servant towards his master, and that was eminently true of God's servant Jesus. He never put off doing His service until tomorrow, nor did He ever move ahead of God's timing. God has a right time for every work of service. We will recall that periodically Jesus said that His time had not yet come according to God's timing (see, e.g., John 7:6-8); but when God's time did come, Jesus never hesitated or held back. He was always right on time; He was immediately faithful and diligent in carrying out all His works of service. Such is the attitude of a true servant, and that is a facet of servanthood which we also ought to learn.

Whenever we are serving God, are we diligent? are we right on time? or are we always five minutes late? Do we postpone our service until tomorrow? When we for certain know the will of God, do we do it right away? diligently? immediately? May we not hesitate or be reluctant to follow through in all our obedience to God's will in doing the one work of God.

God's Work in Us First

There are many other things I could mention, but I would like to conclude with this thought. Jesus is *the* servant of God and as such He teaches us what true servanthood is. He calls us to serve together with Him, and what an honor and a privilege it is. But there is one thing we need constantly to bear in mind: we cannot serve Him and work with Him unless we allow Him to work in us (cf. Philippians 2:13).

Ephesians 2:10 says that "we are [God's] workmanship, having been created in Christ Jesus for good works." Before we can work with the Lord Jesus and before we can work God's work we must realize first that we are His workmanship, that we are His work. That is the reason Jesus explained what the one essential work of God is: that we must believe in Him whom God has sent. Only when we believe in Jesus is God able to work in us. If we do not believe, then He is not able to work in us. Jesus has provided full salvation for us, but if we do not believe, salvation will not become our portion. We are God's workmanship and He is ready to work in us; yet, not only to give us eternal life but also to let that life grow in us in order that Jesus' character may become our character and that we may grow up to be transformed and conformed to the image of God's Son (Romans 12:2b, 8:29a). God is ready to work, but first of all, you and I must cease working and start to believe, because if *we* are working, we do not allow Him to work in us. If we stop working and continually believe in Jesus, we allow God to do all the work in us that is necessary. And after He has worked in us, then He has re-created us for good works (Ephesians 2:9-10). You and I must let God work in us first, and only then can we work out what He has worked into us of His good pleasure (see again Philippians 2:13). Such is the principle of working out God's work.

Today, sad to say, we want to serve God with good intentions and with zeal, and hence, we commence doing this work and that work immediately, instead of waiting and letting Him first do the work that is necessary in us. As a matter of fact, the degree to which we allow God to work in us will be the degree to which we can work out His work. The more we allow Him to work in us, the more we are able to work the work of God.

We do need to look to God in order that we may see the Lord Jesus as *the* servant of God; yet not just see objectively but subjectively see Him in our hearts as God's beloved Servant so that we may be drawn into that servanthood which alone can please God.

Chapter Nine

HIS REJECTION

Matthew 11:20-30—Then began he [Jesus] to reproach the cities in which most of his works of power had taken place, because they had not repented. Woe to thee, Chorazin! woe to thee Bethsaida! for if the works of power which have taken place in you, had taken place in Tyre and Sidon, they had long ago repented in sackcloth and ashes. But I say to you, that it shall be more tolerable for Tyre and Sidon in judgment-day than for you. And thou, Capernaum, who hast been raised up to heaven, shalt be brought down even to hades. For if the works of power which have taken place in thee, had taken place in Sodom, it had remained until this day. But I say to you, that it shall be more tolerable for the land of Sodom in judgment-day than for thee. At that time, Jesus answering said, I praise thee, Father, Lord of the heaven and of the earth, that thou hast hid these things from the wise and prudent, and hast revealed them to babes. Yea, Father, for thus has it been well-pleasing in thy sight. All things have been delivered to me by my Father, and no one knows the Son but the Father, nor does any one know the Father, but the Son, and he to whom the Son may be pleased to reveal him. Come to me, all ye who labour and are burdened, and I will give you rest. Take my yoke upon you, and learn from me; for I am meek and lowly in heart; and ye shall find rest to your souls; for my yoke is easy, and my burden is light.

Matthew 16:13-27—But when Jesus was come into the parts of Caesarea-Philippi, he demanded of his disciples, saying, Who do men say that I the Son of man am? And they said, Some, John the baptist; and others, Elias; and others again, Jeremias or one of the prophets. He says to them, But ye, who do ye say that I am? And Simon Peter answering said, Thou art the Christ, the Son of the living God. And Jesus answering said to him, Blessed art thou, Simon Bar-jona, for flesh and blood has not revealed it to thee, but my Father who is in the heavens. And I also, I say unto thee that thou art Peter, and on this rock I will build my assembly [church], and hades' gates shall not prevail against it. And I will give to thee the keys of the kingdom of the heavens; and whatsoever thou mayest bind upon the earth shall be bound in the heavens; and whatsoever thou mayest loose on the earth shall be loosed in the heavens. Then he enjoined on his disciples that they should say to no man that he was the Christ.

From that time Jesus began to shew to his disciples that he must go away to Jerusalem, and suffer many things from the elders and chief priests and scribes, and be killed, and the third day be raised. And Peter taking him to him began to rebuke him, saying, God be favourable to thee, Lord; this shall in no wise be unto thee. But turning round, he said to Peter, Get away behind me, Satan; thou art an offence to me, for thy mind is not on the things that are of God, but on the things that are of men. Then Jesus said to his disciples, If any one desires to come after me, let him deny himself and take up his cross and follow me. For whosoever shall desire to save his life shall lose it; but whosoever shall lose his life for my sake shall find it. For what does a man profit, if he should gain the whole world and suffer the loss of his soul? or what shall a man give in exchange for his soul? For the Son of man is about to come in the glory of his Father with his angels, and then he will render to each according to his doings.

Authority of Religious Hierarchy Challenged

When Jesus first began His ministry, He was welcomed by the Jewish people. They were amazed at His teaching because He taught with authority and not like the scribes (Matthew 7:28-29). They marveled at the works, miracles and wonders he performed, and they praised and glorified God (see, e.g., Matthew 9:8, 33b; Mark 1:27, 2:12, 7:37; Luke 5:26, 7:16). The Jewish people were expecting the Messiah to come and they now hoped that Jesus was the One (Matthew 12:23; Luke 7:16; John 6:14, 7:40-41, 10:41-42). In fact, large crowds from all over Israel followed Him (Matthew 4:25, 12:15b; Mark 3:7-8, 5:24b); they even wanted to make Him their king (John 6:15). As time went on, however, they gradually began to have doubts about Jesus. Over time they realized that He was not what they had expected Him to be. This was because many of them had come under the influence and mindset of the religious hierarchy (cf. John 9:22b). From the very beginning the religious hierarchy at that time seemed to have been hostile to Jesus. They had their position, their tradition, and their authority; and, fearful of losing all of that, they were always suspicious of anything new, anything different. Hence, from the very outset they were not really favorable or open towards the Lord Jesus (see, e.g., John 7:31-32, 45-49). Their authority had been challenged by Him in many different ways and on many diverse occasions.

The Temple Made a Market Place

When one time Jesus was in Jerusalem and saw in the temple area the sellers of cattle and sheep, and also the money-changers, the zeal of the Lord devoured Him. So He drove out the sellers' animals, turned over the tables of the money-changers, and admonished them, saying that they had transformed His Father's house into a house of merchandise (John 2:12-17).

Now these temple-area activities had been going on for a long time. We will recall from the Scriptures that three times each year the Jews were to go to Jerusalem to the temple to offer sacrifices to God and to pay their tribute money (Deuteronomy 16:16; Matthew 17:24). Because many of the Jews over time had become scattered all over the world, when they came to the temple to offer up their sacrifices, they were not able to bring cattle and sheep from their resident country or villages. So they had to purchase them in Jerusalem, because if they bought their animal sacrifices elsewhere, such animals might not prove to be kosher and thus might not be approved by the priests. Therefore, they could not be sacrificed. So for the sake of convenience and also for their own profit, the priests joined together with the merchants and allowed the latter to sell within the temple area their cattle and sheep that would be approved by the priests.

Moreover, when the scattered Jews came from all over the world to pay tribute money to the temple, it had to be in the form of the shekel of the temple. They had to have their currency changed, and that is why the money-changers were also stationed in the temple area. It was for the sake of expediency, for the sake of convenience, and also, of course, for the profit of the priesthood. So these commercial transactions had been going on for a long time, and thus ultimately everybody had taken it for granted that it was the acceptable thing to do.

But when Jesus entered the temple area that day, He could not tolerate it because the merchants and priests together had transformed His Father's house into a bazaar, a market place, a place of business. There was bargaining taking place, it was noisy, and there was that hidden greediness hovering over the entire area. Therefore, incensed by what He witnessed, Jesus drove the animals away and overturned the tables of the money-changers.

The priests, as the keepers of the temple, confronted Jesus and said in so many words the following: "Give us a sign that You are authorized to have done such a thing. Who are You? Who are You to disturb the peace in the temple? Who are You to challenge our priestly position and authority? Give us a sign that You are the Messiah, that You are the Angel of God who has come into the temple as the purifier, as the refiner's fire. Give us a sign" (John 2:18). Their authority was challenged; their interest was intruded upon. They were not in the least happy with Jesus.

Healing on the Sabbath

On another day Jesus visited Jerusalem's Pool of Bethesda. There were many sick people lying about waiting for the water to be moved by the angel of God because the very first one to step into the Pool would be healed. As Jesus walked through the crowds of the sick and the infirm, He saw one particular man who had been infirm for thirty-eight years; He was there beside the Pool, but was hopeless because no one was present who would carry him into the Pool. So the Lord Jesus asked him, "Do you want to be made whole?" He replied, "Yes; but when the water begins to move, nobody is here to help me, and other people are able to get into the Pool first." Jesus then commanded the infirm man: "Arise, take up your couch, and go." And he did (John 5:1-9).

Now this miracle had occurred on a Sabbath day (5:9b), and not surprisingly the scribes and the Pharisees reacted negatively again, they saying to the man healed that "this is the Sabbath day, the day of rest, and accordingly this should not have been done." Then they inquired of him: "Who told you to carry your couch and walk on the Sabbath day?" He replied: "Someone told me to do this. I do not know who He was" (5:10-13). Later that same day he met Jesus in the temple, who cautioned the man to "go and sin no more" (5:14). It would appear that Jesus often purposely healed on the Sabbath day. He of course healed on any other day of the week as well, but again and again He was to be found healing people on the Sabbath days.

On another Sabbath day Jesus was in a synagogue where was present a man with a withered right hand. All now watched to see what Jesus would do on the Sabbath. He immediately told the man to stand up, and then He challenged the people in the synagogue as follows: "Is it right to do good or to do evil on the Sabbath day? Is it right to save life or to destroy it on the Sabbath?" Everyone remained silent, and according to Mark in his Gospel Jesus became quite angry at the hardness of their hearts. Nevertheless, despite their opposition He told the man with the withered hand to stretch out his arm, and he was instantly healed (Luke 6:6-10, Mark 3:5).

Working on the Sabbath

On yet another occasion Jesus and His disciples were walking through a cornfield together and at one point the disciples became hungry, so they naturally plucked some of the corn, rubbed the kernels together, and ate them. Witnessing this event were some Pharisees and scribes, who said to the Master, "Your disciples violated the Sabbath." According to the Jewish tradition of that day, if someone *plucked* corn from a field, that was not a violation, but if a person then rubbed the kernels together, that was considered to be work, and work performed violated the Sabbath. In response to these Jewish religionists Jesus was moved to explain to them some parallel history from the Old Testament times, as follows: "Are you not aware that when one day David was fleeing from Saul, he had entered the temple, ate some of the showbread which only the priests were allowed to eat, and even gave some to his followers? Have you not read about it? Furthermore, do you not realize that on the Sabbath day the priests work more on that day than on any other and were declared innocent? I say to you all that the Son of man is the Lord of the Sabbath also" (Luke 6:1-5, Matthew 12:5).

Forgiving Sin

Jesus happened one day to be in a house filled with many people, among whom were some Pharisees and scribes who were sitting around the Lord. At a certain moment in the proceedings four men arrived at the house carrying on a couch a man sick with palsy. Because of the press of the people inside they could not enter, so they went up to the roof of the house. In Palestine at that time the roofs were flat and, most likely, the roof on which these men now stood was a temporary one which the homeowner had placed over his residence courtyard. These four men now proceeded to open up the roof and then they let down the sick man lying on the couch and finally brought it to rest directly in front of Jesus. Seeing their faith, Jesus said to the man, "Your sins are forgiven."

Those Pharisees and scribes present, shocked by what they had just heard, immediately began thinking to themselves: "Who, other than God, can forgive sin? Who, then, are You to forgive sin? You blaspheme." Jesus, knowing their thoughts, now said to them: "Which is easier: to say to this palsied man, 'Your sins are forgiven,' or to say to him, 'Get up, take your couch, and walk'? But that you may know that the Son of man has authority on earth to forgive sins, I now say to this palsied man, 'Get up, take your couch, and walk'"; and the paralytic did, just as Jesus had instructed (Luke 5:17-25). As a result, those Jewish religious leaders hated Him because He had not conformed himself to their theological concepts and saw in Him a threat to their very leadership.

Eating with Defiled Hands

On still another day Jesus' disciples happened to have eaten their food with unwashed hands and, again, the Pharisees commented negatively, this time saying that it was not right because according to their tradition, which was the tradition of the fathers, no Jew would eat without first washing his hands. If anyone came from the market place, that person must take a bath before eating. So they asserted that Jesus' disciples had violated the traditions of the fathers. To which Jesus responded by saying: "You violate the commandment of God in order to keep the traditions of the fathers. Be advised that it is not what goes into a man that defiles; rather, it is what comes out of his heart that defiles" (Matthew 15:1-20, Mark 7:1-23).

It would appear that Jesus was always at odds with the priests, the scribes, and the Pharisees. On the other hand, the Sadducees, who were the ruling party among the Jews at that time, were politically oriented. They at first had seriously looked at Jesus, hoping that He was the Messiah for whom they had been waiting and who would be the one who would destroy the Roman Empire, deliver the Jewish people from bondage, and make them the first among all the nations, as promised by the prophets and recorded in the law (Genesis 49:10; Numbers 24:14, 17-19; Isaiah 2:2-4; 11:10; 42:1; Jeremiah 31:33,34; Ezekiel 37:15-24; Daniel 2:44-45). So they watched and observed Jesus very carefully, but eventually they were disappointed in Him because over time they learned that he was not interested in overthrowing the Roman yoke. Indeed, He was not interested in politics at all. His only interest was in souls and in spiritual matters. Hence, they were highly disappointed in Him. They asserted that He was *not* the Messiah, that He was instead an impostor, and they, too, sought to get rid of Him.

The People: Ultimately Disappointed in Jesus

As indicated earlier, the general populace was at first happy with Jesus and were eager to follow Him and to hang on His every word. Especially were they happy with Him when He used those famous five loaves and two fishes to feed well over five thousand people. In fact, even after Jesus sent them away and went to the other side of Lake Galilee, they still followed Him. Upon their finding Him there the next day, He said to them: "You come to Me not because of My word but because of the loaves and fish. Do not work for the bread that perishes but work for the food that is imperishable. I am the bread of life. It was not Moses but God who gave your fathers the manna-bread in the wilderness, and yet they perished; but I am the bread that comes down from above, and if you eat of Me, you shall never die." The people said, "This is too hard a teaching; who can accept such words?" Not only the people in general but even many of His disciples now left Him. They were all highly disappointed in Him because they were looking for physical and earthly results from Jesus, whereas He offered them spiritual and heavenly things. They had no appetite for the spiritual (see John 6:1-66 as source for this paragraph's contents).

Jesus' Countrymen and Kinsmen: Offended by Him

Jesus' Galilean countrymen—that is, the general populace among whom He was reared—and even His own brethren in the flesh did not believe in Him. On the one hand, they marveled and were astonished at what He did and, immediately, they said they knew who He was, that He was the carpenter, the son of Mary. They also said that they knew His brothers, that His sisters were with them. Yet, on the other hand, they wondered but had no explanation as to how He had obtained the wisdom which so readily came out of His mouth. Therefore, they were greatly offended at Him (Mark 6:1-3). In other words, they could not see beyond the natural and were thus bound, they having been blinded by that which was natural. Beyond the natural they could not see that which was supernatural about Jesus, and hence they were offended by Him.

After Jesus had moved among the Jewish people for over two years, we find that gradually and increasingly He came to be rejected by almost all of His Jewish countrymen. They rejected Him because He did not belong to them. And with respect to the Pharisees Jesus had not graduated from any Levitical school; moreover, He did not follow their theology nor fit in with their religious system; furthermore, He did not conform himself to the many traditions of the fathers; and above all else He was not legalistic in any sense as were they, for in rigorously keeping the letter of the law these Pharisees had violated its spirit. In keeping the letter of the law they had violated the very character of God, who grants and desires mercy. Outwardly, they had diligently kept the Sabbath, even having kept it beyond what the law required; and in so doing, the Pharisees had forgotten the very meaning of Sabbath—which is rest.

It can therefore be said that Jesus was rejected by almost everyone in Israel because He was radically different from them. He was heavenly, not earthly. He was spiritual, not materialistic. He was full of compassion and mercy, not legalistic and self-righteous.

Jesus' Reaction to His Rejection

How did Jesus react to His rejection? We read in Matthew 11 that Jesus began to reproach the cities in which most of His works of power had taken place because they had not repented. Jesus, being a man—and a perfect man at that—was sensitive, even highly so. We who are *im*perfect are nonetheless sensitive, perhaps overly sensitive, and sometimes even insensitive; but consider Him who is the perfect Man. All these various rejections were coming to Him, yet not because of any fault of

His but because of the fault of the people pressing upon Him from all directions. Jesus' sensitivity must have been far beyond ours. Of course, He felt their rejection—and felt it deeply. In addition, He was profoundly hurt inwardly: He wondered why they did not understand, why they did not repent after all He had done. Jesus' concern now was centered upon what would happen to the people of these cities. Even with all the mercy and grace that God had so bountifully bestowed upon them, they did not repent. As a result, Jesus greatly mourned for them because their judgment would be even heavier than that of Sodom and Gomorrah, or of Tyre and Sidon (vv.20-24).

Was Jesus bitter? Not at all; for at this very time of rejection He lifted up His eyes and prayed: "Father, I thank Thee. I thank Thee because Thou hast hidden these things from the wise and prudent and hast revealed them to babes. I thank Thee; I praise Thee, because this is Thy good pleasure. Whatever pleases Thee pleases Me" (see 11:25-26). In other words, Jesus accepted all these rejections joyfully as from the hand of His Father.

Did the Lord Jesus withdraw himself from the people because He was rejected? Did He cease to love them and give grace to them because He was rejected? No; for let us remember that He extended an invitation to them, saying: "Come unto Me all ye who labor and are heavy laden, and I will give you rest" (see 11:28-30). And He said these words immediately after He had felt their rejection. By this we realize that His heart did not become narrow because of His rejection; on the contrary, His heart was expanded. Jesus called the people—all those who labor and were heavily burdened down—to come to Him and obtain rest. This was the way the Son of man had responded to His near total rejection.

The World: Also Rejects Jesus' Disciples

Are we disciples of the Lord Jesus? Let us not forget that a disciple is not above his master or a bondman above his lord (Matthew 10:24). And if this is the way our Master, Jesus, suffered, can we at all assume that we as His disciples will or ought to fare better? While He was on earth, our Master was hated and rejected by the world; so should we think we as His disciples will be welcomed by the world? Is it not strange that God's people today are trying to court the favor of the world. Is it not strange that when the world rejects us, we are so hurt as though we are surprised that it should be so. Now the Lord Jesus has chosen and delivered us out of the world. Once we were of the world, but He has called us out of it (John 15:18-21). He has called us to himself so as to be with Him forever. We are in the world but we are not of the world, just as He is not of the world. Like our Master, we do not belong.

Unfortunately, God's people today try to belong to the world; they are afraid to be different. But we do not belong to this world's system; and because we do not belong, we will be hated, we will be despised, we will be rejected (John 15:18-19). If we befriend the world, the world may befriend us, but we become enemies of God (James 4:4). "Love not the world nor the things of the world; if anyone loves the world, the love of the Father is not in him" (I John 2:15). Do we know our place as a Christian? Are we living in the way of following Jesus? If we follow Him, we will be rejected by the world, and not only by the secular world but by the religious world as well. The secular world demands that we conform, and if we do not conform, we should be destroyed. The same thing is true as regards the religious world, for it is just as when Jesus was on earth: for once the religious hierarchy in Israel found out that He would not conform, they sought to destroy Him (Matthew 12:14).

Do we honor the word of God more than the traditions of the fathers? How many things in Christianity today are simply the traditions of the fathers and we take them as God's word. If we really seek to follow God's word, many traditions of the fathers will have to be eliminated. Yet, what happens if we do follow God's word? Will we want to be merciful instead of being legalistic? Will we desire to seek that which is above and not the things below? Will we wish to live supernaturally by the life of Christ in us or live naturally by the life that Adam gave us?

Now if we do follow Jesus and His word, there will not be any other course for us but the way of rejection by the world—both secular and religious. How, though, will we react or respond? Will we develop some kind of persecution complex? Will we become very negative, passive, bitter, and/or exclusive? May the Spirit of Christ Jesus be upon us richly, so that even though the world may reject us, may our hearts be expanded instead of being crushed and becoming narrowed.

In this connection, let us be reminded of what the apostle Paul had confessed when writing to the Corinthian believers who had, to a greater or lesser extent, rejected him: "Our mouth is open unto you, our heart is expanded and enlarged" (see II Corinthians 6:11). The more he loved them, the less he was loved. Nevertheless, for us Christians rejection should expand and enlarge our hearts, not crush and narrow them. Given that kind of positive heart condition, we should love the world, yet not in the sense of once again loving the things of the world but in the sense of God so loving the world that He gave. In *His* rejection, Jesus showed forth His gracious character. May *our* rejection likewise call forth from *our* hearts an expansive and gracious character as true disciples of Jesus.

Jesus' Retreat

The Sadducees and the Pharisees came to Jesus one day wishing to tempt Him by asking Him to show them a sign out of heaven. They pressed Him for a sign and so He said to them: "To this wicked and perverse generation asking for a sign, I tell you that there is no sign to be granted but one to this generation, and that is the sign of Jonah who preached judgment to the people of Nineveh, calling them to repentance. Judgment is coming; therefore, repent; otherwise, there will be no hope for you" (see Matthew 12:38-41). And having said that, Jesus turned away from them and from that time He gradually began to retreat: first from the land of Judea, then from Galilee, and from there to the border of Caesarea Philippi, which we know was situated at the very northern border of the land of Israel and was the beginning of the Gentile country. Having been rejected, Jesus retreated and retreated, waiting for the final crisis of His life to arrive. But that concluding crisis had to take place in Jerusalem; it could not happen anywhere else. So Jesus was biding His time because the Father's time for Him had not yet arrived. Under constant pressure and rejection He retreated until the final crisis would come which must have its beginning in Jerusalem during the Feast of Tabernacles and must end with the Feast of Passover. Till then, meanwhile, Jesus would retreat to the edge of Israel at Caesarea Philippi.

The First of Jesus' Two Questions

But while He was in the villages there (Mark 8:27a) he was moved to ask His disciples the first of two significant questions:

"Who do men say that I the Son of man am?" (Matthew 16:13b) Now let us bear in mind what was the current background here: it was at the time of Jesus' near total rejection, and only a few disciples were any longer with Him when He asked them that question. In having asked it, was Jesus looking for some reassurance? Certainly not! He knew what was coming—the final crisis—and was looking forward to accomplishing His Father's will; but He asked this question for the sake of those few who had remained with Him, many others having deserted Him (see John 6:66). Far from seeking some reassurance of faith in the Father's will for himself, Jesus wanted to reassure and strengthen the faith of these few disciples who had not abandoned Him.

By this time a definite change had occurred in the mindset of many in Israel concerning the Son of man. At the beginning of His ministry men had said that He might be the Messiah, for they had been looking for the Messiah to come. But when, in reply to Jesus' question—"Who do men say that I am?"—the disciples told Him what men now said, it turned out that no one said He was the Messiah. His disciples reported instead: "Some say You are John the Baptist; others, that you are Elijah; still others, Jeremiah because they saw You weeping; and still others more, one of the other prophets" (Matthew 16:14). In short, men's estimation of Jesus by this time had been downgraded from possibly being the Messiah to merely being a prophet.

Jesus' Second Question Elicits the Disciples' Confession

So Jesus asked a second question: "But who do *you* say that I am? You who have followed Me, you who have remained with Me, who do *you* say that I am?" Simon Peter, answering as the spokesman of the Twelve, replied: "You are the Christ, the Messiah, the Son of the living God" (Matthew 16:15-16). What a tremendous confession! Against the backdrop in Israel of an ever increasing doubt over time about Jesus and ultimately a near total rejection of Him, here was a person who confessed Jesus as the Christ, the Son of the living God. By that very confession Simon Peter had separated himself from the world and had become one with Christ Jesus. That is genuine confession.

The Father's Revelation

Jesus said the following in response to His disciple's confession: "Blessed are you, Simon son of Jonah, because this is not something flesh and blood could have taught you. All which flesh and blood can instruct or teach is that I am one of the prophets because flesh and blood can only see what is external. But it is my Father who is in heaven who has revealed this to you (Matthew 16:17). You are blessed because it pleases My Father to reveal His Son in you" (cf. Galatians 1:15).

No one knows the Father but the Son, and no one knows the Son but the Father (Matthew 11:27). Do any of us think we can know God? that we can know Jesus? Flesh and blood cannot teach us who He is. Flesh and blood can only teach us that He might be John the Baptist, Elijah, Jeremiah, or one of the other prophets—that is the extent of what flesh and blood can teach about Jesus: that He is a good man, a man of God, but that is all. For us to see that He is the Christ, the Anointed of God sent with a mission to fulfill, that He is Christ the Savior and Son of the living God, our eyes must be opened by God himself. Such awareness has to come by revelation and nothing else. Thank God, these few disciples received the revelation from God the Father concerning His Son; and they believed what the Father had revealed about Jesus. Moreover, through Peter they all made a good confession to that effect.

Confession is very important. Said Jesus on one occasion: "If you confess Me before the world, I will confess you before My Father and the angels" (see Matthew 10:32, Luke 12:8). By confession we take our stand. By confession our faith is reassured and strengthened. It is therefore important for us that we make that good confession before the world. By our confession we stand with the Lord Jesus; we are on His side; and it therefore constitutes a definite separation from the world.

The Son's Revelation

Now on the basis of that confession Jesus began to reveal something more to Peter and the other disciples: "You are Peter, and on this rock I will build My church and hades' gates shall not prevail against it" (see Matthew 16:18). Let us notice that it was first the Father's revelation. The Father's revelation revealed His Son. Indeed, it is the good pleasure of the Father to reveal His Son as the Christ, the Son of the living God. And as a continuation of the Father's revelation there secondly comes forth the Son's revelation: "You are Peter, and on this rock I will build My church and the gates of hades shall not prevail against it." In the Father's heart there is the Son, and it is His delight to reveal His Son. On the other hand, in the Son's heart there is the church, and it is His delight to reveal His church; but He cannot do that before the Father first reveals the Son. Hence, those who have received the Father's revelation concerning the Son are now open to receive the Son's revelation concerning the church: "You are Peter, and on this rock I will build My church."

It is most instructive for us to note that Jesus was engaging in a play on two closely related words here. As translated into Greek from Jesus' Aramaic tongue, this was what He said to Peter and the other disciples: "You are *Petros*, a little stone. And on this *petra*, this massive rock, I will build My church." There is a similarity and close relatedness there between these two words—stone and rock. Both possess the same nature, but between them there is also a vast difference—not only in size but in function, in use. "You are *Petros*—a small stone, a piece, a mere chip from the *petra*—the much much larger rock. The stone has the same nature as the rock, but it is only a chip; whereas I am the Rock of ages, that massive Rock—indeed, the very foundation of My church."

By confessing the Lord Jesus something happens in you and me. From being mere dust we are transformed into a stone. We were dust, but by confessing Jesus a change comes to us and we become a living stone. Jesus then said to Peter and the others: "With these living stones I will build My church upon that massive Rock." The church is built upon himself, upon His revelation, upon that confession of who He is.

Unfortunately, because of the close relatedness between these two Greek words—*petros* and *petra*—people have misunderstood what Jesus was saying here. Their faulty interpretation of His statement is as follows: "You are Peter, you are a rock, and on this rock—on you, Peter—I will build My church." And hence they have deemed Peter as being the foundation of the church. But if that be so, then *that* foundation was almost immediately afterward violently shaken to its very roots. For those who have embraced this incorrect interpretation have either ignored or else failed to take note of what happened to Peter very shortly after Jesus' revelation of the church to this disciple of His. For Jesus had to confront and severely rebuke Peter to his face, saying: "Get behind Me, you Satan! You, Peter, are a hindrance and a stumbling-block to Me, because you are not minding the things of God but are minding the things of men" (see v.23). Can anyone, having taken into account this confrontation between Jesus and the spokesman-disciple of the Twelve, therefore reasonably assume that Jesus had Peter in mind as constituting the foundation of His church?

Others may nonetheless continue today to assume and advocate that faulty interpretation, but Peter himself well understood what the Lord Jesus had meant. For he wrote the following in his First Epistle: "And coming to Him (Jesus) as to a living stone, cast away by man as worthless, but choice and precious in the sight of God, we also, as living stones, are being built up as a spiritual house for a holy priesthood, to offer up spiritual sacrifices acceptable to God through Jesus Christ" (see I Peter 2:4-5).

Peter well understood and had a correct assessment of who he himself was in relation to Christ Jesus: he was just a small though living stone, possessing the same nature but, nevertheless, only a little stone. Compared to Jesus the Massive Rock we all are little living stones, and He will take hold of us and build us together to be His church.

Let all of us be clear that being saved is not the end; even becoming a living stone is not the end; it is merely the beginning. Living stones are to be built up together and not remain scattered and isolated. *Who* is the builder? Who *can* be the builder? Who is *able* to take all of us and build us together into a spiritual house? Who among all of mankind can do *that*? Certainly not the flawed Simon Peter. There is but one person who can—the Son of man, the Lord Jesus Christ. He therefore rightly declared: "*I* will build My church."

The problem today is that we have too many church builders; and hence, what we end up building is the tower of Babel and not a spiritual house. Jesus said, "*I* will build My church." He thus reserved to himself the right of building His church. He indeed may use us in the process, but He alone is the Builder.

Then, again, we need to ask ourselves, Whose church is it? Jesus clearly answered: "*My* church." The church does not belong to Paul; it does not belong to Apollos; it does not belong to Cephas (another name for Peter) (see I Corinthians 1:12); nor does it belong to Wesley or to Luther or to Calvin. In essence Jesus was saying here: "I will build *My* church, *My* house; and I will build it upon *Myself*." In other words, Jesus' church is to be the extension of himself. It is to be the growth of Christ himself, and when it grows *in Christ*, then the church truly grows. It is to be a glorious church without spot or wrinkle or any of such thing. If, however, the growth comes from the hands of man, there must surely be spots and wrinkles all over; but if it comes from the hands of the Lord Jesus, it will be a glorious church without spot or wrinkle, holy, and without blemish of any kind (Ephesians 5:27). He is a glorious Lord with a glorious church, and the gates of Hades shall not prevail against it. Satan, of course, will open all the gates of Hades and order all the powers of darkness to attack that church; but it is already the church triumphant, built upon the Rock and not upon the sand. That is the church of Jesus Christ.

The Revelation of the Cross

Do we today have a revelation of the church? First, there must be the revelation to us of the Son, and then the revelation of the church. Yet that is not all. Jesus then continued with revealing to His disciples the way by which they were to follow Him, for He began to tell them that He must go to Jerusalem, to be killed by the priests, Pharisees and scribes; but that on the third day He would be raised from the dead (Matthew 16:21). When Peter heard all of this, there ensued the confrontation alluded to earlier between disciple and master. For Peter immediately took hold of his Master and shook Him somewhat and said, "God forbid! You can avoid that." Jesus instantly turned around, faced His disciple, and declared: "Satan, get behind Me, because you, Peter, are not mindful of the things of God but only mindful of the things of man."

In light of what had just then occurred, Jesus now felt compelled to begin teaching Peter and the other disciples what denying oneself and bearing the cross actually meant and why both were necessary for them to experience. Said Jesus: "If anyone desires to follow Me, let him deny himself, take up his cross, and follow Me. He who loves his soul life shall lose it but He who loses his soul life for My sake shall gain it. For what does it profit anyone if he loses his soul and gains the whole world? When the Son of man comes in His glory, He shall recompense each person according to his doings" (see vv.24-27).

This was a further revelation and was the revelation of the cross. Without the cross there can be no redemption. Jesus had to go to the cross, for without it there can be no church. If Jesus had not laid down His life willingly, there could have been no redeemed souls with whom to populate the church. And thus, if we do not deny ourselves and take up our cross and follow the Lord, there can be no building of the church.

Let us therefore hold fast to the eternal life to which we have been called, and let us, too, make a good confession among many people (I Timothy 6:12b). May the Lord Jesus grant us more and more revelation of who He is and what He has done for us. May He show us what He is going to do with us as His own and show us the way of the cross in order that His purpose and work may be accomplished. Here, then, we find in the word of God Jesus' rejection but also redeemed men's good confession concerning Him.

Chapter Ten

His Transfiguration

Matthew 17:1-9—And after six days Jesus takes with him Peter, and James, and John his brother, and brings them up into a high mountain apart. And he was transfigured before them. And his face shone as the sun, and his garments became white as the light; and lo, Moses and Elias appeared to them talking with him. And Peter answering said to Jesus, Lord, it is good we should be here. If thou wilt, let us make here three tabernacles: for thee one, and for Moses one, and one for Elias. While he was still speaking, behold, a bright cloud overshadowed them, and lo, a voice out of the cloud, saying, This is my beloved Son, in whom I have found my delight: hear him. And the disciples hearing it fell upon their faces, and were greatly terrified. And Jesus coming to them touched them, and said, Rise up, and be not terrified. And lifting up their eyes, they saw no one but Jesus alone. And as they descended from the mountain, Jesus charged them, saying, Tell the vision to no one, until the Son of man be risen up from among the dead.

Luke 9:27-36—But I say unto you of a truth, There are some of those standing here who shall not taste death until they shall have seen the kingdom of God. And it came to pass after these words, about eight days, that taking Peter and John and James he went up into a mountain to pray. And as he prayed the fashion of his countenance became different and his raiment white and effulgent. And lo, two men talked with him, who were Moses and Elias, who, appearing in glory, spoke of his departure which he was about to accomplish in Jerusalem. But Peter and those with him were oppressed with sleep: but having fully awoke up they saw his glory, and the two men who stood with him. And it came to pass as they departed from him, Peter said to Jesus, Master, it is good for us to be here; and let us make three tabernacles, one for thee, and one for Moses, and one for Elias: not knowing what he said. But as he was saying these things, there came a cloud and overshadowed them, and they feared as they entered into the cloud: and there was a voice out of the cloud saying, This is my beloved Son: hear him. And as the voice was heard Jesus was found alone: and they kept silence, and told no one in those days any of the things they had seen.

It is always good and helpful, I believe, to turn away from everything else and look solely at Jesus. As we therefore continue considering the life of the Lord Jesus, I would like for us today to consider together in some detail His transfiguration.

The Word became flesh and tabernacled among men, full of grace and truth (John 1:14a, b). When the Son of God came into this world, He took upon himself human flesh, and that flesh served as a veil over Him. This is why when people looked at Jesus during His earthly days, they saw a man but they did not see the glory of the Son of God. Because He was veiled, He walked upon this earth, as it were, incognito. Only those who had received revelation from above—whose inner eyes had been opened by God—could see Jesus' glory, "the glory as of the only begotten Son with the Father." That is the reason why this quoted phrase, which appears in John 1:14, was placed within parentheses; thus indicating that when the Word became flesh and tabernacled among men, the world could not see His *divine* glory—the glory as of the only begotten of the Father. On the other hand, what the world *did* see was that Jesus was full of grace and truth simply because His *moral* glory as the Son of man could not be hidden.

Throughout His life Jesus was under that veil. Only once in His life was that veil opened and His divine glory shone through His human flesh, and that was on the Mount of Transfiguration. It was only for a brief time, and then that veil fell down upon Jesus again until it was rent while He was on Calvary's cross. We recall that when He was crucified, the veil in the Jerusalem temple was rent in two from top to bottom (Matthew 27:51a), and then His glory was fully manifested. So with this as background, I would like for us to consider first what the reason was for His transfiguration having occurred: that is to say, why did it please Jesus at this juncture in His life to grant to His chosen disciples this vision of His transfiguration? And then, I would like for us to consider three further facets to this dramatic event: the fact and the meaning of transfiguration, as well as the effect of His transfiguration upon each of the three chosen disciples and also upon us today.

Why Transfiguration Occurred

In order to understand why Jesus' transfiguration took place, we must look at Luke chapter 9, where we are told: "it came to pass *after these words*, about eight days, that taking Peter and John and James he went up into a mountain to pray" (v. 28). What were these words? They were what Jesus had said to His disciples just days before He ascended the Mount of Transfiguration; and those words do have a distinct connection with the transfiguration event. Now as a help to our understanding of this connection let us briefly review what was shared in the previous message.

We learned last time that when Jesus was rejected, by His people and nation, He retreated northward into the area of Caesarea Philippi, which at that time was at the border between the Jewish and the Gentile territories. And while He was there He asked His disciples, "Who do men say that I am?" After receiving their report He then asked them, "Who do *you* say that I am?" As spokesman for the Twelve, Peter, by means of revelation from the heavenly Father, confessed Jesus to be the Christ—the Anointed and Sent One, the One on a special mission to fulfill—and confessed Him to be the Son of the living God. Upon hearing that confession, Jesus responded with these words: "Blessed are you because this is not something humans can tell you; rather, it is the heavenly Father who has revealed the Son to you." On the basis of that revelation, Jesus proceeded to reveal something more to His disciples, which was the mystery of the church: "On this rock of confession I will build My church, and the gates of hades shall not prevail against it."

Yet, not only did He reveal the church, He also began to tell His disciples that He must go to Jerusalem where He would be rejected, would be crucified, and would die, but that on the third day He would be raised from the dead. And it was at this point—when the Lord began to reveal His future Calvary cross experience to the disciples—that Peter immediately took hold of Jesus and, perhaps even having shaken Him a little, exclaimed: "Lord, this can never be; this should never happen to You!" Whereupon Jesus turned around and declared to Peter: "Satan, get away behind Me, for you are not mindful of the things of God but of the things of man." Peter wanted the Christ without a cross, but by His strong words of rebuke Jesus was making clear to everyone that there could be no Christ if there were no cross; there could be no church if there were no cross.

But then, Jesus began to teach His disciples that not only *He* must go to the cross but also that every one of *them* must go the same way as well. Said Jesus next: "If you love your life, you lose it; if you deny your life for My sake, you gain it to eternity. And I say to you all now that when the Son of man shall come in the glory of His Father, and with the holy angels, He will reward each according to His doing." Now these were the words alluded to which Jesus had uttered just six days before ascending the Mount of Transfiguration; or if one counts both the day He said these words and the day on which He climbed the mountain, then there were "about eight days," according to Luke's calculation.

Interestingly, nothing was recorded in the Gospels as having been said or discussed further between Jesus and His disciples during this six-day interval. Yet it is the belief of some that upon the disciples hearing these momentous words of their Master, it became very difficult for them to take in and absorb all His words. Indeed, that is probably why, on the eighth day, Jesus decided—as an aid to them in understanding what He had said—to take His three closest disciples and ascend what became known later as the Mount of Transfiguration. In other words, this particular mountain experience was not meant to satisfy any purpose of the Lord Jesus other than prayer; for *He* certainly did not need that vision. That vision on the Mount of Transfiguration was given solely for the sake of His disciples. He used that vision to convince them of the paramount kingdom principle—that there is no glory without suffering: that Christ must suffer, and only then can He and will He enter into glory.

This is what the prophets of old had been saying all along but, unfortunately, His disciples could not take this in and understand. His disciples wanted the kingdom and its glory, but they wanted all of it without the cross, without suffering. Jesus therefore used this vision to convince, confirm and strengthen the disciples by showing them *the* kingdom principle and how that principle would work in His life and how that principle will and must work in the life of His own.

Negatively at work also was the fact that Jesus' disciples had an unrealistic, earthly concept of the kingdom of God. Being Jews, they were understandably bound by the dominant Jewish thinking of that day concerning the kingdom. They thought of the kingdom of God in Messianic terms, that when the long-anticipated Messiah would finally come, He would make Israel the first among all the nations of the earth. To the Jewish mindset it was to be all glory and no suffering. And that was the concept in the mind of Jesus' disciples. Hence, Jesus was moved to say this to His disciples: "Some of you standing here, before you taste death, shall see the kingdom of God coming in power." By this means Jesus was intent on showing His disciples the true kingdom reality, what is truly the kingdom of God; which was something they greatly needed to understand. Most likely for these two reasons, therefore, we have described in the Gospels this awesome scene on the Mount of Transfiguration.

The Fact of Transfiguration

On the eighth day, after Jesus had spoken these words, He led three of His disciples onto the summit of a high mountain. Now according to traditional Christianity it has been thought that it was Mount Tabor, but most likely this event took place atop Mount Hermon. The reason for believing it was Hermon is the fact that at this time Jesus was with His disciples in the area of Caesarea Philippi, a place close to Mount Hermon; and hence, it seems to have been quite natural to think that after only six days He would still have been in that vicinity and that Jesus would have simply gone to the high, snow-covered Hermon range of mountains.

Another reason for believing this was the case lies in the fact that Mount Tabor at this time had a fortification situated on it and thus, even if Jesus had been traveling back south during those six days, He would not have gone to a place that was inhabited. He had wanted to get away from people so as to be alone with His disciples for that vision. So it is generally believed today that the Mount of Transfiguration was probably one of the peaks of the Hermon range to which Jesus and His disciples had gone.

And we are told in Matthew's account that Jesus had gone there to pray. We know, of course, that during the earthly life of the Lord Jesus there were special occasions when He had devoted himself to prayer. Yet this does not mean that when he was not setting himself apart to pray He was not praying. Indeed, one could say that the life of Jesus on earth was marked by uninterrupted, unceasing prayer—He prayed without ceasing. There was a communion between the Father and the Son that never ceased. But on special occasions when there was a looming crisis Jesus would usually set himself apart to pray, and this was one of those approaching crises in His life. Another special occasion was when Jesus was being baptized by John the Baptist. We will recall that as He was praying something happened: the Holy Spirit came down in the form of a dove and rested upon Him, with a voice heard from heaven that declared:

"This is My beloved Son, in whom I am well-pleased." Often when Jesus was praying, something remarkable happened.

And in this instance now before us we find that Jesus was going up the mountain to pray. Like at His baptism He was here communing with His Father. We can almost imagine that what He was communing with the Father about was His exodus or exit from the earth. By means of the act of incarnation Jesus had made His entrance upon the earth, and now He was communing with His Father about His exit: how He was going to depart from this earth. He was so one with the Father that as He was praying, the glory that had been veiled within Him broke through and manifested itself without His being conscious of it. In fact, it was something most natural to have happened. As He was communing with His Father about His exit Jesus was so one with His Father about how He was going to exit that the glory simply burst forth.

I think Jesus was probably also praying for His disciples. He had talked with them about the way He was going to exit, but they just could not understand. He therefore wanted to give them a vision so that they would be able to accept what He had told them. Is it not true that we may oftentimes hear something, and yet, we cannot assimilate it? We cannot receive it with understanding until the Lord opens our eyes and gives us a revelation, and then, suddenly, we realize: That's it! That's true! And hence, that is probably the reason He was praying.

Now as Jesus was praying, He was transfigured: His face shone like the sun; His garments were changed and became effulgent bright like lightning—indeed, they were like snow, white and pure. Jesus' glory broke through that human flesh of His. It was as Alfred Edersheim has remarked: "The form of God [broke] through the form of a servant"—he referring to the fact—as explained by the apostle Paul in Philippians 2:6-7—

that though Jesus, prior to His incarnation, was in the form of God, He temporarily emptied himself of that form, it not being that which was to be held on to, and took upon himself when on earth the form of a servant, even that of a bondslave; nevertheless, for the first and only time during Jesus' earthly walk, the form of God could not be held back but broke through the form of His bondslave servanthood in a most extraordinary display of glory.

Now at one point in the vision Moses and Elijah appeared on the scene and talked with Jesus about His exit from the earth. Moses' own exit from atop Mount Nebo was through the natural death process. He saw the Promised Land but he was not allowed by God to bring the people into it nor did he enter in himself; and God was the one who buried him (Deuteronomy 34:5-6). And as for Elijah, he exited the earth by means of a God-arranged chariot of fire: a whirlwind took him away (II Kings 2:11); he, too, not having accomplished his mission. Neither Moses nor Elijah had accomplished their mission before they exited, and that is probably why Moses and Elijah had to be sent back.

However, the exit of Jesus was different. No wonder Moses and Elijah wanted to talk with Him about *His* exit since in His case the work He had been sent to do would be fulfilled: it would be finished on Calvary's cross. Why, then, did Moses and Elijah appear on the scene here? It is because Moses was the representative of the law and Elijah, the representative of the prophets. Both law and prophets had foretold the coming of Jesus and His mission. We therefore find that both the representative of the law and that of the prophets appeared and conversed with Jesus about His exit since that was what both law and prophets had been foretelling all along concerning the Messiah.

Here, then, were Jesus' disciples, who witnessed Him being transfigured in glory. They also beheld both Moses and Elijah talking with the Lord; yet, strangely, they fell asleep. Since they had climbed the high mountain (elevation of the Hermon range at its highest point: 9,232') and it was evening, it was natural for their flesh to need some rest. But more than that accounts for their falling asleep: for when Jesus showed the disciples His glory, it was too much for their flesh. In this connection, let us recall that when Jesus led them to the Garden of Gethsemane, the sorrow over what was soon to take place was too much for them, and they fell asleep. To explain it in Biblical terms, their spirit was willing but their flesh was weak (Mark 14:38b). That, incidentally, is why we need to watch and pray. Yes, their flesh was indeed quite weak; yet, with such glory being manifested on the Mount of Transfiguration, you wonder how they could fall asleep!

For these disciples it must have been as when children, excited over something unusual, do not want to go to sleep, yet they do. Similarly, these disciples could not keep their eyes open. They must have tried very much, but their flesh was too weak. I do believe they tried with great effort to keep awake but they could not. They were too overwhelmed, and so they went to sleep. But just as they awoke from their slumber, Moses and Elijah were about to leave the scene, and that was when Peter stepped into the foreground of this remarkable event.

The Meaning of Transfiguration

The Mount of Transfiguration was an extremely significant event in the earthly life of Jesus, and it has so much to do with us who are His followers. With respect to Jesus himself, He was quite ready to make His exit from the earth via this Mount.

Having come into this world and having walked on the earth for some thirty-three years, He had proved to the world that He is the man whom God had had in mind when he first created mankind. Throughout man's history, in fact, Jesus is the only man whom God has had in mind. Adam was not that man, David also was not that man, even Paul was not that man; as a matter of fact, nobody was. There is only one man who fulfills what was in God's mind—the Lord Jesus. He is the perfect man; and after He walked upon this earth for those thirty-three years, pleasing God to the fullest, heaven was ready to receive back such a man. So far as the Lord himself was concerned, He had fulfilled in His life on earth being the kind of man whom God had had in His mind from even before the Creation: "Here is My man; I at last have My man, and it is the Son of man." And so, after Jesus had finished demonstrating God's kind of man, heaven proclaimed: "Come up; You are qualified."

Jesus could therefore have exited the earth from atop the Mount of Transfiguration; He had that right. And if He had done that, there would finally have been a man after God's own heart in heaven, but there would only have been one man; nobody else. But Jesus refused to exit from the Mount. Yet His refusal to do that was not done for His own sake but for our sake. For Jesus knew that were He to exit in that way, His whole life spent on earth would not have saved anyone but would have condemned everyone, because that is what man should have received: righteous condemnation from God. Instead, Jesus would rather exit *from Calvary's cross* so that He might bring many sons into glory (Hebrews 2:10a). Hence, this was a most important time in Jesus' life. Here we realize that the man Jesus, even after he had been well-nigh totally rejected, was willing to go back down to Jerusalem and die for the world instead of going straight back to heaven—which was His right on the basis of His having lived a perfect life on earth.

Now when the disciples were fully awake and beheld Moses and Elijah beginning to leave, Peter was desperate. It was so good to be there, and he did not want Moses and Elijah to leave. So he just blurted out his desire, without knowing what he was saying: "Lord, it is good to be here. Let us make three tabernacles: one for You, one for Moses, and one for Elijah. We will simply stay here forever, for this is surely heaven." However, at that moment a cloud suddenly overshadowed them, and the disciples were terrified. That cloud was not an ordinary one; it was a bright lustrous cloud. In fact, it was the *shekinah*—that is, the radiance, glory or presence of God. Often when God's glory appears, it is like a very bright cloud; it is the *shekinah*. The glory of God overshadowed them, and a voice from heaven announced: "This is My beloved Son; hear Him."

As it turned out, Peter committed the same error here on the Mount of Transfiguration which he had done only a few days earlier while in the border area of Caesarea Philippi when he had confessed Jesus as being the Christ, the Son of the living God. He was so elated on having received such a glorious revelation. Nevertheless, when Jesus subsequently began to reveal further to His disciples that He must go to Jerusalem and die, Peter boldly rebuked Him, declaring, "No, Lord, You need not and must not do that." Just think of it: at one moment he served as the vessel of God's revelation, but the very next moment he became an instrument in the hands of Satan, because within him was the desire at all costs to avoid suffering and the cross. Because Peter did not relish experiencing the suffering of the cross, he did not want the Lord to experience it either. He desired the glory but not the cross, he desired the kingdom but disdained any suffering. That was the self-centered, selfish mindset in Peter, and because he was like that, he wanted His Master to be like him as well; but Jesus adamantly rejected such a notion. That was what had occurred just days earlier down at Caesarea Philippi.

And here on the Mount of Transfiguration, he was doing the very same thing: "Let us all stay here; for it is such glory with no cross involved; it is the kingdom with not a scintilla of suffering having to be encountered." Having heard Peter blurting forth this self-centered desire of his, God the Father was impelled to interrupt him while he was still speaking. Peter's speaking on the Mount was long-winded, so God had to cut him off. Indeed, Scripture tells us that Peter had to be cut off by God a number of times; as a matter of fact, three times—once each by the Father, the Son, and the Holy Spirit—and this time here on the Mount it was the Father who had to cut him off. While Peter was still speaking, the glory of God overshadowed Jesus' disciples and instantly cut him off: "Hush; you do not know what you are saying. This is My beloved Son, in whom I am well-pleased; you must hear Him. This is not the time for you to talk, it is the time for you to hear."

Peter had not yet grasped what the kingdom is: that the kingdom of God is none else than Christ supreme, none else than Jesus only. In the kingdom of God one does not see Moses; one does not see Elijah; one does not see Peter, John or James; and one most certainly does not see oneself. In the kingdom of God we only see Jesus—*He* is the kingdom of God. And thus, no one can put Moses and Elijah or anyone else on the same footing as the Lord Jesus. That was what Peter was doing here on the Mount in honoring Moses and Elijah. This was not surprising, of course, for all the Jews highly honored Moses and Elijah above all others of God's Old Testament servants; but Peter and Jesus' other disciples had to learn that no one can honor them by placing these two men on the same footing as when honoring the Son of man.

So when Peter blurted forth what he said about making the three tabernacles, God had to dismiss Moses and Elijah immediately: "Go; nobody can stand together with My beloved Son; he is the only One; He is supreme." The implication being for Peter and the other two disciples of Jesus that they must worship Him; see Him; hear Him; listen to Him. For that fundamentally is the kingdom. Hence, if anyone wishes to know what the kingdom of God is, let it be clearly understood that it is Jesus only. Consequently, when the cloud disappeared, Peter and the other two disciples saw no one but Jesus. *That* is the kingdom.

Transfiguration's Effect on Jesus' Disciples

The Effect on Peter

What was the effect of this vision on the three disciples? With respect to Peter, it is necessary to read what he himself wrote concerning this event: "we have not made known to you the power and coming of our Lord Jesus Christ, following cleverly imagined fables, but having been eyewitnesses of his majesty. For he received from God the Father honour and glory, such a voice being uttered to him by the excellent glory: This is my beloved Son, in whom I have found my delight; and this voice we heard uttered from heaven, being with him on the holy mountain" (II Peter 1:16-18).

The entire second letter of Peter was written not long before his departure from the earth. Even as late as just prior to his death, this disciple could still not forget the vision he had seen many years earlier on the Mount of Transfiguration. That vision had caught hold of Peter. Indeed, his entire ministry was concerned with the kingdom of God. In reading his epistles we readily realize that he is entirely focused on the kingdom of God. He shows us in his writings what the kingdom of God is and how we need to enter that kingdom abundantly (e.g., II Peter 1:11 AV): how we must suffer much in order to enter that kingdom. From these epistles of his we can discern that the message which Peter delivers to the church is nothing less than the kingdom of God, and it has its foundation in that Mount of Transfiguration event. Because of what he was shown there, he was willing to die a martyr's death, even to be crucified—with his body, by his own choice, according to church tradition, having been placed upside down on his cross. That was the immense effect which that vision had had on Peter.

The Effect on John

What was the effect of that mountain-summit vision on John? He himself was not so much taken up by the kingdom as he was by the Person who embodied the kingdom; and that was typical of John. He was never bothered about subjects; he instead was constantly occupied with but one subject: the Person of Christ Jesus. He was therefore totally absorbed in focusing on the Person of Jesus as the Son of God: "This is My beloved Son, in whom I have found My delight; hear Him." That in fact is the Gospel of John. In *his* Gospel John is intent on showing and convincing the church that this man Jesus is the Son of God and, believing in Him, a person has life eternal (John 3:16, 20:31). It was in this manner that John was deeply affected by the vision.

The Effect on James

James has not left us with any writing; nevertheless, he was the first martyr of the church among the apostles, with Stephen, of course, having been the first martyr among all believers in the church. James was gripped especially by the glory of Jesus which he beheld there on that mountain. When the divine glory of the Son of God burst forth and shone through the form of Jesus as a servant—when indeed the moral glory of the Son of man came forth in such fullness—he was so deeply touched by that vision that he was willing to give his life. For James, it was worth it.

The Effect on Us Today

That vision on the Mount of Transfiguration had a tremendous effect upon those three disciples. But what effect does that vision have upon us today? The word *transfiguration* and the word *transformation* have the same basic Greek word—*metamorphosis*, or change. But there is a difference between Jesus' transfiguration and our transformation. We must not only be saved, we must also be transformed. As was indicated earlier in this series of messages, when we are saved, something happens in our spirit: he that is born again of the Spirit of God is spirit (John 3:6b). Our spirit was "dead in sins and transgressions" (see Ephesians 2:1); consequently, we had no contact with God—we having been completely shut out of spiritual things. But when we believed in Jesus, the Holy Spirit came in and quickened our dead spirit, making it a new spirit in which the Holy Spirit can now dwell and cry out with us, "Abba, Father" (Romans 8:15b, Galatians 4:6).

That was regeneration for us. But though we have been regenerated and have a new spirit within us, we still have an old soul. We are still *we*. So what we need is to be transformed in our soul on the basis or foundation of regeneration. The Holy Spirit's task is to transform us by transforming our soul, purifying it and rescuing it from the tyrannical domination of self and thus bringing the soul under the dominion and rule of Christ in order that He may be expressed through our thinking, emotion, and will instead of ourselves being expressed. That is the soulish self's transformation. And finally, at the return coming of the Lord Jesus this body is to be transfigured and is to take up a spiritual body (I Corinthians 15:52b-54b; Philippians 3:21).

Transformation is therefore something that is taking place daily in the life of every believer in Jesus. Whereas regeneration happens once and forever, transformation goes on throughout our entire Christian life. We are in the process of being transformed according to His image from glory to glory by the Lord, the Spirit (II Corinthians 3:18). That is what is continually going on today. And hence, the Mount of Transfiguration is an example set before us of what we are to emulate, but there is a marked difference to be noticed.

The Inherent Glory of the Son of God

In us believers *transformation* is an ongoing process but Jesus' *transfiguration* was not a process; it was instead the breaking forth of what He is originally. It was the manifestation of the glory of the Son of God, the glory which is His inherently and which He shares with His Father from eternity. Thus, it is a glory that is not given. Hence, when Jesus came from heaven to the earth, that original glory of His was totally veiled. During

His earthly walk it was always there, but continually covered. So on the Mount of Transfiguration, what occurred was simply an unveiling of His glory as the Son of God, and it just burst forth.

The Moral Glory of the Son of Man

In addition to that, Jesus' transfiguration constituted also the full manifestation of the moral glory of the Son of man, and that is something which throughout His earthly life He was constantly exhibiting—a moral glory full of grace and truth. From the very beginning—at His birth—grace and truth subsisted in Jesus. The law came by Moses but grace and truth came by, or subsisted in, Christ Jesus. In other words, He brought grace and truth into the world and throughout His entire life He proved and manifested the same. Such was His moral glory on earth. Yet, though that moral glory of His could not be hidden, nevertheless, it had its fullest manifestation on the Mount of Transfiguration because by that time He was morally ready to exit the earth from there. We may therefore say that with respect to Jesus' moral glory there was a process which during His earthly life He had been going through: He had to learn obedience; He had to deny himself; He had to experience sufferings of all kinds in order that His moral glory might shine in full brightness (cf. Hebrews 2:10b, 5:7-9). From all this we can discern that His transfiguration had two facets to it—divine glory *inherent* as the Son of *God* and moral glory *earned* as the Son of *man*.

With respect to ourselves, it is that second facet just mentioned—moral glory earned—which we are—or should be—going through and experiencing ourselves. We have life in us, and depending upon the degree to which we deny ourselves and allow the life of Jesus to take control of our life, to that degree will there be a moral glory coming forth from us, and that constitutes our transformation. If as in a mirror we continually look at Jesus' glory with unveiled face, we shall constantly experience being transformed into His image from glory to glory by the Lord who is the Spirit (II Corinthians 3:17a, 18).

Are We Being Transformed?

We must therefore ask ourselves, Are we being transformed? The Mount of Transfiguration event is to be a continuous process for us. It is not to be an ascent of the mountain and shortly thereafter a descent of it only to end and be forgotten. Indeed, it is not meant to be like Moses' experience, who went up Mount Sinai, remained there forty days and nights in the presence of Jehovah God, and upon coming down and returning to the Israelites' camp did not know that his face shone. That glory on Moses' face was not from within but was put on from without and eventually it faded away (see Exodus 34:29-35). With us today, however, the glory which God is depositing in us is different. It is not something external, put on from without; rather, it is an inward transformation which produces glory from within, just as was the manifestation of the moral glory of Jesus while He was on earth.

In this connection, let us take note of the fact that when God created all living things, He clothed them. Whether it was a cat, a dog, a bird, or whatever, it had "clothes"—whether hide, feathers, hairs, etc.; but strangely, man was seemingly created naked. Yet was that true of man? No, I believe that God in creating all things, dressed them all without exception.

Can it therefore be that when God created man He failed to put clothing upon him? I do not think so, for let us recall that Adam and Eve did not discover they were naked until after they had eaten the fruit of the tree of the knowledge of good and evil. So God evidently did clothe man with glory at his creation; but when Adam and Eve sinned, that glory vanished, and they and all of humanity since, became naked. Now, though, God is going to reclothe His redeemed ones with glory, yet not a placing upon them clothing physically, but morally. Man, being God's masterpiece, has to have some kind of glory as his covering, and that glory comes about through the process of transformation.

Regrettably, quite a few Christians today assume that being saved is all that matters. No, that is but the beginning of the believer's walk with the Lord. God's desire is that we be the men and women of His own thought; that we, too, be clothed with glory; that we be conformed to the image of His beloved Son (Romans 8:29a) because the only begotten Son is intended to be the firstborn among *many* brethren (Romans 8:29b): He is to lead *many* sons into glory (Hebrews 2:10a). This, in fact, is the word of God. Let us all therefore keep the Mount of Transfiguration event ever before us.

Let us learn how we can be transformed: it is nothing less than continually beholding the glory of the Lord with unveiled face (II Corinthians 3:18a). In other words, let there be no veil—no separation—between us and Jesus, for the blood of Jesus cleanses and the veil of the temple has been rent. Let there be no distance develop, therefore, between us and the Lord Jesus. Let our attitude be one of wanting always to behold the glory of the Son of God, the glory of the Son of man, the glory of the King of kings and Lord of lords, the glory of His kingdom, and the glory of His majesty. By continually seeing and beholding Him, the Spirit of God can and will effect within us that vital work of transformation and will thus conform us to the image of Jesus that we see and behold. Thank God for what occurred on the Mount of Transfiguration, for it holds out the hope of inner transformation for every follower of Jesus.

Chapter Eleven

HIS TRIUMPHAL ENTRY

Matthew 21:1-11—And when they drew near to Jerusalem and came to Bethphage, at the mount of Olives, then Jesus sent two disciples, saying to them, Go into the village over against you, and immediately ye will find an ass tied, and a colt with it; loose them and lead them to me. And if any one say anything to you, ye shall say, The Lord has need of them, and straightway he will send them. But all this came to pass, that that might be fulfilled which was spoken through the prophet, saying, Say to the daughter of Zion, Behold thy King cometh to thee, meek, and mounted upon an ass, and upon a colt the foal of an ass. But the disciples, having gone and done as Jesus had ordered them, brought the ass and the colt and put their garments upon them, and he sat on them. But a very great crowd strewed their own garments on the way, and others kept cutting down branches from the trees and strewing them on the way. And the crowds who went before him and who followed cried, saying, Hosanna to the Son of David; blessed be he who comes in the name of the Lord; hosanna in the highest. And as he entered into Jerusalem, the whole city was moved, saying, Who is this? And the crowds said, This is Jesus the prophet who is from Nazareth of Galilee.

Luke 19:28-46—And having said these things, he went on before, going up to Jerusalem. And it came to pass as he drew near to Bethphage and Bethany at the mountain called the mount of Olives, he sent two of his disciples, saying, Go into the village over against you, in which ye will find, on entering it, a colt tied up, on which no child of man ever sat at any time: loose it and lead it here. And if any one ask you, Why do ye loose it? thus shall ye say to him, Because the Lord has need of it. And they that were sent, having gone their way, found as he had said to them. And as they were loosing the colt, its masters said to them, Why loose ye the colt? And they said, Because the Lord has need of it. And they led it to Jesus; and having cast their own garments on the colt, they put Jesus on it. And as he went, they strewed their clothes in the way.

And as he drew near, already at the descent of the mount of Olives, all the multitude of the disciples began, rejoicing, to praise God with a loud voice for all the works of power which they had seen, saying, Blessed the King that comes in the name of the Lord: peace in heaven, and glory in the highest. And some of the Pharisees from the crowd said to him, Teacher, rebuke thy disciples. And he answering said to them, I say unto you, If these shall be silent, the stones will cry out. And as he drew near, seeing the city, he wept over it, saying, If thou hadst known, even thou, even at least in this thy day, the things that are for thy peace: but now they are hid from thine eyes; for days shall come upon thee, that thine enemies shall make a palisaded mound about thee, and shall close thee around, and keep thee in on every side, and shall lay thee even with the ground, and thy children in thee; and shall not leave in thee a stone upon a stone: because thou knewest not the season of thy visitation.

And entering into the temple, he began to cast out those that sold and bought in it, saying to them, It is written, My house is a house of prayer, but ye have made it a den of robbers.

Jesus Set His Face towards Jerusalem

After Jesus and His disciples came down from the Mount of Transfiguration He set His face towards Jerusalem. He knew that the hour of His being received up was going to be fulfilled. He therefore set His face toward Israel's capital, even though He had been warned by some of the Pharisees that Herod wanted to kill Him (Luke 13:31). We may recall Jesus as having said the following: "I will continue to cast out demons and heal the sick today and tomorrow, and the third day I shall be perfected; but I must walk today, tomorrow, and the third day, because it is not right for a prophet to perish outside of Jerusalem" (see Luke 13:32-33).

So Jesus went forward with His face set towards Jerusalem, and in light of what awaited Him there those who followed Him were amazed and became much afraid. From Galilee Jesus passed through Samaria, and then He entered the territory of Judea, and from there He crossed over the river Jordan and remained for a time on the eastern side. I do not intend to mention all the details, it would take too long to cover them all; for if you were to read all four Gospels with that in mind, you would be surprised to learn that the greater portion of those Gospels are devoted to recording the many things Jesus had said or done *after* He had set His face towards Jerusalem. But our time together today will be focused solely on His triumphal entry into Jerusalem.

Now it all had begun in the village of Bethany. Jesus sent two of His disciples to a village opposite Bethany which was Bethphage. These were two villages opposite each other and situated very near the Mount of Olives. Whereas the name Bethany means "the house of dates" or "the house of affliction," the name Bethphage means "the house of unripe figs." Now before Jesus sent His two disciples to Bethphage He had told them they would notice an ass tied there along with its colt and that they were to loose them and bring them to Him. Moreover, if anyone should ask them why they were doing this, they were simply to say, "The Lord has need of them," and the owners would let them go.

We know for certain that Jesus had entered Jerusalem a number of times. He had nearly always entered the city privately and, once, He even entered it secretly. This latter instance we will recall from John 7. The Feast of Tabernacles was approaching while Jesus was still in Galilee. It was then that His brothers, who did not believe in Jesus, had advised Him, saying: "If You want to make a name for yourself, you must go to Jerusalem where the people are. Don't hide yourself here in Galilee." But the Lord's response was: "Your time is always ready, but My hour has not yet come. You go." So Jesus stayed behind. But after they themselves left for Jerusalem, His hour came; and it was on this occasion that He went and entered secretly into the city. In the middle period of the days-long Feast He showed himself to the people, and told them on the last day of the Feast that if anyone was thirsty, he could come and drink of Him, and out of his innermost being would flow rivers of living water (vv. 14, 37-38).

So whereas Jesus had previously entered Jerusalem many times in His life—yet, either nearly always privately or else secretly—this present instance was the only time that He entered Jerusalem in a public way. Not only that, if one reads the Gospel narratives carefully, one finds that Jesus had actually planned and made arrangements for it. It was not an event which just happened. This we see evidence for in the fact that He sent two disciples in advance to get an ass and its colt and bring them to Him. So they went and brought to Him the ass along with its colt. All the disciples then took off their outermost garments, placed them on the ass and the colt, Jesus proceeded to ride on the colt, and the entire entourage headed towards Jerusalem.

They started from Bethany and Bethphage and a crowd followed them. At about the same time as they and the crowd began to come down from the Mount of Olives, another crowd commenced coming out from the city of Jerusalem. Now the members of this latter crowd were not inhabitants of Jerusalem because, as we would say today, they were too sophisticated and condescending in their attitude for that. Rather, these were out-of-town pilgrims who, having arrived from all over the land of Israel for the Passover Feast and had heard especially about the raising up of Lazarus, began coming out from the city to meet Jesus upon their hearing that He was coming (John 11:55-56, 12:9, 12). Evidently, these two crowds met together at the descent of the Mount of Olives—a place where the city of Jerusalem could be seen beginning to come into view. So when these two crowds met, the people comprising them—but especially the disciples of Jesus—rejoiced enthusiastically. They were so excited that they began to shout: "Hosanna to the Son of David. Blessed is He who comes in the name of the Lord. Behold, the King is coming; behold, the kingdom of David is coming. Hosanna, glory in the Highest."

But some of the Pharisees who were in the crowd turned to Jesus and said, "Rebuke your disciples." For the first time during this event the Lord Jesus opened His mouth and said the following: "Were these people to remain silent, the very stones would cry out." So the procession continued.

Then there was a turn and Jerusalem was out of sight for a few minutes. But as they began to ascend towards a ledge of smooth rock, suddenly, the city of Jerusalem appeared before them again, and this was the moment when Jesus beheld Jerusalem and wept. This was an altogether different kind of weeping from what Jesus had manifested when He learned that Lazarus was dead (see John 11). Mary was weeping, and those who came to comfort her were weeping, and Jesus wept, too (v. 35). But it was a silent weeping which He exhibited over the loss of His friend Lazarus, whereas upon now viewing the city of Jerusalem, Jesus wept aloud: "Jerusalem, you do not know what is going to happen to you. Had you only known, yet you have refused. You shall be leveled to the ground and utterly destroyed, for there shall not be left in thee a single stone resting upon another."

Nevertheless, Jesus and the crowds continued on till they finally entered Jerusalem. The whole city was moved, and people there began to ask: "Who is this fellow? Who is this man?" And the crowds answered: "This is Jesus of Nazareth, the Prophet." After entering the city Jesus looked all around and thereafter left and returned to Bethany. Such, then, is a brief account of Jesus' triumphal entry into Jerusalem.

Reasons for Jesus' Public Entry into Jerusalem

Yet why did Jesus deliberately enter Jerusalem at this particular juncture in His life and in this way? He had never done it in this manner before. Why did He do it in this way at this moment? Did He not know that he was to be rejected? Did He not know that he would be crucified? Of course He did, for back on the Mount of Transfiguration, He had been discussing it with Moses and Elijah. Furthermore, on three different occasions He had told His disciples that He would be going to Jerusalem, would be rejected and crucified, but that on the third day afterwards He would be raised from the dead. So why *did* Jesus enter Jerusalem in such a public fashion? I think there are at least three reasons.

Presented Himself Publicly As King

The first reason has to do with Jesus' Kingship. We know from Scripture that He was born a King—even born the King of the Jews (John 18:33-37). He was born to be the Savior of the world and thus His name was to be Jesus, the One who takes away the sin of the world. He was the promised Messiah who would come to rescue God's people. Throughout Jesus' life, however, He had never previously claimed publicly His Messiahship, His Kingship. Nevertheless, throughout His life—especially during the last three or so years—He had demonstrated to the people that He is the promised Messiah, the Son of David, the King of the Jews. He had demonstrated His Messiahship and Kingship by His life, by His words and by His works, but He had never publicly claimed this as being His position among God's people. The people should have been able to recognize it, but they failed to do so. So finally, at the last minute, as it were, Jesus presented himself to the people, both formally and publicly, as their Messiah-King. This became necessary for the sake of testimony. There could be no yea or nay in this matter, for Jesus was indeed the Jewish people's Messiah-King. If they received Him, they would be saved; if they did not, they would be judged. Hence, the first reason Jesus must enter Jerusalem in the way He did was because He needed to present himself publicly as a testimony to the Jews that He is the promised Messiah and that He is their King.

Jesus' Entry: a Fulfillment of Prophecy

The second reason was for the purpose of fulfilling the prophecy found in the book of Zechariah which had promised some five hundred years before Christ that the Messiah-King of the Jewish people would eventually come, and would do so in the following manner: "Rejoice greatly, daughter of Zion; shout, daughter of Jerusalem! Behold, thy King cometh to thee: he is just, and having salvation; lowly and riding upon an ass, even upon a colt the foal of an ass" (9:9).

With extraordinary accuracy and in great detail, this long-ago prophecy had described how Christ the King would enter Jerusalem in the presence of His people and how they would respond. Let us carefully note that prior to King Jesus, there had never been any king in history who had ever ridden upon an ass or ass's colt.

In this connection, there is a true story about a donkey-driver who was saved because of that verse in Luke 19 which says that no one before this moment had ever ridden upon the colt mentioned there; thus signifying that it had never been broken in. Now if a beast of burden has never been broken in, is anyone able to ride upon it? The answer is, No. So when the donkey-driver heard the narrative of Jesus having ridden upon that colt which had never been broken in, he remarked that Jesus must be divine because no man can do that. The wonder of wonders is the fact that the colt had allowed the Lord Jesus to ride upon it without any complaint, resistance, or outright rejection.

If you know anything about an ass you know that it is a very tricky animal. When I was young, my family did not have a car. So when my father would come home from the railroad station, he would always ride a donkey; and all the children liked to have a ride on it. Even so, riding a donkey or an ass can be a very tricky affair. But here in the case of Jesus, that colt upon which He rode into Jerusalem quietly and meekly allowed Him to do so most smoothly. Even with all the excitement which went on around this colt along the entire route, it never got excited in the least. It is indeed a wonder of wonders!

The Lord Jesus rode into Jerusalem on this colt the foal of an ass, and that was a tremendous fulfillment of Old Testament prophecy. His riding on that colt also reveals what kind of King He is, it indicative of how greatly different is *His* Kingship from all the other kingships of the earth. It was the fulfillment of prophecy. In fact, the life of Jesus was a continuous, unfailing fulfillment of all the prophecies in the Bible, and this event in His life was no exception.

Jesus' Entry: Demonstrating the Love of God

The third reason Jesus had to enter Jerusalem in such a public display of himself as the Jewish people's Messiah-King has to do with the love of God. We may recall Jesus having spoken a parable about the man who planted a fig tree in his vineyard. For three years there was no fruit. So finally, the owner said to the vinedresser, "Destroy it; it does not bear any fruit. What is the use of letting it occupy the land?" But the vinedresser said, "Allow it to remain; let me work on it just a little more. If it bears fruit, fine; if not, then cut it down" (Luke 13:6-9). Jesus had been presenting himself and working among the Jews for three years already. Figuratively speaking, He had been trying to tend that fig tree, which was a symbol of the Jewish nation, by constantly attempting to give it spiritual nourishment. Yet, for three years there was no fruit, only leaves. It was time for it to be cut down, but Jesus' response was similar to that vinedresser's in the parable: "Allow Me to make one last effort. I will try again. If still no fruit comes forth, then the nation must be cut off." Formerly, He had never publicly proclaimed himself as the Jewish nation's Messiah-King. Now in order that there be no misunderstanding and no excuse, He presented himself to the nation, as it were, as her Messiah-King. This was Jesus' last effort and the last expression of God's love; but when that love was rejected, that nation, as represented by the parabolic fig tree, had to be cursed (cf. Matthew 21:18-19) and judgment had to fall upon the Jewish nation.

It can be stated, therefore, that the Lord Jesus entered Jerusalem in triumph for three very good reasons.

The Lesson for Us from This Event

What is the message to us? What lesson does God want us to learn from this event? I believe He wants us to learn much concerning the Kingship of Jesus. As the Son of God, all things were created in Him, by Him, and for Him. He is the Sovereign over all things and the heir of all things. He is their Majesty, their King. This was and is His original, inherent right. Yet, His Kingship and His rulership was challenged by the rebellion of the archangel Lucifer (Isaiah 14:12-14) and also by the sin of humanity's forefather, Adam. Because of this, Jesus' Kingship was rejected. But in the fullness of time the Word became flesh. The Son of God came to the earth to be the Son of man. He was born of the royal family of David and was thus born the King of the Jews; but He was born in a small town, Bethlehem, and not in Jerusalem, the prestigious capital. Nor was He born in a palace but was born in a manger. He was raised in the Galilean town of Nazareth, that hilly, obscure, out-of-the-way place. Moreover, He had never attended any rabbinical school, and yet He was King.

The Son of God came as the Son of man to save the world. He came to serve and not to be served. He came to die for the sins of the world, to redeem and to restore the world back to God. This Jesus was a totally different King since He was neither a king according to the world's concept nor according to the concept of the Jews, who during the time of the Messiah-King had thought He would come with overwhelming power, overthrow the Roman yoke, and make Israel the first among all the nations of the earth; they also believed their Messiah would be a King who would sit on David's throne, issue orders, and be served and not serve. Now that was the Jews' concept of what their Messiah-King would be like and what their concept of a kingdom would be like. However, when Jesus came into the world, He was indeed the King, but He offered to God's people a different kind of kingdom: it was the real kingdom—a kingdom of light, a kingdom of righteousness, a kingdom of love. Jesus offered himself as their King who would serve and not be served—indeed, a Servant-King.

Even when Jesus as the Son of man entered Jerusalem, presenting himself as the Jewish nation's King, He did not ride on a magnificent white horse; He instead rode on a colt the foal of an ass. That is a true picture of *His* Kingship—a Servant-King. A colt is a beast of burden, thus indicating that Jesus came to labor: that is to say, to serve and not to be served (Mark 10:45). He had to bring in and demonstrate the spiritual reality of what His kingdom is all about before that kingdom could be publicly manifested in this world; but the Jews at that time did not understand Him. And because the Son of man was not a King according to their concept, He was rejected by them, was crucified, and the nation entered into judgment.

Thank God, however, that on the third day following His crucifixion, Jesus was raised from the dead. He appeared to the disciples for forty days, teaching them about the kingdom of God, and then He ascended up on high. Revelation 5 lays out the scene of His ascension, it being a replay to the apostle John of the scene of His ascension. There in heaven the Lord Jesus, as the Lamb newly slain, stands before the throne of God, where is manifested the fact that He is the only one who is worthy to take up the little book that is the title deed to the entire universe. He takes it up into His hands, opens its seals, and executes the Father's will—thus bringing all things back to God and inheriting from the Father the nations as His rightful inheritance. This is parallel to what Psalm 2 records of what Jehovah God declares: "Ask of Me and I will give You the nations as Your inheritance" (see v.8). This is what happened when the Lord Jesus ascended back to heaven. And He is now sitting there on the right hand of the Majesty, executing the will of God His Father until that day when He shall come back to the earth—*this* time indeed mounted upon a white horse—to destroy His and our enemy and establish His kingdom here on the earth.

Yet even while He was still on the earth, Jesus was gathering His disciples around himself. Then, after His ascension He sent His Holy Spirit down, and 120 of His disciples were baptized by the Spirit into one body (Acts 1:15, 2:1-4). Throughout these twenty centuries since then, and wherever the gospel has been preached, many have been brought into the body of Christ. To them the Lord Jesus is their

Messiah and Savior-King. He saves us by giving His life for us. He shows mercy and grace to us. He brings us into His kingdom. However, He never, ever forces us with any strong, heavy hand into obeying Him and submitting ourselves to His Kingship. Jesus will never do that. Yet, this does not mean that He never lays His claim upon us as our King. Indeed, He does. Nevertheless, what He uses is His love by which to constrain us in causing us to willingly submit ourselves and accept Him as our King—not only as our Savior but also as our King.

Individually, We Must Respond

One day the claim of His Kingship will come upon you. It will be much better if it comes to you at the time you are saved. It should; unfortunately, however, the gospel is not for the most part being preached fully; instead, we preach the Gospel according to Luke—that Jesus Christ comes to save and to forgive our sins. Yes, we must thank God that the Lord Jesus is our Savior. But we do not likewise preach the Gospel according to Matthew—that He is our King; which is to say that we are not only to believe in Him but also to obey Him. That is a more complete gospel. We must not only accept Him as our Savior but also as our Savior-King. We need to yield our lives to Him. This should happen at the time all believers are saved but, sad to say, because they have not heard the full gospel, many of God's people are saved but they still do not surrender their lives to the Lord Jesus and accept Him as their King, their Sovereign, their Ruler. They are still masters of their lives. But the day will come when the claim of His Kingship will descend upon all who have only believed but have not yet obeyed.

One day the claim of the Lord Jesus upon you as your King will come to your life, and when that day of His claim comes, how will you respond? Will you respond in the way of the Pharisees and the rulers of the Jews? The Lord Jesus does not use force nor does He set himself up as a tyrant; rather, He exhibits meekness and lowliness. He will never fit in with any earthly concept of kingship which we may have; therefore, though you may be saved, you will begin to despise Him. You will think you can treat Him any way you want to: if you need Him, you will call upon Him; on the other hand, if you do not agree with Him, you will ask Him to depart from you. Thus, you will want to have your own way. Is that the way you are going to respond to the claim of the Lord Jesus as your King? Or are you going to respond to Him as those householders in Bethphage had done? When the Son of man was in need of a colt, they willingly—even gladly—released their colt into the hands of the Lord.

Moreover, will you respond to the Lord's claim as the King in the same way which that colt had done? Figuratively speaking, we each of us are that colt whom the Lord Jesus needs. He needs to ride upon each of us in His triumphal entry into Jerusalem. Are we willing to submit ourselves to Him as did that colt? How true it is that no one has ever ridden upon us; for we are unbroken. Should anyone attempt to ride upon us, we shall be quick to shake him off of us. That is the way too many of us are.

Permit me to ask, Has the love of God ever tamed you, restrained you? Nobody has ever ridden upon you, but are you willing to let Christ Jesus ride upon you? Are you willing to carry Him in triumph as King to Jerusalem? Nobody would ever have remembered that colt had not the Bible mentioned it. What happened to that colt afterwards? No one knows; nevertheless, it was wonderfully used by Jesus to fulfill a tremendous prophecy—that of the King of kings coming to His people. Are you therefore willing to be like that colt?

Allow me to ask this of you as well: Are you like that crowd of people in the streets of Jerusalem who cried out: "Hosanna to the Son of David"? Or are you like those Pharisees who said to Jesus: "Forbid them"? How shall you respond?

Individually, we each of us must respond. I believe that that claim of the Lord Jesus will one day come upon you. If it has not come yet, it will surely come; and how are you going to respond to His claim as your King? Is He really your King? Are you allowing Him to rule over your life? Are you giving yourself over to Him, obeying and submitting to Him in all things?

We Must Also Respond Corporately

On that day two thousand years ago when Jesus entered Jerusalem and presented himself to the Jewish people as their Messiah-King, they ended up crucifying Him, and their ancient city of Jerusalem was eventually destroyed in 70 A.D. The temple was destroyed, with not a stone left resting upon another stone; that is to say, God's judgment fell upon it. But are we not the new Israel of God today? (Galatians 6:16) Are we not the new Jerusalem which God is building? One day the new Jerusalem shall descend from heaven with the throne of God and of the Lamb in the midst of it (Revelation 21:2, 9-10; 22:3b). There, Jesus, the Lamb of God, is exalted as the sovereign King and is joyfully received. But how about today? Jesus once said, "Where two or three are gathered together unto My name, there am I in the midst of them" (see Matthew 18:20). What does it mean—"two or three gathered in My name"? It means that where two or three or more are gathered together, thus placing themselves corporately under the name of the Lord Jesus—that is to say, under His authority, Kingship, and Lordship, allowing Him to be the Head and themselves the body—Jesus shall be in their midst, thus enthroned in the midst of His people. In such a circumstance as that, the King shall be in their midst and there shall be the shout of the King in the midst of the congregation (cf. Numbers 23:21b).

Is this true with all of us believers today? How many so-called Christian congregations there are where the name of the Lord Jesus is not honored, His word is not kept, and His throne is not set. Instead, men themselves sit upon the throne; and at the same time tradition rules. But the King is coming, meek and lowly, and riding upon a colt. Are we willing to accept Him corporately and let this Servant-King sit in the midst of the new city—New Jerusalem?

I do believe this event in the life of Jesus is not only a "must" message meant for the nation of Israel but is also recorded in God's word as a message to us all today. And so, I shall conclude with Psalm 24:7-10, a Messianic psalm: "Lift up your heads, ye gates, and be ye lifted up, ye everlasting doors, and the King of glory shall come in. Who is this King of glory? Jehovah strong and mighty, Jehovah mighty in battle. Lift up your heads, ye gates; yea, lift up, ye everlasting doors, and the King of glory shall come in. Who is he, this King of glory? Jehovah of hosts, he is the King of glory."

Chapter Twelve

THE LAST SUPPER

John 13:1-5,34-35—Now before the feast of the passover, Jesus, knowing that his hour had come that he should depart out of this world to the Father, having loved his own who were in the world, loved them to the end. And during supper, the devil having already put it into the heart of Judas son of Simon, Iscariote, that he should deliver him up, Jesus, knowing that the Father had given him all things into his hands, and that he came out from God and was going to God, rises from supper and lays aside his garments, and having taken a linen towel he girded himself: then he pours water into the washhand basin, and began to wash the feet of the disciples, and to wipe them with the linen towel with which he was girded.

A new commandment I give to you, that ye love one another; as I have loved you, that ye also love one another. By this shall all know that ye are disciples of mine, if ye have love amongst yourselves.

John 14:1,15-18—Let not your heart be troubled; ye believe on God, believe also on me.

If ye love me, keep my commandments. And I will beg the Father, and he will give you another Comforter, that he may be with you for ever, the Spirit of truth, whom the world cannot receive, because it does not see him nor know him; but ye know him, for he abides with you, and shall be in you. I will not leave you orphans, I am coming to you.

John 15:1-8—I am the true vine, and my Father is the husbandman. As to every branch in me not bearing fruit, he takes it away; and as to every one bearing fruit, he purges it that it may bring forth more fruit. Ye are already clean by reason of the word which I have spoken to you. Abide in me and I in you. As the branch cannot bear fruit of itself unless it abide in the vine, thus neither can ye unless ye abide in me. I am the vine, ye are the branches. He that abides in me and I in him, he bears much fruit; for without me ye can do nothing. Unless any one abide in me he is cast out as the branch, and is dried up; and they gather them and cast them into the fire, and they are burned. If ye abide in me, and my words abide in you, ye shall ask what ye will and it shall come to pass to you. In this is my Father glorified, that ye bear much fruit, and ye shall become disciples of mine.

John 16:33—These things have I spoken to you that in me ye might have peace. In the world ye have tribulation; but be of good courage: I have overcome the world.

John 17:1,11,25-26—These things Jesus spoke, and lifted up his eyes to heaven and said, Father, the hour is come; glorify thy Son, that thy Son may glorify thee.

And I am no longer in the world, and these are in the world, and I come to thee. Holy Father, keep them in thy name which thou hast given me, that they may be one as we.

Righteous Father,—and the world has not known thee, but I have known thee, and these have known that thou hast sent me. And I have made known to them thy name, and will make it known; that the love with which thou hast loved me may be in them and I in them.

In meditating together on the life of the Lord Jesus we considered last time His royal entry into Jerusalem, which event commenced what many in the church have come to call the Passion Week. Much has been recorded in the four Gospels concerning that last week in Jesus' life before His resurrection from the dead. It was a most important week, but because of time constraints we are not able to delve into all that happened; we shall therefore select only a few of the many events and meditate together on those few, beginning this morning with the last supper Jesus had with His disciples.

On the fourteenth day of the Jewish month of Nicene, the Passover Feast was observed. For the first and only time in Jesus' earthly life He himself prepared this Passover Feast for His disciples. For it so happened that in the past He had been a guest in the home of some family, but on this occasion Jesus now gathered His disciples around Him as His own family and, as the head of the family, He prepared this Passover Feast himself.

He commanded two of His disciples, John and Peter, to go into Jerusalem, and were told by their Master that when they saw a man with a pitcher of water, they were to follow that man to his house and ask the owner: "Where is My room that I may eat My Passover Feast with My disciples?" (see Luke 22:7-11)

It seems that throughout Jesus' life He was always borrowing something from His friends. For instance, when He was born He had borrowed a manger because the innkeeper in Bethlehem was not that friendly and said that there was no room in his inn (Luke 2:7). Or when he was about to have this last supper with His disciples, He borrowed a room from one who loved Him. Then, too, we are aware that after Jesus died, He as it were borrowed the tomb which Joseph of Arimathea had prepared for himself (Matthew 27:57-60). All these instances demonstrate for us the grace of God because Jesus—who was rich and the Creator of the entire universe and who thus owned all things—became poor for our sake that in His voluntary poverty we ourselves might be enriched (II Corinthians 8:9).

So it seems that Jesus was always borrowing things from people. As a matter of fact, in this present instance of Jesus asking His disciples to find a room for Him and them to celebrate the Passover Feast, let us notice that the Greek word for room or guestchamber appearing in Luke 22:11 of the Greek New Testament is *kataluma*. What is pictured for us here by the use of this Greek word is an open area such as a courtyard where travelers' beasts of burden can be unloaded of their burdens and where travelers' staffs, shoes, and other dirty belongings can be laid down. In other words, this open camp-like area was a very common place for resting—even probably the *worst* place on the grounds of a given homeowner's residence; nevertheless, that was all which Jesus requested to be set aside for His use.

So Jesus only asked for a very common, low-quality space for observing the Passover Feast. But having requested this from a friend of His—a man who loved Him—what did that man give the Lord? He gave Him the upper room—*anagaion* in Greek—which was the best room in the house (Luke 22:12): a large chamber that was often situated over a porch or connected with the home's roof and where meals were served and which provided great privacy.

Let us observe that whenever the Lord asks something from us, He always asks what is the minimal, the lowest, the very least from us. Yet how do we react to Him? Do we say there is no room in our inn, or do we give Him the upper room? The upper room was very important because it was not only where Jesus had His last supper with His disciples, it was also the place where the church began when on the day of Pentecost those 120 disciples of Jesus were gathered there and the Holy Spirit came down upon them and in one Spirit they were baptized into one body (Acts 1:15, 2:1-4).

This Passover Feast observance by the Lord Jesus with the Twelve was the first and only time that Jesus offered up a sacrifice (cf. Luke 22:7-8). Previously He had never offered up a sacrifice, but on this occasion He did so because His time had come. In fact, He himself was the Paschal Lamb sacrifice. In that one offering Jesus offered up himself and that offering epitomized the substance of this last supper. After *that* supper there was no more Passover provided by God because the spiritual reality of the Passover observance had finally been fulfilled in that our Passover (Paschal) Lamb had been sacrificed.

Washing the Disciples' Feet

Jesus gathered His own around himself and, during that last supper, He stood up. We are told by authorities on the subject that during the Passover Feast observance there are a number of specifically named cups which were to be drunk. The first cup was called the cup of thanksgiving which the head of the family would raise up and bless. The next thing to occur was for the family head to arise and wash his hands before the family could continue with beginning to eat the real supper. It needs to be mentioned that Jesus did not follow this outward ritual but actually transformed it by adding real and practical elements to the observance of Passover. Instead of washing His hands, Jesus rose up, took off His outer garment, attached a linen towel to His waist, poured water into a basin, and commenced to wash His disciples' feet.

Why did He do that? John 13 informs us that Jesus loved the Twelve who, though they were in the world, were nonetheless His own, and that He loved them to the end. Therefore, before He would leave them, He would once again demonstrate His love for them by washing their feet. The Greek word for the English word end here conveys more in its meaning than simply the idea of time—to the last; it also conveys the idea of quality—to the uttermost: Jesus has loved us to the very last, and He has loved us to the most extreme degree. In other words, He has done everything for us that He could to bring us to His fullness, and hence there is nothing more He can do.

We need to realize that the Lord was not observing a ritual here; He never did; rather, He was expressing His love for His own—the Twelve—and wanted to do everything necessary for them. As a matter of fact, these disciples' feet had not yet been washed upon their entering that upper chamber. It was usually the case among the Jews back then that whenever anyone was invited to a meal in someone's home, there would be a maid at the door to wash that guest's feet. This was because at that time there were no paved roads and, hence, the roads were extremely dusty and dirty. And because, further, people wore sandals instead of shoes, much dirt would have attached itself to the guest's feet and thus meaning that the first thing which must be done was for the guest's feet to be washed. It was a work done by girl servants and slaves and, given the nature of this particular work, it was considered to be the lowest form of work. Oddly enough, that evening when His disciples entered the upper room, all things had been provided by their Master for their feet to be washed, except that there was no maid!—the water was there; the basin was there; the towel was there; but there was no maid. Most likely, this was a purposeful prearrangement made by the Son of man.

These disciples had all come into that upper room expecting, by custom, that a maid would instantly come forward to wash their feet—to refresh them—so that they could enjoy the Passover Feast, but there was no maid to be seen. Moreover, when the Twelve entered that upper chamber, they were once again arguing among themselves concerning the matter of "Who [was] the greatest?" Even at this late date in the life of their Master these disciples were still quarreling and striving among themselves as to who of them was the greatest! So upon entering the room and seeing no one available to wash their feet and because none of them would ever think of washing the others' feet, they all reluctantly seated themselves at the table in an un-refreshed state. More than likely each of them tried to assume the highest seat. As a matter of fact, it is believed that Judas Iscariot secured that seat of honor for himself. This, then, was the kind of atmosphere which now pervaded the room: not only their feet were dirty, their souls were dirty as well. Out of His great love, therefore, their Master and Teacher was most willing to humble himself at the feet of His disciples and wash their soiled feet. Love is willing to descend to the lowest place and do the meanest job.

The Bible scholar, Alfred Edersheim, has attempted to draw a picture for us of where he thought the disciples were sitting and, for him, Simon Peter was seated at the end of the Feast table and was probably the very first one to have his feet washed. Now when Jesus came to him intending to wash his feet, Simon said, "Lord, do You intend to wash my feet? Never!" Though he was too proud to wash the others' feet, he knew this much—that it most certainly was not the task of the Lord Jesus to do such a thing. But Jesus answered: "What I am doing, you do not understand now, but you will understand afterwards."

Peter, not satisfied, and becoming increasingly uncomfortable, told Him, "No, never! You can never wash my feet." So Jesus replied, "If I do not wash you, you can have no part with Me." Hearing this word from the Master, Peter told Him: "Lord, I want to have all parts with You; therefore, wash not only my feet but also my head, my hands, and everything else." To which Jesus said, "No; those who have bathed themselves have no need to wash anything again except the feet." So Jesus began to wash Peter's feet. He in fact washed the feet of all of them and wiped them dry; and after He had finished with everyone, He put back on His outer garment, sat down at the feast table, and began to speak: "Do you understand what I have done to you? If not, then you shall know now. You call Me Teacher and Lord—and so I am." Jesus knew who He was. As a matter of fact, He knew at that time that the Father had given all things into His hands (John 3:35, 13:3a); that He is the Lord of all. He could therefore say to His disciples: "As your Teacher and your Lord I have washed your feet. And thus I have set an example for you: Wash the feet of one another."

A New Commandment

Jesus also said, "A new commandment I give to you. As I have loved you, love one another, and then you will be disciples of Mine." And this act of washing the disciples' feet was an expression of Jesus' love. It tells us how He loved the Twelve and how He loves us today; and, in just the way He loves us, He wants us to love one another and wash one another's feet.

Why, though, does Jesus call this a *new* commandment? Now we know that in the Old Testament there is this commandment: "Love your neighbor as yourself" (see Leviticus 19:18b). Yet here Jesus declares that what He is giving His disciples is a new commandment; and it is indeed new because the love that He requires of us is not our natural love; rather, it is the love that He has already given us; for Jesus said to His disciples: "I have loved you; I have given My love to you; now use *that* love—and not your natural love—to love one another."

From this we realize that this New Testament commandment which Jesus now made known to His disciples is more than a command, order, or obligation of *law*—which is quite typical of the Old Testament commandments; for in addition, Jesus' new commandment is marked by *grace*, since along with the command there is the capacity or ability to obey because Jesus has already given us the love with which to love one another. To put it another way, on the one hand, we do not by nature have within us the love which Jesus' new commandment requires of us to express in loving one another; on the other hand, that love has been graciously given to us by the Lord Jesus and thus we now have the ability to love one another with *that* love and not with our natural love. This latter love was what the Old Testament commandment had reference to when it ordered the people to "love your neighbor as yourself." We all do in fact love ourselves, but what exactly is that love? It is self-love and, therefore, according to this Old Testament command, it is enough to simply love your neighbor as you love yourself. But the commandment which Jesus has issued is this: "You are to love one another even as I have loved you." Hence, the love in view here is one that is totally different in *kind*: not self-love but divine love; it is God's *agape* love, the love of Christ. Therefore, commands Jesus, use *that* love to love one another.

Yet who are the neighbors whom Jesus has in mind here when He says, "Love one another"? These are all who belong to Him. We who believe in the Lord Jesus are the "one another." We are to love one another. It is brotherly love that He commands us to express. This brotherly love, this "love one another," is the sign—the mark—of the disciples of the Lord Jesus. If we demonstrate *that* love, then we demonstrate and prove that we are His disciples. If we do not demonstrate His love, how will the world know that we are disciples of Jesus? How, then, do we demonstrate that love? We do so by washing the feet of one another.

The Defilement of the World

Thank God, we have all been washed. When we were baptized, we were immersed into the water and we were all washed, cleansed by the word of God; but as we have contact with this world in our daily life, as our feet touch this world, its dirt will begin to accumulate upon our feet. Is it not true that as we walk through this world and have contact with it, we feel defiled? We may not fall into sin, but in our heart and spirit we are not fresh and living. There seems to be some kind of cloud, some kind of darkness, some sense of uncleanness that descends upon us, and our fellowship with the Lord seems to be dimmed if not totally broken.

Early in the morning, when you get up and have your time with the Lord, you are so refreshed, and you go out into the world refreshed. But in the evening, when you return home, you are not as fresh before the Lord as previously. Perhaps you are struggling and find that your soul is burdened: there seems to be some weight upon you, something is unclear. You cannot say you have sinned; indeed, you may not have sinned through the day; nevertheless, you sense that you have been defiled by the world: your feet are dirty and you need to be refreshed; you thus need to be washed. If we as the children of God love one another, we will need to wash one another's feet. When your brother or sister is low in his or her spirit, when there seems to be a kind of cloud in their fellowship or in their relationship with the Lord, then you will need to go and wash their feet—that is to say, you will need to try to refresh them and bring them into a clear fellowship with the Lord. That is what is meant by washing the feet.

Let me illustrate this somewhat more practically. Suppose you come to a prayer meeting which occurs after a long day's work when you are very tired; you have been touched by the world and all kinds of things have crowded into your mind. So when you arrive at the meeting, probably you feel very heavy and have no desire to pray. But during the meeting, you hear a chorus or a hymn being sung and, suddenly, you find you are washed, you are refreshed, your spirit rises up. Or perhaps a brother or a sister prays, and that prayer lifts you up. Perhaps a testimony is also given, and that testimony refreshes you. This is washing one another's feet. Not only should this be taking place in the meeting but likewise in our daily life, when we are in contact with brothers and sisters; and so, if we really love one another, we should try to lift the spirits of our brethren. We should try to wash and refresh them so that their fellowship with the Lord will be transparent and that they may go on to enjoy Him. This is love.

We learn from Numbers 19 that God made provision for the children of Israel while they were traveling through the wilderness. He commanded them to bring a red heifer to be burned to the point of total ashes. The ashes were then to be put in a clean place outside the camp. Whenever an Israelite touched a dead body, either consciously or unconsciously, he was considered defiled and had to be purified with the water of purification. They put some of the burnt heifer's ashes into a vessel and added living water to it, and then a clean person would sprinkle this water of purification upon the defiled person so that he would be purified. Otherwise, he would be excommunicated and would have to go outside of the camp. He would be unclean; therefore, were he to remain in the camp he would make the entire camp unclean. In our New Testament era the washing of the feet for cleansing and refreshment performs the same function as did the ashes of the red heifer for purification in the Old Testament times.

We today are a part of the house of God. Yes, we have been washed; yes, we are a clean people. But in our contact with the world we touch something dead, and anything that is dead defiles. We may even touch the dead in ourselves, that is, in our flesh. We may also touch death around us in the world or even in our brothers and sisters, and whenever we touch death we are defiled. We need to be purified and this comes about, figuratively speaking, by the application of the burnt heifer's ashes and the living water. Now the ash is the last form of that burnt red heifer. In other words, it represents the finished work of Christ that is always there and ready to be applied. Jesus does not need to go to the cross many times—only once and for all. The ash is death, but the Spirit of life—a picture for us as the living water—applies the finished work of Christ upon our souls and we are washed clean and refreshed.

Who is to do that for us today? On that last Passover night it was Jesus himself who was doing the washing, but today it is His body that continues that cleansing work. It is more than an obligation or a duty; it is the love of God with which we must wash one another's feet by sharing with them in the power of the Holy Spirit the finished work of Christ. We are like that clean person, helping to purify the unclean, and this is an expression of the love of God.

The Lord Is Purifying the Church

The Lord loved His church and gave himself up for it, and He sanctified it, purifying it by the washing of the water by the word, that He may present that church to himself a glorious church without spot or wrinkle or any of such sort (Ephesians 5:25b-27). The Lord is washing us. He is washing His church all the time; and that is by the Spirit of life. He is sanctifying and purifying His church by the water with the word; that is the finished work of Christ. He is always purifying us. How the church needs to be sanctified and purified all the time, in order that He may present us to himself as a glorious church without spot or wrinkle.

This washing of the feet is also fellowship. The Lord said to Simon Peter, "If you do not allow Me to wash you, then you have no part with Me." What is fellowship? Fellowship is imparting Christ to one another, and when we impart Christ to one another, we purify one another.

Let us not be too proud to be washed. Sometimes we are too proud: we may feel we do not need Christ; that we do not need our brothers and sisters. Let us be humble enough to receive washing from others. Let us not be like Peter at the very beginning of his transaction with Jesus on that Passover night.

He did not want to be washed, and the Lord's response was: "If I don't wash you, you have no part with Me." On the one hand, we as brothers and sisters must always be ready to wash our brethren's feet, to do the lowest work, to share Christ with them, to lift them up. On the other hand, we must always be humble enough to receive washing from them, for we need fellowship with one another.

The Betrayer

Now Jesus and His disciples began to partake of their last supper together, and the Lord began to be troubled in His spirit. He told His disciples that one of them was going to betray Him. He felt sorry for that person, knowing it would be better if that person had never been born. He was not thinking at all of himself here but felt extremely sorry for the betrayer. At this point all the disciples began to inquire: "Is it I? Is it I?" Peter, being at the other end of the table from Jesus, made signs to John to ask who the betrayer might be. John was on the left side of the Lord, and when he reclined, he could easily have had his head resting on the bosom of Christ. So John looked up and said, "Who is it?" Jesus replied: "He it is to whom, after I have dipped the morsel, I give it." Judas was on the honorable side—the right side—of Jesus, and so he whispered to Him: "Is it I?" Jesus dipped the morsel and gave it to him.

According to Jewish tradition, whenever a family began to partake of the supper, the head of the family would take a morsel, which was bread wrapped up with bitter herb (today, it is a wrapped piece of lamb), dip it in a sauce of apple and almond, and then give it to the first person to receive it and who would be the honorable guest. Jesus therefore took that morsel, dipped it, and when Judas asked, "Is it I?" He gave it to him. To the very last moment, the other disciples did not know it was Judas. It was Judas all along, of course. For when Jesus first chose him, He knew that Judas would be the betrayer; nevertheless, it was the Father's will for Him to choose Judas as His disciple, who would watch Him all those years and then betray Him. Jesus knew, but never once did He reveal it to His other disciples. Even at this very last moment when He said, "When I dip the morsel and give it to the person, that is the one," the disciples could not understand Jesus' words since the morsel was going to be given to the honorable guest! So they were utterly confused. They thought because Judas had the money bag that Jesus wanted Judas to go out and buy something for the feast or, probably, to give to the poor. They did not know that when Judas took that morsel, Satan immediately entered into him. That was the last chance the Lord gave to Judas, but he did not repent. Satan entered into him, and so the Lord said to Judas: "Go; what you intend to do, do quickly." So he left. And the Bible record marked this moment in the event by saying that it was night (see John 13:21-30).

The Giving of the New Feast

After Judas went out Jesus resumed partaking of His last supper with the disciples. Towards the end of the meal He took up bread, blessed it, broke it, and, giving it to His disciples, said, "This is My body." Then He took up the cup. We are told that this was what is known as the third cup of the Passover Feast; it is called the cup of blessing. So Jesus took up this third cup, blessed it, and, giving it to the disciples, said, "Drink it; this is My blood of the new covenant." So far as God's people in the church today are concerned, that Passover Feast was the final one required to be observed since it was fully fulfilled in Jesus, who became *the* Passover Lamb that in this instance was offered up by Jesus himself on Calvary's cross. Indeed, Jesus had now given His church a new feast—known as "the Lord's Supper" (I Corinthians 11:20) or "the Lord's Table" (I Corinthians 10:21). The Lord's Supper is the fulfillment in type of the Passover because the sacrifice has already been offered up. The blood has been shed; the body has been broken; the work of redemption has been accomplished. We today are to celebrate the finished work of Christ, to celebrate His love for us.

Let us realize that the Lord's Supper or the Lord's Table has been instituted by Jesus himself as, first of all, a *commemoration*—a remembrance of what He has done for us. We are to remember Him (I Corinthians 11:24-25): to remember how He loves us; to remember how He emptied himself of the glory of His being on an equality with God in the Godhead; to remember how He came down to this earth, took up the form of a bondslave, and—being in the fashion of a man—humbled himself in obedience to His Father even to the point of death, and that the death of the cross. And now the Father has highly exalted Him, has given Him a name which is above every name, and that to that name every knee shall bow and every tongue confess that Jesus is Lord (see Philippians 2:6-11). Let us ever and always remember this. We are here to commemorate and to exalt Him.

The Lord's Table is also a *communion*. It is a present reality. In other words, when we partake of the loaf and of the cup, we by faith are in communion in our spirit with the Lord Jesus. Each time we drink this cup we know our sins are forgiven; each time we take of the loaf we know He lives in us. We thus are in communion with Him (I Corinthians 10:16-17).

The Lord's Supper or Table is a *confirmation* as well. Every time we come to the Lord's Table the new covenant is being confirmed. God has made a new covenant with us (Luke 22:20, I Corinthians 11:25b); and it is also an eternal covenant (Hebrews 13:20; Ezekiel 37:26a,b; Jeremiah 32:40a).

The Lord's Supper is also an *anticipation*. We today are looking forward to the day when Jesus shall return (I Corinthians 11:26). And in view of that expectation the church will continually keep this Lord's Supper until Jesus' coming again. As He himself said: "I will never again drink of this fruit of the vine until that day when I drink it new with you in the kingdom of My Father" (see Matthew 26:29). And hence, every time we partake of the Lord's Table we are looking forward to the Marriage Feast of the Lamb. That is what we are always looking forward to today. How the church needs to honor the Lord's Table and not neglect it.

Comfort for the Disciples

Then Jesus said, "Let not your heart be troubled." This was part of the last discourse He would have with His disciples. These were some of His parting words to them. His disciples were troubled because, somehow, they had sensed and now knew that He was leaving them, and they sadly thought they would be left as orphans (cf. John 14:18a). Who would take care of them? So Jesus comforted them with these words: "Let not your heart be troubled; ye believe on God, believe also on me" (John 14:1). Then He later added: "If you love Me, keep My commandments; and I will beg My Father, and He will give you another Comforter. This Comforter will be with you forever. The world cannot receive Him because it does not see or know

Him, but you know Him because He abides with you and He shall be in you" (see John 14:15-17).

Yes, Jesus was indeed departing from His disciples, but He would not and did not leave them as orphans, for He said to them: "Yes, I am going away, but I am sending another Comforter to you." When Jesus was with His disciples, He was their Comforter. This English word comforter is the Greek word *paracletos*. It means: "One who comes alongside to help and to protect." This Greek word conveys the idea of a person who is to represent you, who is going to protect your name, plead your cause, and manage your affairs. When the Lord was on earth, He himself was the Comforter, the *Paracletos*, of His disciples. How he defended them! How He protected them! How He took care of them! How He managed their affairs! He was always there taking care of them, but Jesus now said to them, "I will send you *another* Comforter, just like Me." That word another signifies "another of the *same* kind," not another of a *different* kind. "This Comforter will be just like Me. He is the Spirit of truth, the Holy Spirit, and He will be with you forever." When Jesus was on the earth with them, He was alongside them, but with the Holy Spirit coming, He would be *in* them and not just alongside. The greatest gift of God to the world is His Son; and the greatest gift of the Son to us is the Holy Spirit.

On that Passover night, it was a promise—and this promise was fulfilled on the day of Jesus' resurrection—and to us, it is now a reality. Thank God, that promise has been fulfilled in us; for we have another Comforter—the Holy Spirit—who is in each one of us. Is He there representing *you*? No; He is there representing His client, the Lord Jesus. He is representing Him in you; He is protecting the Lord's name in you; He is pleading the cause of Christ in you; He is managing the affairs of Christ in you because you are His property. So the Holy Spirit who is in us as another Comforter is representing the ascended Christ; and the ascended Christ, who is now seated at the right hand of the Father, is our Advocate, even our Paraclete with the Father. There at the Father's right hand Jesus is representing us. He is protecting our name, defending our cause, and managing our affairs.

With such a dual help granted to us by the Lord Jesus, what else could we want or need? It is so wonderful. What provision the Lord has given to His own! It is all because of love.

A New Relationship

It is recorded at the end of John chapter 14 that the Lord said to His disciples, "Rise up, and let us go from here." Most probably that was the end of the Passover Feast, so they rose up and went out with the Master. Now there have been two, perhaps three, different interpretations put forward here. One is that they left the upper room and began heading towards the outskirts of Jerusalem on their way outside to the Garden of Gethsemane. And while on the way there Jesus began to share with them the contents of what is now chapters 15 and 16 of John's Gospel. Bible scholars of this interpretation have also surmised, in more specific detail, that while yet within Jerusalem itself Jesus most likely happened to have caught sight of a large vine growing somewhere along the path they were taking; and so, these scholars believe, Jesus used that vine to begin teaching His disciples the lesson about the vine and the branches, which is the subject of the opening verses of chapter 15. These scholars also believe that before crossing to the other side of the Kidron (Cedron) river valley where was the Garden of Gethsemane into which they would soon enter (see John

18:1a), Jesus and His disciples stopped at a certain spot along the way where He offered up what is often referred to as His "High Priestly Prayer" that forms the entire content of John chapter 17.

A second interpretation has it that after the Passover Feast Jesus took His disciples to the temple on a return last visit there; for according to the custom of the Jews back then, some of them would return to the temple immediately after concluding their Passover Feast for one final visit before departing back to their homes. And hence, in keeping with *this* interpretation, the Master is believed to have probably taken His disciples there, and that in the temple atmosphere, Jesus commenced speaking forth to them all the contents of chapters 15 and 16 of John. In support of their interpretation these scholars have pointed out that on the door of the temple there was worked into it an elaborate decorative golden vine; and when Jesus saw this, it most likely moved Him to commence speaking what is the content of chapter 15, which begins with His vine-and-branches teaching. Moreover, say these scholars, because the temple had been one of the places where Jesus had encountered persecution, He also spoke the contents of the latter half of chapter 15 and the opening verses of chapter 16, all of which consist of Jesus' warnings of coming persecution for His disciples as well.

Be all that as it may, we find recorded in chapter 15 the fact that the Lord Jesus shows and explains to His disciples (and, by extension, to us also) a new relationship which was soon to come into being. Their and our relationship with the Lord Jesus is no longer to be an external one, for anything external can only be temporal in nature. Let us be mindful of the fact that in view of Calvary the relationship of the Lord with His disciples was henceforth to become an inner one. This is clearly borne out by what Jesus now said to them: "I am the vine; you are the branches. You are in Me, and I am in you." Could there be any relationship more intimate than that? Jesus is the whole vine—not just the root but the entire vine—and we are the branches: we are therefore parts of Him, which thus makes it possible for Him and us to be one—He in us and we in Him. Such has now become our relationship with the Lord Jesus. And it is because the Holy Spirit has come that this new relationship could be formed.

But Jesus also made it clear that with this new relationship there arises a new responsibility on the part of all His disciples, for He then said this: "You must abide in Me and I in you." In other words, because Jesus is in us and we are in Him, therefore, we should abide in Him, stay in Him, make our home in Him, be with Him constantly. In our daily life we are to abide in Christ Jesus, and then He will abide in us. It means that His very life—Christ himself—and all His riches are ours. By this means and only by this means can we bear much fruit, and thus we will be fruitful disciples of His. How wonderful!

We are in Christ because God has put us in Him and, furthermore, God has made Him our wisdom, righteousness, holiness, and redemption (I Corinthians 1:30). That is an eternal fact based as it is upon the finished work of Christ. And thus that fact never changes. But, then, the crucial question arises: What is our experience? Are we constantly abiding in Christ? How do we abide in Him? We are told in I John 2 that if we obey the teaching of the anointing of the Spirit within us, we shall abide in the Son and in the Father (see vv. 24-28a). That in essence is what we find in the first part of John chapter 15.

Overcoming the World

We should take thoughtful note of how Jesus, as told of in John chapter 15, applied to His disciples the prophetic words concerning himself which He quoted from two Messianic psalms of David (35:19b, 69:4a): "They [people of the world] hated Me without [any] cause" (15:25); and, Jesus made clear to His disciples, "The world will hate you, too, because you are not of the world, since I chose you out of the world. Moreover, you will be persecuted because they persecuted me first" (see 15:18-21). But, then, at the very end of all of Jesus' teaching to His disciples, whose words we have in chapters 15 and 16 of John, He again makes reference to the world and what they could expect from it: "You will encounter all kinds of trouble and tribulation in the world; but take courage from the fact that in Me you may have peace since I have overcome the world" (see 16:33). Though we are still in the world we who follow the Lord Jesus are not of the world and that no matter what happens, we may rest in the peace which only Christ can give because He has already overcome the world. What a comfort that is!

The Lord's Prayer

Having taught all these things to His disciples, Jesus then raised His eyes and prayed to His Father. Now this which we have in John chapter 17 is truly the Lord's prayer. We call the prayer recorded in Matthew 6 the Lord's prayer but, actually, that is the church's prayer. This chapter 17 of John is truly the Lord's prayer, and this prayer of Jesus is so rich. In verses 1-5 is the text of what He was praying to His Father for himself. It was a personal prayer offered up for himself: "Father, glorify Me that I may glorify You." What did He mean by this? He meant: "Let Me finish the work which You have sent Me to do, which will glorify Me; and by so doing, You will be glorified. When the work is finished, then receive Me back to the glory that I had with You before the world existed." In other words, He was to return to the glory of the Godhead. Everything about Jesus' personal prayer is full of glory and nothing but glory.

Then, verses 6-24 consist of His prayer for His own. It was not only for the Eleven who were around Him at this moment (v. 9) but also for all those who would believe in Him through their word (v. 20). To describe this another way, Jesus was here praying for the church; and in the course of praying these sentiments to the Father He offered up these significant words: "Holy Father, sanctify and set them apart through Your truth which is Your word."

The church is holy; it is set apart from the world. The church is one as the Lord Jesus and the Father are one—one Head, one body, one Lord, one church. That was—and continues to be—His prayer for the church: that the church will not in any way sink into the world and allow the world to come into her and drown it; that the brothers and sisters, God's people, will not be divided; that they will be one as the Son and the Father are one. That oneness is an inward oneness since it is a oneness founded in life—even in the life of God; it is the unity of the Spirit that we need ever to maintain, as Paul wrote in Ephesians 4:3.

Finally, we are told in verses 25-26 that Jesus prayed, "O righteous Father." The Father is righteous. So Jesus the Son asked the Father to love the Eleven—to whom Jesus had revealed the Father—just as the Father had loved Him, and prayed further that the Father's love might be in the Eleven and that Jesus himself might be in them. In other words, the Father will reward us with His love: He will love us just as He loves His beloved Son.

Such was the prayer which the Lord Jesus prayed to the Father on that same evening after having eaten His last supper with His disciples. What now awaited Jesus still later that evening was His earthly life's final and severest crisis. It would take place in the Garden of Gethsemane.

Chapter Thirteen

THE GARDEN OF GETHSEMANE

Matthew 26:36-46—Then Jesus comes with them to a place called Gethsemane, and says to the disciples, Sit here until I go away and pray yonder. And taking with him Peter and the two sons of Zebedee, he began to be sorrowful and deeply depressed. Then he says to them, My soul is very sorrowful even unto death; remain here and watch with me. And going forward a little he fell upon his face, praying and saying, My Father, if it be possible let this cup pass from me; but not as I will, but as thou wilt. And he comes to the disciples and finds them sleeping, and says to Peter, Thus ye have not been able to watch one hour with me? Watch and pray, that ye enter not into temptation: the spirit indeed is ready, but the flesh weak. Again going away a second time he prayed saying, My Father, if this cannot pass from me unless I drink it, thy will be done. And coming he found them again sleeping, for their eyes were heavy. And leaving them, he went away again and prayed the third time, saying the same thing. Then he comes to the disciples and says to them, Sleep on now and take your rest; behold, the hour has drawn nigh, and the Son of man is delivered up into the hands of sinners. Arise, let us go; behold, he that delivers me up has drawn nigh.

Mark 14:32-42—And they come to a place of which the name is Gethsemane, and he says to his disciples, Sit here while I shall pray. And he takes with him Peter and James and John, and he began to be amazed and oppressed in spirit. And he says to them, My soul is full of grief even unto death; abide here and watch. And, going forward a little, he fell upon the earth; and he prayed that, if it were possible, the hour might pass away from him. And he said, Abba, Father, all things are possible to thee: take away this cup from me; but not what I will, but what thou wilt. And he comes and finds them sleeping. And he says to Peter, Simon, dost thou sleep? Hast thou not been able to watch one hour? Watch and pray, that ye enter not into temptation. The spirit indeed is willing, but the flesh weak. And going away, he prayed again, saying the same thing. And returning, he found them again sleeping, for their eyes were heavy; and they knew not what they should answer him. And he comes the third time and says to them, Sleep on now, and take your rest. It is enough; the hour is come; behold, the Son of man is delivered up into the hands of sinners. Arise, let us go; behold, he that delivers me up has drawn nigh.

Luke 22:39-46—And going forth he went according to his custom to the mount of Olives, and the disciples also followed him. And when he was at the place he said to them, Pray that ye enter not into temptation. And he was withdrawn from them about a stone's throw, and having knelt down he prayed, saying, Father, if thou wilt remove this cup from me:—but then, not my will, but thine be done. And an angel appeared to him from heaven strengthening him. And being in conflict he prayed more intently. And his sweat became as great drops of blood, falling down upon the earth. And rising up from his prayer, coming to the disciples, he found them sleeping from grief.

And he said to them, Why sleep ye? rise up and pray that ye enter not into temptation.

In continuing on with the life of Jesus I would like for us next to consider together His experience in the Garden of Gethsemane. After the last supper was concluded Jesus led His disciples out of Jerusalem, across the river Kidron (Cedron), and to the Mount of Olives (Matthew 26:30, John 18:1). As they were on their way there, He told His disciples that He as the Shepherd would be smitten and they as the sheep would be scattered, but that He would rise again and go ahead of them to Galilee and meet them again (Matthew 26:31-32). In having spoken these words Jesus actually quoted Zechariah 13:7: "Awake, O sword, against my shepherd, even against the man that is my fellow, saith Jehovah of hosts: smite the shepherd, and the sheep shall be scattered."

Peter immediately remonstrated and said that even if all others would be offended and fall away because of Jesus, he would never do so; in fact, Peter added, he would never deny the Lord and would even be willing to die with Him. The Lord said, "Before the cock crows today, you will deny Me three times" (Matthew 26:33-35a). The Lord also said to Peter: "Simon, Simon, Satan has demanded to have thee, to sift thee as wheat; but I have prayed for you that your faith fail not; and when you have been restored, strengthen your brethren" (see Luke 22:31-32).

The Battle in the Garden

Jesus, of course, knew what was coming; and further, His disciples themselves had a sense that a terrible thing was about to happen. Indeed, it seemed as though all the powers of darkness were closing in upon Jesus. He therefore sought out a secluded place, a place where He could go and fight the battle. And he chose the Garden of Gethsemane.

This immediately reminds me of the first garden to be mentioned in God's word. We will remember that in the Garden of Eden Satan had tempted Adam, the first man, and won that battle. Adam not only lost that battle for himself, he also lost that battle for all of mankind who would come after him. The second Man and last Adam—Jesus the Son of man—now entered the Garden of Gethsemane and there He fought His own battle with Satan; and, thank God, this Man won the battle. He won it for mankind. Throughout Jesus' entire life Satan assaulted Him and tried to defeat Him again and again. We will recall how Satan tempted Jesus in the wilderness and exhausted all his temptations upon Him until another opportunity might later present itself (Luke 4:13). Throughout His life Jesus was tempted in all things; yet He was without sin (Hebrews 5:13). That means that during His life on earth Jesus was totally victorious over Satan, and that is why on the Mount of Transfiguration He was ready to depart this world and could have returned to heaven because He had won the victory. By the entire way Jesus had lived while on the earth He had demonstrated to the world the man of God's heart, the man of God's purpose, the man whom God had desired even before Creation.

Nevertheless, Jesus had come into this world not only to demonstrate to it what was the kind of man whom God had desired, He also had come to this world to save the lost; and hence Jesus did not exit the earth while atop the Mount, but descended the Mount and soon thereafter entered Gethsemane's garden for His final conflict with Satan where, for the sake of lost mankind, He would fight and win victoriously the battle against God's enemy.

Now after Jesus entered Gethsemane He took farther into the Garden for watching and praying with Him His three closest disciples—Peter, James and John—and left the other eight behind, asking them to be seated at a place that was most likely near the entrance. Something now quite out of the ordinary commenced happening to Jesus while He and the three disciples made their way farther into Gethsemane. Two of the Gospels describe how "he began to be amazed and oppressed in spirit," that "he began to be sorrowful and deeply depressed"—in fact, so "very sorrowful," He said to the Three, that His "soul [was] full of grief even unto death."

Let us be reminded, if need be, that the Son of man had been quite calm and composed throughout this entire evening's many activities. By this time He well knew that He was to exit the earth and return to His Father. By this time He knew that His Father had given all things into His hands. So Jesus was able to comfort His disciples who had been sorrowful during their last supper with Him. Said Jesus to them: "I leave joy with you; I give My joy to you" (see and cf. John 15:11). In other words, the Lord knew what was about to happen to Him, and yet He was so calm, so composed, and so sure of the outcome that He was able to comfort others. He knew this was the hour for Him for which He had long waited; nevertheless, suddenly, at this moment in the Garden, it seemed as though Jesus had lost His composure. Did He not realize that this was the hour for which He had come into the world? Did He not know that what was about to occur on Calvary was the very cup the Father had given Him to drink? Why, then, did Jesus recoil from entering into its experience? Why did He ask, "If it be possible let this cup pass from Me"?

The Hour for Which Jesus Came

Throughout His life Jesus had mentioned a number of times that His hour had not yet come, which meant that He was continually waiting for that hour to arrive. In fact, He had come into the world and was born for that very hour; Jesus said as much to His disciples shortly before He would go to Calvary: "The hour has come,… and what shall I say?—'Father, save Me from this hour'? But it was for this hour that I came to this earth" (see John 12:23, 27); and yet, before that hour came, nothing definitive related to redemption could happen. Now to what did that hour refer? That hour referred to His glorification, and His glorification began at the cross (see again John 12:23, and also 12:28). He was actually waiting for, and looking forward to, that hour of His death because His death would be the occasion of His glorification. By His death He glorified the Father and the Father glorified Him. Recall, too, that when His two disciples, James and John, came to Him requesting that they be able to sit one on His right and one on His left in His kingdom, Jesus inquired: "Are you able to drink the cup that I am going to drink?" (see Matthew 20:20-22) In other words, Jesus knew already that He was going to drink the cup of suffering on the cross. So why is it that at this moment in Gethsemane it seems that Jesus suddenly lost His composure?

I feel this scene in Gethsemane's garden is really too sacred to be talked about or described. It is a scene that should remain hidden from the world. It can be likened to when after the seven thunders had spoken forth, John on the isle of Patmos was about to write down what they had uttered, but God said, "No, what they have uttered is to be sealed up and kept secret" (Revelation 10:1-4). For me I have often felt that what occurred that night in the Garden of Gethsemane between Jesus and His

Father ought to have remained a secret because of its sacredness. Nevertheless, it has pleased God to reveal that scene to us in order to unveil to us what tremendous cost Jesus paid for our salvation.

The conflict was so terrific that Jesus' spirit was oppressed. His soul was sorrowful. His body was under such agony that He sweat drops of blood that fell upon the ground. An angel had to appear to strengthen Him physically because, without that strengthening, He might have died in the Garden.

In Philippians 2 we are told concerning Jesus: "He who was equal with God did not consider that equality to be something to be grasped at or held on to, but he emptied himself of that and took upon himself the form of a slave; and being found in appearance as a man He humbled himself and became obedient to His Father even to the point of death—and that to the extent of death on a cross" (see vv. 6-8). Jesus is the eternal Son of God and is thus one with God and is God. From eternity He has lived in all glory with His Father; yet, because of His love for us He emptied himself of all the glory, majesty, and honor associated with God. Jesus emptied himself of all these attributes of deity (but *not* Deity himself) and took the humble form of a man. Now *that* is love—divine love.

Even so, He having done all that, it did not affect Jesus' character. It is important for us to be clear in understanding that Jesus remained pure, holy, loving, and everything else that God is in His nature; and also that He remained in His humanity everything that God has always desired in a man. Jesus' emptying himself of his equality with God did not affect His divine and human character as both Son of God and Son of man. Nevertheless, something terrible—even horrific and appalling—happened.

The Bitter Cup

"My Father, if it be possible let this cup pass from Me." Cup in Scripture speaks of portion. Psalm 16:5 says: "Jehovah is the portion of mine inheritance and of my cup. Thou maintainest my lot." Psalm 23:5 reads: "My cup runneth over." Cup speaks of portion. It speaks of God's will; and in the present context, therefore, cup denotes God's will for His Son. At that very moment in Gethsemane's garden God's will for His Son was for Him to become a sin offering.

As noted earlier, from all eternity the Son and the Father have always been one: between Them there was such harmony, such oneness, such love, such purity. There was never a cloud, never a shadow. Even when the Son of God came into this world to be a man, during His thirty-three years of life on earth as the Son of man there was not a hint of shadow, shade, or distance between Him and the Father because He pleased God in all things. Jesus always did the Father's will, and the Father was always with Him. Indeed, He said concerning himself, "I am never alone. My Father is with Me" (see John 16:32b). There was no separation, only perfect harmony and oneness. But in the Garden of Gethsemane the cup which the Father now delivered to Him was the bitter cup of curse. In other words, He who knew no sin was now to be made sin for us that we might become the righteousness of God in Him (II Corinthians 5:21).

Let us pause and simply meditate on *this* for a few moments: We are far from being pure as Jesus was pure while on earth. But if some terrible sin is mentioned in our hearing, even *we* will shrink from it as though it were too dreadful, too defiling. However, contrast that with what was about to happen to Jesus who was Purity Incarnate—the One who while on this corrupted planet knew no sin, who did not even know what sin is, who from all eternity had never sinned. He always pleased the Father, and yet at this Gethsemane moment, the cup delivered to Him was to make of Him sin constitutionally! On the one hand, yes indeed, all the sins of the world which were and will ever yet be committed were to be piled upon Him—your sins, my sins and all future sins yet to be committed in the world Jesus was now to bear in His body. That in itself would have been horrible enough for anyone to bear! On the other hand, what Jesus was about to endure was far, far more horrible than even that: He was to be made sin itself! No wonder Jesus was oppressed in His spirit. No wonder He was sorrowful even to the point of death.

How could He who was and is sinless perfect submit himself to become sin itself? How could He who was the Person on earth the most sensitive to sin bring himself to tolerate such a gross offense to His very nature; for He who is Absolute Holiness Come in the Flesh would now be totally defiled. Just think of this and wonder at the severe magnitude of it all, that this Pure Human Will that abhorred and automatically recoiled from sin in all its forms—and yet it was the Father's will that His Beloved Son willingly offer himself to become, as it were, Sin Incarnate!! Now *that* in its most appalling terms was the cup which Jesus was now being called upon by His Father to drink.

From the various Gospel descriptions which we have of what happened to Jesus personally there in the Garden, it would appear that all the powers of darkness had descended upon the Son of man and surrounded that pure human will of His, inwardly taunting Him thusly: "Save yourself; don't allow yourself to be defiled; for You are holy, You are pure. Therefore, keep Yourself whole and intact. Most surely, You are not one to be defiled." Thus have we been given a glimpse by God into the nature and severity of the battle which raged momentarily within Jesus' soul.

Yet that was only part of the struggle which was occurring within Jesus' heart and mind at this very time. For it must not be overlooked that He—who had pleased the Father without exception throughout His entire earthly life and for whom, from all eternity, there had never been even the slightest separation from His Father but only sweet communion and fellowship between them—He nonetheless knew that were He to drink this cup of curse it would likewise mean separation from the Father. Such a separation, no matter how brief, would for Jesus be like experiencing hell, even like experiencing eternal death. And hence, because of the love He so deeply cherished with His Father, Jesus was at this moment recoiling from the very thought of being separated from Him. Nevertheless, Jesus also knew that the Father's will for this hour in His life was that He should drink this cup: a cup of curse *and* of separation.

Therefore, we can perhaps now see that the battle in the Garden of Gethsemane was over this issue of the cup. From the perspective of His pure human will, Jesus greatly desired this cup to pass. He did not want either to be defiled or to be separated from His Father. That was the cry of Jesus' heart at this moment. Yet He humbly bowed before God and prayed: "Not My will but Thine be done. If it is your will that I must drink of this cup, then so be it." He yielded His perfect human will to the Father's will, and the battle was won.

When salvation comes to us, it is free and, sometimes, we may entertain the impression that salvation is cheap because it costs us nothing. True, it is given to us freely, but God does desire us to know how much it cost Him and how much it cost His beloved Son. In the words of the hymn of remembrance, "Lead Me to Calvary": "Lest I forget Gethsemane, lest I forget

His agony, lest I forget Thy love for me, lead me to Calvary." I do believe that the reason this almost unspeakable scene has been revealed to us is for the purpose of showing us the deep love for us of God the Father and the equally deep love of God the Son so that we may never forget how much God loves us. That, in fact, is the very foundation of our salvation.

In Hebrews 5 we are told that while Jesus was in the days of His flesh, He offered up supplications and entreaties to the One who was able to save Him from death; He did so with strong crying and tears, and He was heard because of His reverent submission; for after being perfected, He became to those who obey Him the author of eternal salvation (vv. 7, 9). That was Gethsemane.

Oil Press

The proper name Gethsemane actually means "oil press." We do not know who owned that garden, but it must have been one of Jesus' friends because He had free access to it. Some people think that John Mark's father may have owned that property. It was a place to which the Lord often went (John 18:2b).

It can be said, I believe, that Jesus, while on earth, was like an olive and full of oil; for, spiritually speaking, He had been born of the Spirit and had been filled and anointed with the Spirit. We can say that throughout His life He was like an olive—so perfect, so complete, so pleasant; and yet that Olive must be pressed and broken so that the oil of the Spirit could flow forth for the healing of man. It can also be said that there in Gethsemane's garden that perfect outward man known as Jesus the Son of man was crushed and broken so that the life of

God could flow from Him for the healing of the nations. That was Gethsemane.

Gethsemane serves as more than only an event of history; it also serves as a spiritual principle. Let us recall again the question Jesus had put forth to the two sons of Zebedee: "Are you able to drink the cup that I am going to drink?" They said they could, but they really did not know what that meant or signified. Nevertheless, Jesus continued by saying: "Yes, you will indeed drink My cup" (see Matthew 20:22-23); thus meaning that the cup which Jesus would drink was also to be our cup to be drunk.

Now what was His cup? At that crucial moment in the Garden of Gethsemane it was for Jesus the bitter cup of curse; and because He drank that bitter cup of curse, He has left us with the cup of blessing. Whenever we remember the Lord at His table, it is a cup of blessing which we bless, and the reason is because Jesus has drunk the bitter cup of curse so that we now have the sweet cup of blessing (I Corinthians 10:16a). But with respect to the cup itself, let us be reminded that it represents the Father's will. At that moment in the Garden of Gethsemane the cup for Jesus was the Father's will; and for us who believe in the Lord Jesus the Father's will is also now our cup—and no matter its contents, whether bitter or sweet.

Yielding Our Will to God

When we first believed in the Lord Jesus we were united to God in life. We received a new life, the life of the Son, God's very own life; and we were united with God in life. We became children of God, but that was just the beginning. Spiritual growth is a growing into union with God in *will*—not only in life but in will. Our will is being brought into one with God's will. The highest union which man can ever have with God is the union of two wills. It is not His will that we have no will. God is the supreme will, and He created man with a will; but it is the will of God that our human will be so submissive to the divine will that there will be a union of wills. That is the highest Christian experience. And to that end we find that the operating principle throughout our Christian growth is this: "Not my will but Your will be done."

True, it is extremely difficult for us to yield our will to God's will, for our natural will is not pure like the human will of Jesus. Jesus' will while on the earth was perfect; and yet, though His human will was pure, even with that pure will, He experienced a tremendous battle in yielding that will to the Father's will in oneness—"Not my will but Your will be done." Now if that was true with Jesus, how much more we need to yield our will to God's will!

One's Good Will Cannot Substitute for God's Will

Our will is so selfish, so self-centered, so self-interested, so protective of our self. We want to keep ourselves intact, whole. Even the best will we may have cannot substitute for God's will. How often we think our good will is God's will. In fact, we assume that God ought to be pleased with our will; to our surprise, however, we come to realize that our good will—even our best will—cannot substitute for God's will. Indeed, oftentimes our good and best will is an enemy of God's will. Eventually we must come to the point that we must acknowledge: "Not my will"—not even my best will, even my good will—"but Your will be done."

Let us consider Peter once again. He had just received a great revelation, confessing Jesus as the Christ, the Son of the living God; to which Jesus responded: "Simon Barjonah, you are blessed because this that you have rightly confessed was not shown you by means of flesh and blood but it was revealed to you by My Father in heaven. And now I declare to you that you are Peter—just a stone—and yet I will build My church, composed of like stones, upon the truth of this 'confessional' rock, and the gates of hades shall not prevail against it." But then, the Lord Jesus began to reveal to Peter and His other disciples that He must go to Jerusalem where He would be rejected and denied; where, too, He would be sentenced to death and die on a cross; but that on the third day afterwards, He would rise from the dead. Now let us notice that Peter had received praise from the Lord Jesus at first; but having become so elated emotionally by that tremendous revelation from heaven, he now lost all rationality. Taking hold of Jesus, Peter shook Him a little and said to Him: "Not so, Lord. Be good to Yourself. You need not go to the cross"—an example of human good will. Jesus' strong and stern reaction, however, was this: "Satan, get behind Me" (see Matthew 16:13-23). Oh, how often our good will is nothing but Satan's suggestion.

Then later, during the last supper with His disciples, Jesus rose up and began to wash their feet, with Peter most likely being the first one to be washed; and Peter said, "No, Master, You are the Lord. How can You possibly be the one to do that?" Surely, that was very reasonable on Peter's part. The Lord, though, declared this to His disciple: "If you do not allow Me to do this, you will have no part with Me." To which Peter said, "Well, then, wash my hands, my head, every part of me." But the Lord responded with these corrective words: "You do not need that kind of cleansing" (see John 13:1-10). *A good will—even a reasonable will—is not necessarily God's will.*

Recall also that occasion when on the tanner's roof in Joppa, Peter, while in a trance, saw in a vision a sheet coming down out of heaven full of unclean animals. And then a voice commanded: "Peter, rise, kill, and eat!" Peter said, "Not so, Lord; I have never eaten anything unclean." This scene and voice occurred three times, but each time he refused to do what had been commanded from heaven: "Not so, Lord" (see Acts 10:5-6, 9-16). What a contradictory will Peter still possessed!

That was Peter in his earlier days as a disciple of the Lord. Yet is this not what we too often are ourselves? Indeed, we may have been guilty of conducting ourselves in this way during much, if not all, the time in our Christian life! This is perhaps a great temptation, perhaps even the greatest temptation confronting us: "My will, not Your will, Lord. Let Your will be *my* will, not my will be *Your* will." The submission of our wills to God's will is a most important principle for our life which we must learn to follow. We need to learn always to say: "Not my will but yours be done." Only thus can we grow spiritually.

Full of the Holy Spirit

I would remind us once more what the meaning of Gethsemane is: oil press. And as was mentioned earlier, unless the Christian's outer man—like an olive—is pressed and crushed, no oil of the Spirit can flow forth for the healing of man and of the nations. Jesus was crushed and life consequently flowed out from Him for our redemption. In that very regard, He stands alone. Yet it is the will of God that we do not simply grow into a pleasant, perfect and complete ripe olive. It is quite true that we need to grow; and by that I mean that we need to be filled with the Spirit. This matter of spiritual growth is not only having the Spirit of God *dwelling* in us, which we all have minimally by virtue of our having repented and believed in the Lord Jesus—which is to say, our new birth. But we also need to allow the Holy Spirit to *fill* us.

We should be like those two olive trees mentioned in Old Testament prophecy. We may recall in the prophetic book of Zechariah the vision which that prophet of God saw of a golden lamp and two olive trees—one each standing on the left and right of the lamp—which were symbolic of "the two sons of oil" mentioned there and that were supplying the needed oil to the lamp (4:2-3, 12-14). The will of God is that we believers should be like those olive trees that produce olives which when crushed provide the needed oil. In other words, we disciples of the Lord Jesus should be full of the Holy Spirit, just like those two sons of oil. Yet, without the pressing and crushing of those two trees' olives, those sons of oil would have been empty of any oil. Like those olives, therefore, we need to be crushed in order that the oil of the Spirit of life may come forth for ministering resurrection life to others. And that is the very message of II Corinthians 4:7-12, which Scripture passage will be discussed more fully shortly.

God's will is not merely for us to receive and receive and receive. Thank God, He has placed us in the Promised Land. And that is a good land, flowing with milk and honey—symbolizing the Lord Jesus himself and all the riches of Christ which we are enjoying of Him. Thank God for that, but that is not the end purpose of His salvation. Rather, God wants us who have received such riches from Him to distribute those riches—that is to say, to give to others what we have received of His resurrection life for the healing of the nations. But how can we give out and share unless we are put into the olive press? That, in essence, is the principle of the cross in operation. That is the reason Jesus instructed His disciples: "Deny yourselves, take up your cross, and follow Me." As a matter of fact, such self-denial, if put into practice, is a sign of genuine Christian discipleship. Are we willing to deny ourselves? Such a decision is an issue of the will. If we are willing to deny ourselves, that is, to deny our will—"Not my will but Yours be done"—then the Holy Spirit will arrange our circumstances—to place us, as it were, in the olive press. Whether those circumstances come in the form of people, events, or issues of life, it is not according to our will but according to His wisdom. He will arrange our circumstances in order to crush us and break our outward man so that the life divine within us can flow out to others.

Now within God's arranged circumstances you may at times find yourself surrounded by all kinds of pressure and demands being placed upon you, but be encouraged: you have not been crushed to the point of being finished. Yes, if you find yourself hard pressed on every side, you may think you are indeed finished. Nevertheless, please be advised that there is an *upward* way by which you can still continue on. Like Jacob of old, you may have come to your wits' end—but not life's end. Like Jacob, you may have even planned and plotted and schemed your whole life long; but now—like him—you are facing *your* "brother Esau," who comes at you today, not—like Esau had done—with four hundred men but with four hundred different challenges, problems and pressures. And so, you find yourself at your wits' end as to how to deal with the situation. Nevertheless, take heart, fellow Christian, you are not in the least at life's end but at life's beginning—that is to say, at the beginning of *resurrection* life. Indeed, like Jacob, you may, in God's wisdom, have been crippled by Him; even so, that just may be the beginning of resurrection life for you in service to

God (see Genesis chapters 32, 33). In the words of God's bondservant Paul which are found in II Corinthians 4: "We are handicapped on all sides, but we are never frustrated; we are puzzled, but never in despair. We are persecuted, but we never have to stand it alone: we may be knocked down but we are never knocked out! Every day we experience something of the death of Jesus, so that we may also know the power of the life of Jesus in these bodies of ours" (vv. 7-10 Phillips).

The Holy Spirit will discipline us, using an environment that may be unexpected, perhaps unwelcome, even strange and unimaginable; yet the Holy Spirit knows what He is doing. He knows there is the oil of spiritual life there that needs to be released. If there is no oil of the Spirit there, there is no need for crushing. Some believers have never been crushed because they are empty of the Spirit's filling. But if there is oil of the Spirit within, the Father's will is for that olive life of yours to be crushed. This, in fact, is "the slaying of Jesus" which Paul further mentioned in II Corinthians 4: "I bear in my body the slaying [or, dying] of Jesus, so that the life of Jesus may be at work in others." Furthermore, "though our outer man may be decaying and wasting away," added Paul, "our inner man is being renewed day by day" (see vv. 10, 12, 16). Such is the secret of spiritual ministry for all of us who are Jesus' disciples.

Watch and Pray

To repeat, Gethsemane is more than an event of history; in addition it represents a foundational principle which Jesus has victoriously demonstrated to us; and He is calling us to watch with Him for an hour: "Watch and pray, that ye enter not into temptation." The only way we can overcome our will and will God's will is to watch and pray. The enemy is trying very hard to tempt us to hold on to and exert our own will. We must therefore watch and pray; but because we are often not able to, we must look to the Lord Jesus, who will supply to us whatever is needed. He is the author of our eternal salvation, and because He has overcome, therefore, His victory is ours, and we too may overcome. If we obey Him, we will not fall into temptation, but we will be able and willing to drink the Father's cup, be it sweet or bitter. Let *God* choose for us; let us ourselves not choose.

On that night in Gethsemane's garden even the three disciples closest to the Lord were so overwhelmed with grief that they fell asleep, and that is the reason they fell into temptation: they all scattered; and Peter even denied the Lord. Consequently, the word of the Lord for us today is: "Watch and pray, that ye enter not into temptation." The temptation is to follow our own will rather than embrace God's will. That is the battle each of us must fight and win, as did the Lord Jesus on that crucial night in Gethsemane's garden.

Chapter Fourteen

HIS CRUCIFIXION

Luke 23:33-49—And when they came to the place which is called Skull, there they crucified him, and the malefactors, one on the right hand, the other on the left. And Jesus said, Father, forgive them, for they know not what they do. And, parting out his garments, they cast lots. And the people stood beholding, and the rulers also with them sneered, saying, He has saved others; let him save himself if this is the Christ, the chosen one of God. And the soldiers also made game of him, coming up offering him vinegar, and saying, If thou be the king of the Jews, save thyself. And there was also an inscription written over him in Greek, and Roman, and Hebrew letters: This is the King of the Jews.

Now one of the malefactors who had been hanged spoke insultingly to him, saying, Art not thou the Christ? save thyself and us. But the other answering rebuked him, saying, Dost thou too not fear God, thou that art under the same judgment? and we indeed justly, for we receive the just recompense of what we have done; but this man has done nothing amiss. And he said to Jesus, Remember me, Lord, when thou comest in thy kingdom. And Jesus said to him, Verily I say to thee, To-day shalt thou be with me in paradise.

And it was about the sixth hour, and there came darkness over the whole land until the ninth hour. And the sun was darkened, and the veil of the temple rent in the midst. And Jesus, having cried with a loud voice, said, Father, into thy hands I commit my spirit. And having said this, he expired. Now the centurion, seeing what took place, glorified God, saying, In very deed this man was just. And all the crowds who had come together to that sight, having seen the things that took place, returned, beating their breasts. And all those who knew him stood afar off, the women also who had followed him from Galilee, beholding these things.

John 19:25-30—And by the cross of Jesus stood his mother, and the sister of his mother, Mary the wife of Clopas, and Mary of Magdala. Jesus therefore, seeing his mother, and the disciple standing by, whom he loved, says to his mother, Woman, behold thy son. Then he says unto the disciple, Behold thy mother. And from that hour the disciple took her to his own home. After this, Jesus, knowing that all things were now finished, that the scripture might be fulfilled, says, I thirst. There was a vessel therefore there full of vinegar, and having filled a sponge with vinegar, and putting hyssop round it, they put it up to his mouth. When therefore Jesus had received the vinegar, he said, It is finished; and having bowed his head, he delivered up his spirit.

Matthew 27:45-54—Now from the sixth hour there was darkness over the whole land until the ninth hour; but about the ninth hour Jesus cried out with a loud voice, saying, Eli, Eli, lama sabachthani? that is, My God, my God, why hast thou forsaken me? And some of those who stood there, when they heard it, said, This man calls for Elias. And immediately one of them

> *running and getting a sponge, having filled it with vinegar and fixed it on a reed, gave him to drink. But the rest said, Let be; let us see if Elias comes to save him. And Jesus, having again cried with a loud voice, gave up the ghost. And lo, the veil of the temple was rent in two from the top to the bottom, and the earth was shaken, and the rocks were rent, and the tombs were opened; and many bodies of the saints fallen asleep arose, and going out of the tombs after his arising, entered into the holy city and appeared unto many. But the centurion, and they who were with him on guard over Jesus, seeing the earthquake and the things that took place, feared greatly, saying, Truly this man was Son of God.*

In the Garden of Gethsemane Jesus drank the cup which the Father gave to Him. He yielded His pure will to the perfect will of God. He was willing to be defiled, to be made sin for us. He was willing to be separated from His Father with whom He had had uninterrupted communion from all eternity. He drank that bitter cup so that we may have the cup of blessing. Jesus' hour had come. He had accepted the cross, so He rose up and—while still in the Garden—went forward to meet those who now came to arrest Him. He was bound; judged unrighteously; and condemned to death by *the Jews* because He claimed to be—and rightly so—the Son of God. He was also condemned by *the Gentiles* because He rightly claimed as well to be the King of the Jews, even the King of truth. So the Roman authorities led Him to Golgotha's hill, otherwise known as The Place of the Skull, to be crucified.

Crucifixion had commonly occurred as a form of punishment two thousand years ago, but the concept of the cross had long before been conceived in eternity past in the council of the Godhead. It was part of the eternal plan of God. We know that He had purposed an eternal purpose even before the foundation of the world; and His purpose was none other than to make His beloved Son, His only begotten Son, the heir of all things. He also had purposed to give His Son a helpmate: the church. But in His wisdom God, being omniscient, knew what would happen over time in the universe; and because of this foreknowledge He had laid a plan, and in that plan was included the cross.

Let us be clear, however, that the cross of the Lord Jesus was not in God's eternal *purpose*; rather, it was in His eternal *plan*. There is a great difference between these two. In the eternal purpose of God He had not purposed the rebellion of the angels or the fall of man; for had God purposed these developments, then he would have been responsible for such to have occurred. But God is omniscient: He knows the end from the very beginning. He therefore knew well in advance that there would in fact *be* rebellion in creation, both celestial and terrestrial; accordingly, in order for His eternal purpose to be fulfilled, He formulated an eternal plan, and in that plan the cross has a central place; nevertheless, the cross was never intended to be the end but was only intended to be the *means* to that end or purpose. So let us be clear that the cross was never God's eternal purpose; instead, it was part of His eternal plan, and by means of that plan His purpose would be fulfilled.

Jesus is called the Lamb slain from the foundation of the world (Revelation 13:8 AV). He is not the Lamb slain *before* the foundation of the world, but *from* the foundation of the world. Had He been slain before the foundation of the world, then the cross would have been in the eternal purpose of God. Only after the foundation of the world was set could He then in fact be the Lamb slain.

Now after man had sinned in the Edenic garden God clothed him with skins which were obtained from a slain animal, probably a lamb. From that first lamb slain in the Garden of Eden until the last lamb offered in the temple in Jerusalem, those countless, numberless lambs were but types of *the* Lamb—the Lamb of God. Hence it was that John the Baptist declared: "Behold the Lamb of God, who takes away the sin of the world" (John 1:29b).

We who believe in Jesus know that He was born to die. He came to be crucified. That was the central part of God's plan. Throughout His life Jesus was conscious of the cross. When He stepped into the water of the river Jordan to be baptized, He offered himself as a substitute for mankind. He continually had the cross in view. No wonder that the heavens opened and the Father was heard to say, "This is My beloved Son, in whom is My delight." The Holy Spirit came down upon Jesus as a dove and dwelt in Him (Luke 3:21-22, John 1:32), because by the eternal Spirit He was to offer himself spotless to God (Hebrews 10:14b). During His life He again and again alluded to "My hour: there is an hour coming to Me; My hour has not yet come, I nonetheless have come for that hour." That hour was not the time of Jesus' ascension for returning to His Father. That hour especially pointed to the time of His crucifixion because He always looked upon His crucifixion as the hour of His glorification (cf. John 17:1b).

Jesus never shared with His disciples concerning the cross until Peter confessed Him as the Christ, the Son of the living God. Only then did He begin to share with His disciples that He must go to Jerusalem where he would be rejected and killed, but that on the third day thereafter He would rise from the dead. At least three times he shared with His disciples regarding His death. According to Matthew 16, it was after Peter's confession that Jesus for the first time said, "I must go to Jerusalem and there I will die, but I will be raised up on the third day." We learn from Matthew 17 that in Galilee He again told His disciples what would happen. Finally, from chapter 20 we learn that as He and His disciples were approaching Jerusalem He again shared with them that He was to die. Jesus knew exactly what was going to happen to Him. And, therefore, in the Garden of Gethsemane He yielded His will to His Father and willingly accepted the cross.

Seven Words Spoken on the Cross

We are all familiar with the story of the crucifixion, so I will not discuss that event in detail here. If you want to know about His suffering on the cross, there is the prophetic Psalm 22 which described well beforehand concerning the sufferings of the cross of the Lord Jesus. If you want to know the meaning of the cross, you can read Isaiah 53, because there the meaning of His crucifixion was prophesied. Jesus' crucifixion is mentioned in all four Gospels, but for our consideration today I would like for us to try to enter into the inner meaning of the cross. And I believe there is no better way to gain an understanding of the inner meaning of the cross than through the seven words Jesus uttered while on the cross. These seven words are like seven windows that can open to us a glimpse into the inner reality of the cross.

The First Word

The Roman authorities led Jesus to Golgotha. There they crucified Him along with two criminals—one crucified on his right and one, on His left. After Jesus was lifted up upon His cross the first word He uttered was this: "Father, forgive them, for they know not what they do." Jesus was on the cross for a total of six hours. He was crucified at the third hour of the day—that being at 9:00 in the morning, and He expired at the ninth hour, or at 3:00 in the afternoon. During His crucifixion's first three hours—from 9:00 a.m. to 12:00 noon—Jesus uttered three words; and from 12:00 noon to 3:00 p.m. He uttered four words.

The three words which Jesus spoke forth during those first hours were utterances with man in view, because during those hours of being nailed to the cross He suffered terribly physically. Yet, it was not only physically that he suffered during those hours but also emotionally and psychologically. This was because the place where He was crucified was just outside the city and thus many people were passing by during these proceedings. And when they passed by, many laughed at Him, scorned Him, and sneered at Him. The Jewish rulers and the Pharisees joined themselves in with the multitude and scorned Him in mocking fashion by saying: "You who saved others, save yourself. If You come down from the cross, we will believe You are the Christ. You trust in God, now let God save You." The soldiers, too, made fun of Him, and gave Him vinegar to drink. Even one of the malefactors who was crucified with Him ridiculed Him, saying: "If you are the Christ, save Yourself and save both of us." In short, during those first three hours on the cross Jesus was being rejected, ridiculed, mocked and sneered at by the world that He loved so much.

Not only that, but behind those people all the powers of darkness were surrounding Him and attacking Him with all the force of hell; and thus, Jesus suffered tremendously. Even so, His Father was with Him. So Jesus' first word from the cross was, "Father." Man may have rejected Him, but He was not alone. His Father was there with Him on the cross. So He prayed: "Father, forgive them, for they know not what they do."

"How can man be just before God?" (see Job 9:2) This has been an agelong question that we find mentioned in the writing of Job, the first Bible book to have been written. Man being what he is—unjust, sinful, rebellious, an enemy of God—how can he be just before God? How can a just God justify—or make righteous—a sinner? How can He be just and at the same time justify us? Humanly speaking, there is no way; but, thank God, He has made the provision in His Son. So when Jesus was on the cross, the first word He uttered was, "Father, forgive them." He could pray to the Father to forgive us because He was being crucified in our stead. He was the Lamb slain.

There is no greater sin than the sin of rejecting the Son of God. There is no greater sin of man than to crucify the Son of God. Can you think of any sin greater than that? There at Calvary man committed the greatest sin in the whole universe. Throughout the ages that has been deemed to be the greatest sin in the universe; and yet, there, God manifested the greatest act of love. Against the backdrop of man's greatest sin, God reveals to us the secret of redemption. Christ died for us, and because He died in our stead, He bore all our sins in His body. On the basis of that fact Jesus prayed to the Father: "Father, forgive them; they do not know what they are doing" (see Luke 23:34a). Love always tries to explain, always covers; and it is because of this prayer of Jesus that we are forgiven.

Forgiveness is therefore the very spirit of the cross. That is why throughout the centuries—from the time of the first Christian martyr, Stephen, to the last one who shall ever be killed during this present age of grace—whenever a martyr is about to expire, the prayer on his/her lips is, and always shall be, "God, forgive." Martyrs never ask for vengeance but for forgiveness. Again I say, that is the spirit of the cross.

Therefore, we who have received forgiveness need to forgive one another; we need to forgive even our enemies.

The Second Word

One malefactor turned to the Lord Jesus and said, "If, as You have said, You are the Christ, then save yourself and save us." The other malefactor turned to his fellow criminal and rebuked him, saying: "We deserve our judgment. We know what we have done, and we should be crucified; but this Man has done nothing amiss." Evidently, this criminal must have heard of Jesus before this moment. Most likely when Jesus had been traveling and preaching and teaching, this malefactor must have personally heard Him or at least heard about Him. Then, too, when he now noticed how Jesus was being crucified and heard Him say, "Father, forgive them," his eyes were doubtless opened. He saw that He was the Savior of the world. So he turned to the Lord Jesus at this critical moment and said, "Remember me in Your kingdom."

As a whole the Jews did not believe that Jesus was the King; but here was a criminal about to die, and God gave him such revelation, showing him that Jesus was indeed the King; that this One who was hanging on the cross was none other than the King of the universe, and that his kingdom shall one day appear on earth. What a revelation! So he petitioned Jesus, saying, "Remember me in Your kingdom." And the Lord told him: "Verily, verily, I say unto you, today you shall be with Me in paradise."

This malefactor was obviously only thinking of the future: "When Your kingdom comes, remember me." But the Lord said, "No, today, even right now, you shall be with Me in paradise." Paradise is the place where the blessed dead go and rest until they are called back in resurrection life. So Jesus assured him that he would be with Him in paradise.

The prayer of Jesus—"Father, forgive them"—was answered right there on the cross; for that criminal was saved, his sins were forgiven, and he had the assurance of salvation: "Today, you shall be with Me in paradise." What a blessing!

Can we ever doubt our salvation? Do we need to wait until we die and, as people say, go to heaven's gate and there decide whether we can go in or not? We do not. Thank God, Jesus' prayer to the Father has been answered, even right there on Calvary's cross. The one forgiven was a thief and an outcast, and throughout the ages those, fallen people like him, who believe in the Lord Jesus, if they should die before Jesus returns, will be in paradise. That is the assurance of salvation and that is the cross: the cross gives us assurance.

The Third Word

Towards the end of these first three hours Jesus saw some women standing at the foot of His cross. There was His mother, Mary; there was Mary's sister, Salome; there was also Mary the wife of Clopas; and Mary of Magdala was there as well; and also, His beloved disciple John was there. So Jesus looked down towards His mother and said, "Woman, behold, your son." Then He looked at John and said, "Behold, your mother." And from that very hour, John took Mary to his home.

When Jesus was undergoing such tremendous pain and suffering, He was not thinking of himself. Rather, He was thinking of the world, of those very people who were right then crucifying Him. He was also thinking of that thief and saved him at the last minute. He was thinking of His mother, too: to the very last breath of His earthly life, He faithfully fulfilled His duty as a son to His parent.

The Bible commands: "Honor your father and mother" (see, e.g., Exodus 20:12a, Mark 7:10a, Ephesians 6:2). Even to the last minute Jesus was still taking care of His mother. That ought to be a lesson for us all to learn. We who are the Lord's need to honor our father and mother. We need to look after them. There on that cruel cross Jesus committed His mother to His beloved disciple John.

Let us consider this third word more closely. Jesus looked upon His mother and said, "Woman, behold, thy son." He did not call her "mother" but "woman." I believe we all can recall reading that Jesus had used that word woman before when referring to His mother. At the beginning of His ministry, when he was at Cana in Galilee attending a marriage feast, a moment had arrived when there was no more wine; and Jesus' mother came to Him and said, "Son, they are short of wine; do something for them. I know You can do it. Save the situation." And recall that in response He had said to her, "Woman, My time has not yet come" (see John 2:1-10).

This Greek word translated as woman is not to be understood as being a harsh term of address. If we want to put the translation into more accurate English, it would probably be correct to say: little woman. It is a very affectionate term. Hence, Jesus while on the cross did not call His mother "mother" but called her "little woman," because the relationship on a fleshly basis had come to an end. From then on, all relationships would be on a higher—that is to say, spiritual—level. With regard to the marriage feast at Cana, Jesus had said, "Woman, My hour has not yet come." Here His mother was putting her hand into His work, and so, in essence Jesus was saying that "in My work no fleshly relationship can be involved." And in a corresponding way, on the cross Jesus was finishing the work of redemption; so that henceforth His relationships were all to be on a spiritual basis, including even His relationship with His earthly mother. He therefore said to her: "Little woman, here is your son." His reference to son here did not refer to himself but to His disciple John: "Look at your son, little woman; this is now your son."

Then Jesus looked at John and said, "Here is your mother." On the ground of redemption a new family relationship was at this moment being established: from now on we who are followers of Jesus belong to one family—some of us being as mothers, some of us being as sons, and some as brothers and sisters; it is a new relationship, even the family of God; and this is all the result of the cross. "From that hour" John took Mary to his home (John 19:27b). Jesus, it is believed, did not want His earthly mother to see His agony during the last three hours. He wanted to spare her because her heart had already been pierced (cf. Luke 2:34-35). Therefore, at that moment John took Jesus' mother home in order that she would not have to see and hear Him cry out, "My God, My God, why hast Thou forsaken Me?" What tender love there was in the Lord Jesus.

The Fourth Word

From the sixth hour beginning at 12:00 noon, suddenly, it became dark everywhere. The sun, as it were, hid its face. For three hours Jesus was there alone. He was "treading the wine press alone" (Isaiah 63:3). These were not the hours during which mankind crucified Him; these were not the hours when the powers of darkness attacked Him—He had already overcome all these during the first three hours on the cross. Instead, this was the time in which His Father proceeded to crush Him. He had now become the sin offering. He was now made sin for the sake of the entire world. During these last three hours on the cross the Father cut off His relationship with His Son Jesus. The Father is the righteous God, the God who judges the sin of the world; so during these hours Jesus could not say, "Father, My Father"; for it was no longer true that God was His Father; instead, He could only cry out in anguish: "My God, My God." It was as a man, even as the representative of creation, that Jesus at this moment could only address God as His God and not as his Father: "My God, My God, You made Me; You created Me. Why do You now forsake Me? Have You separated yourself from Me? Why?" (see Psalm 22:1)

At this point in our consideration of this fourth word of Jesus, we need to ask ourselves, What actually is death? Physical death is but a shadow; whereas *real* death is what the Bible has termed the second death, which is what the "lake of fire"—another Biblical term—represents (Revelation 19:20, 20:6a, 10). Real death is therefore eternal separation from the living God. And that was what was taking place during Jesus' final three hours on the cross.

Let us remind ourselves again that the Lord Jesus had been with the Father from eternity. There was such unity, such harmony, such love between Them. Indeed, there was never a moment of shadow or shade. Even when for some thirty-three years He was in this world as a man, He pleased His Father in all things. And because of this, Jesus was never alone; His Father was always with Him. Even during those first three hours on the cross, His Father was there, supporting Him, standing by Him; but during these last three hours Jesus was made sin for us—in that God bruised Him, made Him suffer, and crushed Him (Isaiah 53:10a). It was, as it were, eternal separation from the Father. Jesus could bear all the sufferings from the world,

He could bear all the sufferings from the evil forces, but when it came to His being separated from His Father, He could not bear *that* suffering. So at the ninth hour, which saw the conclusion of God's crushing of Jesus, He had to cry out in a loud voice, asking: "Why?" The answer is, of course, you and me. We are the answer. It was an act of tremendous love, an act of amazing love. Can we ever doubt the love of God when considering that He gave His only begotten Son to us? God's love was surely manifested here at Calvary.

The Fifth Word

Jesus knew all things were about to be finished. In order that the prophetic Scripture from the Psalms might be fulfilled, He cried out, "I thirst." Physically speaking, when a person loses blood, he becomes thirsty. Jesus was approaching the end of His suffering. He had lost almost all His blood, and for the first time, He thought, "I am thirsty, I thirst." That shows His sufferings were real. He suffered to the very end. It was to fulfill Psalm 69:21: "For My thirst, they gave Me vinegar to drink."

As for myself, however, I believe there must be a deeper meaning to this fifth word than that. I believe when Jesus said, "I thirst," He was addressing God. It reminds me of Psalm 42: "As the deer panteth after the water, so my soul panteth after Thee, O God. My soul thirsteth after the living God" (see vv. 1-2). In other words, though He was crushed by God, He was still thirsty for Him. I am reminded also of Job's declaration of his ongoing faith in God no matter what He might do to him: "Though You slay me, yet I still hope, trust, and believe in You" (see Job 13:15). That was the attitude of Jesus on the cross as expressed by this fifth word of His.

The Sixth Word

After receiving the vinegar Jesus uttered the sixth word: "It is finished." It was as though, having been strengthened by the vinegar, He had gathered up all His remaining strength and uttered a great shout: "Finished!" That shout of victory resounds throughout the whole universe from that hour to eternity to come: the work of redemption is now totally finished. There is nothing to be added nor anything to be taken away. It is the word of victory over sin, over death, over the old creation, over the flesh, over the enemy, over everything in opposition to God. It is a loud shout of triumph. Thank God, all the redemptive work of Jesus is done and, today, we stand in the good of it all.

The Seventh Word

Crying out in a loud voice, Jesus uttered His last word from the cross: "Father, into Your hands I commit My spirit" (cf. Psalm 31:5a) That relationship of oneness and harmony with God His Father was now resumed. These last three hours were those of atonement. There on the cross He died a vicarious death. His death atones for our sins, and it was all accomplished within that three-hour period; Jesus' relationship with God His Father was once again renewed, for He could now say, "*Father*, receive My spirit." Then He bowed His head and dismissed His spirit into the Father's hands.

We know God's salvation is perfect. There is no doubt about it because Jesus' relationship with His Father was renewed and therefore the salvation which from eternity God had planned was now complete. Moreover, if you read the Gospel narratives very carefully, you will find that throughout the entire period of His crucifixion, and despite such terrific sufferings, Jesus' head was always held erect: not once did He ever bow His head until at the very last moment He bowed His head and dismissed His spirit. This thus indicates that nothing and no one took His life from Him (John 10:18): on the contrary, Jesus gave His life away voluntarily. That was Jesus' crucifixion; and that, I believe, unveils to us the deeper meaning of the cross.

On that cross we see the absolute awfulness of sin. There has been no place on earth which displayed the ugliness and the sinfulness of mankind's sin more than on the cross of Jesus. On that same cross, however, we also see displayed the glorious love of God and the amazing grace of God. If we truly see and understand even a little of the cross of Jesus, can we possibly glory in anything else? Jesus' cross is our salvation; it is our glory. By His cross our sins have been forgiven. It is because of His cross that our old man was crucified with Him (Romans 6:6a); nevertheless, it is no longer we who live but it is Christ Jesus who lives in us (Galatians 2:20a). And this means that the former things have all passed away; all things are becoming new; and it has all been done by God through His Son Jesus on the cross (II Corinthians 5:17-18a). Furthermore, it is because of the cross that the world is now behind us, for the cross separates us from the world (cf. Galatians 6:14). Moreover, it is by that same cross that we have victory over Satan and all his evil forces. Therefore, the cross of the Lord Jesus is indeed our glory (cf. I Corinthians 1:31 AV). So may we be like the apostle Paul who determined to know nothing but Jesus Christ and Him crucified (I Corinthians 2:2).

Chapter Fifteen

His Resurrection

Matthew 28:2-10—And behold, there was a great earthquake; for an angel of the Lord, descending out of heaven, came and rolled away the stone and sat upon it. And his look was as lightning, and his clothing white as snow. And for fear of him the guards trembled and became as dead men. And the angel answering said to the women, Fear not ye, for I know that ye seek Jesus the crucified one. He is not here, for he is risen, as he said. Come, see the place where the Lord lay. And go quickly and say to his disciples that he is risen from the dead; and behold, he goes before you into Galilee, there shall ye see him. Behold, I have told you. And going out quickly from the tomb with fear and great joy, they ran to bring his disciples word. And as they went to bring his disciples word, behold also, Jesus met them, saying, Hail! And they coming up took him by the feet, and did him homage. Then Jesus says to them, Fear not; go, bring word to my brethren that they go into Galilee, and there they shall see me.

I Corinthians 15:3-5—For I delivered to you, in the first place, what also I had received, that Christ died for our sins, according to the scriptures; and that he was buried; and that he was raised the third day, according to the scriptures; and that he appeared to Cephas, then to the twelve.

On the fourteenth of the Jewish month Nisan a lamb was to be sacrificed for each and every Israelite family. On that very same day Jesus was crucified; Christ the Paschal (Passover) Lamb was sacrificed. Because this was the Preparation Day before the great Sabbath, the Roman soldiers assigned on Calvary made sure the crucified ones there were dead. They broke the leg bones of the two malefactors who were crucified with Jesus in order to speed up their deaths. But when they came to Jesus they found that He was already dead. To make certain He was truly dead a soldier thrust a spear into His side, and out of His broken heart came blood and water.

Christ the First Fruits

Joseph of Arimathea asked the Roman Governor permission to take possession of Jesus' body. He and Nicodemus, the one who early on in Jesus' ministry had come to see Him at night, came with a hundred pounds of ointment and hurriedly embalmed Jesus and placed His body in a tomb in a garden that was nearby to Calvary. It was a tomb that Joseph had prepared for himself. They buried Jesus there with only a few women present who saw where He was laid to rest. When this small mourning party was returning to Jerusalem, a noisy crowd was coming out from the city, led by the Jewish elders. It was the Preparation Day for the Feast of First Fruits, and so the crowd was going out of the city across the river Kidron (Cedron) to an appointed field. The harvested first fruits of the fields were already bound; for instance, there was a sheaf of barley standing there, ready to be cut. And hence, this crowd led by the elders were coming out to witness the cutting of the sheaf. Three men with sickles and baskets arrived as expected at the field and cut that sheaf of barley and prepared it to be offered on the day after the Sabbath as the first fruits to God, because unless that was offered, no one could eat any corn or barley recently harvested. Such was the Feast of First Fruits (see Leviticus 23:9-14).

Now it so happened that the third day following Jesus' crucifixion was to be the very day on which the Jewish priest was to offer up a *homer* of the first fruits to God; and, of course, that was the same day on which Jesus was raised from the dead because He himself, as Paul wrote, is the first fruits of resurrection: "Christ the first fruits, and then those who are His at His coming" (see I Corinthians 15:23). So we are given to understand here that Christ Jesus is our Passover and also He serves—by virtue of His resurrection—as the First Fruits. Moreover, Jesus' resurrection is typified in the Old Testament not only by the Feast of First Fruits but also in the offering up by Abraham of his only begotten son Isaac (Genesis 22:1-18). Indeed, that event serves as a type of God the Father offering up His beloved Son for us and, like Abraham receiving back as from the dead his only son Isaac, His receiving to himself back from the dead His only Son Jesus.

The psalmist David said in one of his Messianic psalms: "Thou wilt not leave my soul in Sheol, and thou wilt not allow thy Holy One to see corruption" (see 16:10). Thus Jesus' resurrection was being prophesied here. Likewise, in Isaiah 53:10-12, having first noted that the Messiah—as the Suffering Servant—would be made an offering for sin by God, the passage goes on to speak in resurrection terms concerning the Messiah: "He shall see His offspring, He shall prolong His days, and He shall be satisfied with the result of the travail of his soul. He will also divide the spoil with the strong." There are many other places in the Old Testament where the resurrection of Jesus was clearly prophesied.

When Jesus was on earth He, too, predicted His death and resurrection. Let us review again those instances. After Peter had confessed Jesus as the Christ, the Son of the living God, He told them He must go to Jerusalem, be ill-treated by the elders, scribes, and Pharisees, and be killed; but that on the third day thereafter He would rise from the dead (Matthew 16:21). When He was in Galilee He again told His disciples that He would be killed, but that on the third day following He would rise from the dead (17:22-23). Then, too, on His final journey to Jerusalem, Jesus again shared with the disciples that He was going to Jerusalem to die, but that on the third day He would rise from the dead (20:17-19). It seems that Jesus never spoke of His death without at the same time mentioning also His resurrection.

After Jesus had held His Passover Feast with His disciples and His conversation with them, they left the upper room and went on their way to the Garden of Gethsemane, and again He told them that he would die but that He would rise back to life and meet them again in Galilee (26:31-32). But somehow His disciples could not take it in. They were grieved because they knew something was going to happen to their dear Master, but when he told them He would be raised from the dead, it did not sink in. As a matter of fact, they did not believe it. Is it not strange that His disciples did not believe that their Master would be raised from the dead but somehow the hostile priests and Pharisees believed it? For we may recall that after Christ was crucified and buried, these Jewish leaders went to Pilate and said: "We heard this deceiver say that on the third day He would be raised from the dead; and if the disciples steal His body and say to the people, He is risen from the dead, that will deceive even more people." So they asked for guards to guard that tomb lest this should happen (see Matthew 27:62-66).

Somehow, they had the premonition that it just might happen, but the disciples themselves did not believe it.

In the early morning, on the first day of the week, suddenly, there was an earthquake, and an angel of the Lord came down from heaven and rolled back the huge stone that served as the gate to the tomb. The guards were frightened at the angel and, evidently, they fled (Matthew 28:2-4). But on that early morning some women came to anoint the Lord. Jesus' body had been embalmed very hurriedly by Joseph and Nicodemus. It was not properly done, so these women who loved the Lord prepared spices and were intent on using these spices to reanoint Jesus' dead body (Mark 16:1-4). It would appear from Scripture that all the various visitors to the tomb did not come together as one group but came in various groups of two or more.

Mary of Magdala loved the Lord so much. She was probably the first one who arrived at the tomb, and when she approached, she found that the stone was rolled away. Immediately, she turned and went to find Peter to tell him that something had happened (John 20:1-2). So Peter and John ran to the tomb (v.3). But while they were going to the tomb, some other women arrived, went into the tomb, and saw an angel there. The angel said, "Fear not; I know you have come here seeking the crucified One, but He is not here. He is risen as He said. Come and see the place where He lay. Go and tell His brethren that He will go to Galilee and there they shall see Him." So, with fear and joy, they ran to tell the disciples (see Matthew 28:5-8, Mark 16:1-7).

While they were going away, Peter and John arrived. John, being younger, ran faster, and Peter arrived later. But when John reached the tomb and looked inside, he, being very timid, did not enter. But Peter rushed into the tomb. And so did John eventually. They both saw the burial cloth lying there, and the handkerchief for the head in another place; thus indicating that their examination of the tomb was not something done hurriedly. But the body was not there. They saw the empty tomb and believed, though as yet they did not understand the Scripture that said Jesus must rise from the dead. So they returned to their homes (John 20:3-10).

As these two disciples went back, Mary of Magdala arrived at the tomb a second time. She looked into the tomb while sadly weeping. She then heard a voice behind her: "Woman, why are you weeping?" She thought the man standing behind her must be the gardener, so she said, "Where did you take Him? I will go and get Him." In response the voice said, "Mary." She turned towards the man and said in Aramaic, "Rabboni," meaning Teacher. The risen Jesus then said, "Do not touch Me; for I have not yet ascended to My Father. Go and tell My brethren that I ascend to My Father and your Father, to My God and your God." So Mary left (see John 20:11-18a). As some of the women were on their way to see and tell the disciples what they had seen and had heard from the angel at the tomb, the risen Lord met them. He allowed them to clasp hold of His feet and worship Him, and then said to them: "Fear not, but go and tell My brethren to meet Me in Galilee" (see Matthew 28:8-10).

That same day two disciples, one of whom was named Cleopas, were quite disappointed because—having believed that Jesus was indeed the Messiah—He was nonetheless now dead. So they left Jerusalem and were walking back to their home village of Emmaus, greatly saddened by what had happened to Jesus. Suddenly, a Man appeared and joined them in their walk. He asked them, "Why are you so sad?" They replied: "Do you not know what has happened in Jerusalem? There was a Man by the name of Jesus whom we believed was the great Prophet of Israel, yet He was killed, crucified. But a strange thing happened. Some women came to us from Jesus' tomb and reported that they had seen Him risen." The Man who was walking along with them said the following: "Oh, foolish and dull in heart. Do you not understand that He who died and suffered had to die and suffer before he could enter into glory?" Then He explained to them from the Psalms, the Law, and the Prophets about himself (see Luke 24:13-27).

Eventually, these two and the Stranger arrived at Emmaus as evening was approaching, and the Stranger was seemingly intent on going on farther. So they urged Him strongly to stay with them, which He did. They went into the house and prepared for supper. At the table the Man took a loaf, gave thanks, broke it, and gave it to them; and at that moment their eyes were opened and they recognized that this Man was the Lord Jesus. And with that he disappeared from their sight. They said to each other that when he was talking with them on the road, their hearts were greatly warmed by what He had told them. Immediately they returned to Jerusalem, and when they arrived there, the Eleven reported to them that "it was true, and that the Lord has indeed risen and has already appeared to Peter." Moreover, while all of them were still talking about all of this, Jesus himself appeared and stood among them and said, "Peace to you" (see vv. 28-36).

After that, during the next forty days Jesus appeared a number of times to His various disciples. He appeared to Peter; He appeared to the twelve apostles; He appeared on one occasion to more than 500 brethren at the same time; He appeared to James. And Paul wrote that "last of all He appeared to me, who am like an abortion, and who am not worthy to be called an apostle. Jesus was indeed raised from the dead on the third day according to the Scriptures" (see I Corinthians 15:3-9).

Evidence of Resurrection

There was no doubt that Jesus was risen from the dead. There was one highly significant piece of physical evidence—the empty tomb. There were the testimonies of those who saw Him after his resurrection. Over time their testimonies were challenged, they themselves were persecuted, but their testimonies stood. Not only that, their lives were changed. After Jesus was crucified, at first those disciples of His were gathered in a room with the doors locked because they were full of fear of the Jewish leaders (John 20:19a, 26), but after they saw the risen Lord, they were completely changed. This transformation was not only true with the disciples who saw Him physically, bodily, in resurrection, but that transformation has been witnessed throughout these twenty centuries since then by countless people of all backgrounds from all over the world. How their lives were completely changed because they believed in the risen Lord. That is, in fact, the best evidence that Jesus is alive.

Doctrinally speaking, Jesus must have been raised from the dead because, He being the Son of God and the Originator of life, how could He possibly have been held by death? On the contrary, He went into death, robbed death of its power, and came out in victory (I Corinthians 15:54-55). Jesus is proven to be the Son of God by having been raised from the dead (Romans 1:4). In truth, He is indeed risen!

Resurrection As an Article of Our Faith

What is our faith? What is the gospel—the good news to all humanity? The apostle Paul summed it up for us when he wrote: "For I delivered to you, in the first place, what also I had received, that Christ died for our sins, according to the scriptures; and that he was buried; and that he was raised the third day, according to the scriptures" (I Corinthians 15:3-4).

His death, burial, and resurrection are the three cardinal articles of our faith. We believe in His death, we believe in His burial, and we believe in His resurrection. This is the gospel. We read in the book of Acts that when the gospel was first preached on the day of Pentecost, Peter stood up and delivered the first gospel sermon. He mentioned about the death of the Lord, but His whole emphasis was on the resurrection of Jesus. The people in Jerusalem knew that He was dead because it had just happened fifty days earlier, but they did not know about His resurrection. That was known only to those who were His. So when Peter preached the gospel that day, it was resurrection that was emphasized. In fact, resurrection became the focus of conflict between the apostles and the Jewish priests, Pharisees, and scribes because the apostles had borne bold witness that Jesus was alive. Yes, He had died, they testified, but He is now alive; He is living.

Then later when Peter preached in the house of Cornelius, he began speaking about the life and ministry of Jesus, then went on concerning His death; but when he came to the resurrection of Jesus, the Holy Spirit fell upon all listeners, and they were all baptized in the Spirit (Acts 10:34-47). When Paul preached the gospel in Antioch of Pisidia, he began with the story of Israel. Then he came to the life of Christ, His death, and concluded with His resurrection (Acts 13:14ff.). That is the gospel.

When Paul was in Athens he was asked to speak on Mars Hill in the city auditorium that was there. So he spoke, saying, among other things, that God has appointed a Man to justly judge the entire world one day, and the Man He has appointed has been proven to be such by God having raised Him from the dead (Acts 17:30-32a). In other words, whenever the gospel is preached, it is resurrection that is to be emphasized.

The Bible tells us that people must not only believe in Jesus' death but also in His resurrection; for if we read the Bible carefully, we learn that we are commanded to believe in both these articles of faith, yet the emphasis is upon the resurrection of Jesus. In Romans, for example, it says that the word of faith is not far from you; in fact, it is near you—even in your mouth and heart; and that if you confess with your mouth Jesus as Lord and believe in your heart that God has raised Him from the dead, you shall be saved (Romans 10:8-9). The gospel is the good news of the risen Lord, of the living Christ. Obviously, people must believe in Jesus' death, for without death there is no resurrection. But believing in His death alone is not enough. I have sometimes wondered why, when the gospel is preached today, there is not that accompanying power. Is it because preachers do not mention, or emphasize enough, the resurrection of the Lord Jesus? Yes, indeed, Jesus has died for us, but on the third day, He rose from the dead. That is the gospel we believe, and that is the gospel we must faithfully preach. He is risen!

Resurrection As a Daily Experience

What is Jesus' resurrection to us today? It is not only an historical fact—He having been bodily raised up from death. The resurrection of the Lord Jesus is not only an article of our faith that we believe in; it is to be, as well, our daily experience; in fact, it is everything. There is no Christian life if the Lord is not risen. Paul declared this: "If the Lord is not risen, then in vain do we preach and in vain do you believe" (see I Corinthians

15:14, 17). If Jesus was not raised up from the dead, then our preaching will be false and therefore powerless; and people's belief will be vain and worthless. Nothing can be accomplished if Christ be not risen from death. Moreover, if Jesus had not been raised from the dead, how would we ever know that God had accepted Jesus' voluntary offering of himself as a sin offering for us? The fact of Jesus' resurrection proves that God *did* accept His Son's offering.

On the yearly Day of Atonement in Old Testament times the high priest in either tabernacle or temple would enter the holiest space of all behind the veil, bringing with him the sacrificial blood with which to sprinkle before the mercy seat, along with the smoking incense to cover him—for who could come into the very presence of God and come out alive? When once every year the high priest was there in the holiest of all making atonement for the sins of all the people, the people themselves would be standing outside in fear and trembling. Why were they standing there? They were there listening for the bells to ring that were attached to the fringe of the garment which the high priest wore. For as he walked, the bells would ring; but if there was no sound of the bells ringing, then it was assumed that the high priest must have been smitten dead in the presence of God, the blood sacrifice not having been accepted and the atonement therefore not having been made. So the people listened for the bells to ring, and if they did hear them ringing, then they knew that the atonement for all their sins had been made and thus they were relieved to know that they were safe for another year (see Exodus 28:33-35).

Romans 4 informs us that Christ "was delivered up for our offenses, but He was raised for our justification" (see v. 25). Jesus was offered up for our offenses as a sin offering, but He was raised for our justification. How do we know we are justified? How do we know God has accepted Jesus' offering of himself on our behalf? We know for certain because God has raised Jesus from the dead. His offering of himself has been accepted; therefore, we are justified. If Christ be not risen, wrote Paul, then in vain we preach and in vain people believe.

Furthermore, Paul also wrote this: "If we have hope in Christ only in this life, then we are the most miserable of all men" (see I Corinthians 15:19). If Christ is not risen but we nonetheless believe in Him, what does that signify? It signifies that we admire His moral condition. We take Him as our model. We want to imitate Him. We want to live as He lived. In order to imitate Him, however, we have to forsake the world. Even so, we will never arrive at a point in our life that we can claim we are like Him. In other words, the more we try to imitate Jesus, the less we are like Him. In short, we are condemned, we are accused; our conscience can never be at peace; and thus we are the most miserable of all men. People who do not believe in Jesus can go to the world and enjoy themselves, but we who desire to follow Him cannot. So if there is no resurrection, all is in vain.

Yet, we can rejoice because Christ *is* risen! Because He is risen from the dead, we are justified; and not only justified, but sanctified. If Jesus by His sacrificial death died for our offenses, then how much more shall we be saved by His life (Romans 5:10 ASV). Because He is risen, therefore, He becomes our life—Christ is our life (Colossians 3:4a ASV). He gave His life to us. We have His life in us, and by this life of His, we live; by this life, we are separated; by this life, we are sanctified; by this life, we are glorified, transformed, and are being conformed to the image of himself (Romans 8:29-30). In a very real sense, therefore, Jesus' resurrection is the very foundation of our life. It is the secret of Christian living. There can be no Christians if

Christ is not raised from the dead. There can be no Christian living if it is not the risen Christ who lives in us.

The problem today is that even though we believe in the resurrection of Jesus, for some reason it is merely an article of faith which we confess instead of it being our daily, living experience. What is a Christian? And what is Christian life? A Christian is one who believes in the Lord Jesus—in His death, burial, and resurrection. A Christian life is simply this: Christ in you and me, and He is our hope of glory (Colossians 1:27b). Jesus' death is our death, for when He died on the cross, we died in Him and with Him. In other words, Jesus by His death concluded the old creation: for when He died to sin once and for all, we too died to sin; when He died to the world, we also died to the world. In short, the entire old creation died when Jesus died, so our old man died with it. His death therefore concluded us as part of the old creation. And now, Jesus' resurrection life begins the Christian's real life (see Romans 6:3-10). The apostle Paul declared: "For for me to live is Christ"; and, "I am crucified with Christ: and no longer live I, but Christ lives in me" (Philippians 1:21a, Galatians 2:20a-b). Christ himself is now our very life (see Colossians 3:4a).

Life Out of Death

Does that spiritual fact register deeply in you? What is resurrection? Resurrection is life out of death. Resurrection is life that enters into death, robs death of its power, and comes out the other side in victory. Whatever has not gone into death and is able to come out is not resurrection; that is merely a surviving element of the old creation. Let us be clear and stand upon the fact that the old creation entered into death when Jesus died on the cross, and it was buried there in

Jesus' burial, *forever*. Therefore, the old creation can never come out. Only the divine life that enters into death, conquers death, and comes out in victory is resurrection. Jesus himself declared: "I am the resurrection and the life" (John 11:25a); which is to say that His life is resurrection life. And that is the only life that can be called resurrection life. All other life will enter into death and be conquered, for it lacks the power to come out. Hence, the resurrection life of Jesus is the only life by which we live as Christians.

Have we discovered and entered into the reality of the secret of Christian living? Or are we still struggling to live a Christian life by means of our old life and serving the Lord by the energy of the flesh? If we are doing that, we do not know what resurrection is. Whatever is not animated and energized by the resurrection life of Christ is not of God and is therefore not acceptable to Him. God is not pleased with it because His verdict is that the old creation died and must remain dead. All the old things have passed away and all things have become new; for all these things are from God who has done it all; it is indeed a new creation, for if anyone be in Christ He is in fact a new creation (II Corinthians 5:17-18a). But how often we still live as though we are living *before* resurrection and not after resurrection. Not only do we try to *live* before resurrection, we also try to *serve* before resurrection.

We need to ask ourselves, Is there the mark of Jesus' cross upon our life? The apostle Paul could say "Yes" to that inquiry, for he wrote: "From now on let no one disturb me for I bear on my body the brand-marks of Jesus" (Galatians 6:17). For Paul it was the mark of the cross, and that mark exhibited the fact that he was no longer living by his old life; it had been dealt with long before. But it also exhibited further the fact that he was living altogether by the resurrection life of the Lord Jesus.

Such is the only *life* which counts and such is the only *service* which counts.

I fear for myself and for my brethren that we do not really know what resurrection is. Whatever is not lived out by the resurrection life of the Lord Jesus is not Christian, and any work done for God that is not by the power of His resurrection is not Christian service. In I Corinthians 15 Paul made it very clear concerning resurrection, for there He argued and explained as follows: "If it is true that the dead are not raised at all, then why do I allow myself to face death daily in service to God and His people? If, indeed, the dead do not rise, why not, as it was said of old, 'let us eat and drink, for tomorrow we die'? If there is no resurrection, why bother to live and work rightly? There is no sense to it all; therefore, why not enjoy ourselves." But because of the fact of resurrection, Paul was willing "to die daily" in the cause of Christ; and he therefore did not himself dare to be careless in his own Christian walk, and went on to warn the Corinthian believers themselves not to be deceived or misled by anyone, he quoting the Greek philosopher Menander who said: "Bad company corrupts good character." So in view of resurrection being a fact, Paul concluded by urging the believers at Corinth to return to a sober and righteous life, and to "stop sinning" (see I Corinthians 15:29-34).

In that same chapter 15 of I Corinthians—that tremendous short treatise on resurrection—Paul in so many words raised this question and gave answer to it: "Why should we apostles labor? It is because there is resurrection in view." One day, it will be Christ the first fruits; then we all who are Christ's at His coming will be resurrected (see vv. 1-24), and at that time we shall receive our reward. This body of humiliation will be transformed into a body of glory, for we groan within ourselves, eagerly waiting for our adoption as God's sons at the redemption of our body (Romans 8:18-23). In the future there will be the resurrection even of our physical body; but now, we can experience resurrection every day, in that we can live by the resurrection life of the Lord Jesus.

Paul wrote elsewhere concerning himself in relation to the resurrection life of Jesus: "I have the sentence of death in me that I may live not by depending on myself but by depending on the One who raised Jesus from the dead" (see II Corinthians 1:9). Is that our testimony?

The Church Is on Resurrection Ground

Resurrection has everything to do with us, not only individually but corporately; and with respect to the latter, the church is built on resurrection ground. Christ is "the head of the body, the church," and He "is the beginning, [the] firstborn from among the dead" (Colossians 1:18). Resurrection is the foundational building block of the church, for God builds up the resurrection life of Jesus in you and in me, and with that resurrection life in us He builds the church. That is the reason why Jesus when on earth declared: "I will build My church upon this rock, and the gates of hades shall not prevail against it" (see Matthew 16:18). The Lord Jesus can indeed build His church because that resurrection life of His has already overcome hades.

Today, though, we see the church so weak, so fragile, so defeated, so broken up. And why? Is it because it is not built upon resurrection ground? If it is built on *that* ground, the gates of hades cannot prevail against it. The church is the church triumphant; it is never defeated. The enemy is already defeated, and the greatest and last enemy is death; and yet it, too, has been overcome (I Corinthians 15:26-27).

Whenever we bring something other than resurrection life into the church, that something will corrupt the church; it gives the enemy opportunity to harm and destroy. How we therefore need to be before the Lord that it is His resurrection life which animates and energizes everything having to do with our personal walk and with the church. In other words, it is to be Christ in all things individually and corporately, because it was Jesus who declared: "I am the resurrection and the life" (John 11:25a). And if that be true of all of His saints, then there will be the church triumphant.

So we Christians believe in the resurrection of Jesus as an historical fact, as an article of our faith, and as the theme of the gospel we preach. More than that, however, we take Jesus' resurrection to ourselves personally, for His resurrection is our very life. But we also take His resurrection to ourselves collectively, because Jesus' resurrection life is the only thing which can build the church. So may God enable each of us to do our part both individually and corporately.

Chapter Sixteen

HIS APPEARING FOR FORTY DAYS

I Corinthians 15:1-11—But I make known to you, brethren, the glad tidings which I announced to you, which also ye received, in which also ye stand, by which also ye are saved, (if ye hold fast the word which I announced to you as the glad tidings,) unless indeed ye have believed in vain. For I delivered to you, in the first place, what also I had received, that Christ died for our sins, according to the scriptures; and that he was buried; and that he was raised the third day, according to the scriptures; and that he appeared to Cephas, then to the twelve. Then he appeared to above five hundred brethren at once, of whom the most remain until now, but some also have fallen asleep. Then he appeared to James; then to all the apostles; and last of all, as to an abortion, he appeared to me also. For I am the least of the apostles, who am not fit to be called apostle, because I have persecuted the assembly [church] of God. But by God's grace I am what I am; and his grace, which was towards me, has not been vain; but I have laboured more abundantly than they all, but not I, but the grace of God which was with me. Whether, therefore, I or they, thus we preach, and thus ye have believed.

Acts 1:1-5—I composed the first discourse, O Theophilus, concerning all things which Jesus began both to do and to teach, until that day in which, having by the Holy Spirit charged the apostles whom he had chosen, he was taken up; to whom also he presented himself living, after he had suffered, with many proofs; being seen by them during forty days, and speaking of the things which concern the kingdom of God; and, being assembled with them, commanded them not to depart from Jerusalem, but to await the promise of the Father, which said he ye have heard of me. For John indeed baptised with water, but ye shall be baptised with the Holy Spirit after now not many days.

Introduction

Over these past weeks we have been considering together the life of the Lord Jesus; and today I would like for us to look into this matter of His appearing which occurred over many days following His resurrection but before His ascension. And I would like for us to do so in some detail.

In I Corinthians chapter 15 the apostle Paul announced to the Corinthian believers what he had received from the Lord: "Of first importance are these following points: first, Christ died for our sins according to the Scriptures; second, He was buried; third, He was raised from the dead according to the Scriptures; fourth, He thereafter often appeared" (see vv. 3-5ff.). Here are mentioned two significant combinations of events—His death and His burial; His resurrection and His various appearings. And that, in summary, is the gospel or glad tidings on which we Christians stand and by which we are saved.

Jesus' death is essential to our salvation because He bore our sins in His body, and thus we receive forgiveness of our sins by His death on the cross. His burial is likewise essential because by that event our old man was finished, buried out of sight. Moreover, Jesus' resurrection is highly significant because by His having been raised from the dead He is able to give us a new life. And lastly, Jesus' appearing is also very important because by His various appearings He shows us a new way of living. So we see, on the one hand, that Jesus' death is according to the Scriptures, and His burial is intended to support and reinforce the fact of His death. And on the other hand, we see that Jesus' resurrection is according to the Scriptures as well, and His appearings are intended to strengthen our belief in the fact of His resurrection.

These four events are the essentials of the gospel, the doctrinal foundation on which we stand. I think we know, more or less, of His death, of His burial, and of His resurrection, though admittedly there is so much more about them which we need to know; strangely, however, it is as though we neglect completely the matter of Jesus' appearings. We do not think much about them, and yet the apostle Paul includes that event as being among the four points which in his view are essential in constituting God's glad tidings. Hence, I would like for us to focus our attention on the frequent appearing of Jesus to His varied disciples.

Having been raised from the dead on the third day following His crucifixion, Jesus did not ascend publicly to God immediately; for between His resurrection and public ascension there was a forty-day interval. That does not mean, however, that during those forty days Jesus never ascended to His Father. It is true that when He first appeared to Mary of Magdala, He had said to her: "Do not touch Me for I have not yet ascended to My Father" (see John 20:17a). Yet a little while later, He allowed the other women to clasp hold of His feet (Matthew 28:8-9). So we are sure He must have ascended during that short period, even though His *public* ascension did not occur until forty days later.

As a matter of fact, in resurrection there are no such factors as time and space. When Jesus was in His physical body He was limited by time and space, as we all are. If He was in Jerusalem, He could not be in Galilee. Jesus was reared in Nazareth, and when He grew up to maturity He traveled around preaching the gospel; and He was therefore restricted everywhere He went by time and space. But in His resurrection Jesus took upon himself a spiritual body; or to phrase it another way, He was thereafter in the spirit, thus transcending the time and space factors. No longer bound by either time or space, Jesus is everywhere and is always present—thus leading our brother T. Austin-Sparks to put the matter this way: "In the resurrection of our Lord Jesus, it is no longer a matter of come and go; it is simply a matter of appearing and disappearing." In other words, it is simply a matter of His being seen or being unseen. Jesus is always here, because He is living and lives forevermore. If you have faith, you see Him; if you do not have faith, you do not see Him. Nevertheless, whether one has faith or not, the fact remains that Jesus is everywhere, ever living and living forever. That is resurrection.

Hence, because Jesus is no longer limited by time and space, He could appear to his numerous disciples for forty days in many different places without any difficulty before His public ascension. The number forty in the Scriptures has a very special meaning; it symbolizes "testing." It is a time of testing for people. The first mention in Scripture of this number forty is found in Genesis 7 where is told of the rain which came down for forty days and nights—causing the universal flood.

Moses went up to the mountain to receive the Ten Commandments and the pattern for the construction of the tabernacle. He was there forty days and nights. Then he went up again for forty days and nights more—after the two original stone tablets had been broken—in order to receive the Ten Commandments a second time. We also will remember the spies who went forth to spy out the Promised Land for forty days during the time of Moses. We can recall as well that Elijah journeyed across the desert for forty days to Mount Sinai, sustained by heavenly food. Let us be reminded, too, that Jonah went to Nineveh and told them that in forty days the city would be destroyed if the people did not repent. Jesus was in the wilderness for forty days and nights, fasting, being tempted, and overcoming (Exodus 34:1-2, 28, Numbers 13:25, I Kings 19:8, Jonah 3:4, Matthew 4:1-11).

Now after He was raised from the dead, He appeared to His disciples during these forty days about which we are now discussing. And like all the aforementioned instances of testing, it was now a time of testing for His disciples. Jesus was bringing them out from that which was physical into that which is spiritual, out of that which was earthly into that which is heavenly—a forty-day period of testing.

A Description of Jesus' Recorded Post-Resurrection Appearings

We know from God's word that the risen Jesus appeared a number of times during those forty days. Immediately after he was raised from the dead He appeared to Mary of Magdala. Because of her intense love for Jesus, He had to appear to her immediately after He was raised from the dead. His message to her was: "Do not touch Me; for I have not yet ascended to My Father. But go and tell My brethren that I go to see My Father, your Father, My God, your God" (see John 20:17). A short time later He met several other women—Mary the mother of James, Joanna, and others with them. He now allowed *them* to clasp hold of His feet and said, "Fear not; go and tell My brethren that they may see Me in Galilee" (Luke 24:9-10, see Matthew 28:8-10).

Next we recall those two disconsolate disciples, one of whom was named Cleopas, who, having been perplexed and greatly saddened by Jesus' crucifixion, had left Jerusalem and were walking on their way to their home village of Emmaus. And while they were talking about what had happened in Jerusalem, Jesus suddenly appeared and began walking with them, but they did not recognize Him. Eventually Jesus opened their understanding of the Scriptures, and when He expounded the Scriptures to them concerning himself, how their hearts were greatly warmed. When they arrived at Emmaus, they earnestly urged Jesus to stay with them. And as they were at supper, the Lord Jesus broke some bread, blessed it, and gave it to them, and their eyes were opened to see the risen Jesus; but He immediately disappeared from their sight (Luke 24:13-32).

These two went instantly back to Jerusalem, and when they came to the house where the apostles and the others were gathered, they were told that Jesus had appeared to Simon Peter (vv. 33-34). (Now we do not know what happened during *that* appearing; it must have been so intimately personal that it was not recorded; but I believe in that private appearing that Jesus restored Peter completely.) While they were still talking together in the house, suddenly, Jesus appeared and said, "Peace be unto you." He showed them His hands, His side and His feet, and He breathed into them and said, "Receive the Holy Spirit" (Luke 24:36, 40; John 20:19b-22). Thomas, who was not there, subsequently announced: "Unless I put my finger in His wounds, I will not believe" (see John 20:25b).

A week later, in the evening, he was there and, suddenly, the Lord appeared. The doors were locked shut, but as was noted earlier the spiritual body is not limited by time or space or material things. The Lord appeared to them and said, "Thomas, here are My hands; put your finger here and see. Do not be faithless but believe." Thomas said, "My Lord and my God" (see John 20:26-28).

In John chapter 21 we are told that seven of the apostles were in Galilee, and at one point Peter said to the other six, "I am going fishing, I have nothing to do." The others said they would go with him. So they all went fishing, but they could not catch anything all night. In the morning Jesus was standing on the lake shore, and He said, "Children, you have no fish, do you?" They said, "No." So He said, "Cast your net on the right-hand side of the boat," and consequently they caught 153 large fish. John said, "It is the Lord." The others could not recognize Him, but John did. Peter threw himself into the water and went to the Lord. There, Jesus asked Peter three times: "Do you love Me more than these? Do you love Me? Are you really attached to Me?" I believe it was at this particular appearing that the Lord restored Peter publicly before his companions and commissioned him to tend and shepherd His sheep (see vv. 1-17).

Paul tells us that on one occasion the resurrected Jesus appeared to more than 500 of His Christian brethren all together at one time; and I personally believe that this must have occurred at the mountain in Galilee which Jesus had designated as the place to which the Eleven should go to meet Him after He would rise from the dead (see Matthew 28:16). For prior to His arrest Jesus had instructed His disciples that they were to go to Galilee where, He added, "I will meet you" (e.g., see Matthew 26:32). When they went to that Galilean mountain,

Jesus did indeed meet them; and I believe further that it was there that He gave them the Great Commission which we find in verses 18-20 of Matthew 28.

It was most likely after that that Jesus appeared to James, His brother in the flesh. We are told in John 7:5 that even His brethren in the flesh did not believe in Him before His death; however, after Jesus' crucifixion, burial, resurrection, and later His appearing to His brother James, the whole family turned to the Lord.

Jesus then appeared to "all the apostles." I believe the place of that appearance was at the Mount of Olives from where Jesus ascended into heaven (Acts 1:9-12). I believe that 120 believers saw Him ascend from atop the Mount and from where they were commanded to return to Jerusalem and wait for the promise of the Father—the gift of the Holy Spirit—so that they might receive power from on high to be His witnesses in Jerusalem, in all Judea and Samaria, and to the ends of the earth (Acts 1:4-5, 8).

These, then, are the recorded appearings of the risen Lord during these forty days following His resurrection. But Paul, in concluding his recounting the various appearings of Jesus, added that He also had appeared to him "last of all"—though Jesus' appearance came, "as it were, to one untimely born." Indeed, confessed this apostle, he was unfit to bear the title of apostle because he once persecuted the church of God (I Corinthians 15:8-9). Nevertheless, the resurrected Jesus appeared to Paul. So, these are the Biblical facts concerning the Lord Jesus' various appearings after His resurrection.

Why Jesus' Post-Resurrection Appearings Are Important for Us

His Appearings Revitalized the Faith of the Disciples

Now what exactly did Jesus do during those forty days of appearing? What did He teach during that period? Why is it that those forty days are important for us today? First of all, I believe His appearings were for the purpose of revitalizing the faith of His disciples. When Jesus was arrested, His disciples scattered. After He was crucified and buried, they were in mourning—and, in fear. They locked themselves inside the house where they were gathered. Even when the news came to them from those several Christian women that Jesus had risen, they could not bring themselves to believe it. They were weeping, mourning, fearful, and trembling. Their faith was challenged; in fact, it wavered; it was greatly weakened. It therefore took the appearings of Jesus to revitalize their faith.

When we talk about resurrection today, we probably do not have the same feeling as that of those disciples of old. For them, however, the resurrection of Jesus was the first case of genuine resurrection. Though in the Old Testament period there had been people raised, and though in the New Testament period Jesus had raised people from the dead, these were not truly genuine resurrections. That is because those people who were raised from the dead still remained in their mortal bodies and later in their lives still died afterwards; but the resurrection of the Lord Jesus was the first instance of real resurrection.

What, then, *is* resurrection? Resurrection is a going into death, overcoming death, coming out of death, and living forevermore. Jesus was the first one who was able to enter into death, rob it of its power, then come out of death and live forevermore. Such an event had never happened before. So we cannot blame those first disciples for not being able to believe that their Master had indeed been raised from the dead. It required Jesus' resurrected appearings to convince them that His resurrection was true. Even though He could go through walls, His resurrection was nonetheless real. He was not a ghost, not a spirit, but a real living person. He had flesh and bone, but such was not material flesh and bone. Moreover, He had no blood and there would thus be no decay. He was resurrected a spiritual body; nevertheless, He was a real person: but unbounded, omnipotent, omnipresent, omniscient. That is the risen Jesus. Gradually, through His several appearings, this fact dawned upon the disciples. They realized that He was genuinely risen from the dead, and what a glorious thing it was: Jesus is now Lord of all, He is now living forever, He is now all-powerful because He had overcome death and all other obstacles. That restored their faith. That changed them, transformed their emotions form mourning to joy, from fear to courage. It was the Lord Jesus appearing to them which showed them who He really is.

As recorded by John in the first chapter of Revelation, Jesus testified of himself that He is the Alpha and the Omega, the beginning and the end, the first and the last; He is the living One, the One who had gone into death but who is now alive and lives forevermore and holds the keys of death and Hades (vv. 8, 17b-18). This is the testimony of Jesus, the living Christ; and by His appearings, this was assured and reassured to the apostles. No wonder there was such a transformation occurring within these early disciples. Such, then, is what I believe was the first reason for His various appearings during those forty days.

Do we really believe that the Lord Jesus is alive? Do we truly believe He is here, and everywhere else? Do we really believe that no matter where we may be, He is with us, that He has never left us, that He is always there with us? Jesus is no longer limited by time and space, so we have Him all the time.

However, many times you do not see Jesus; many times you think the risen Lord is not there; many times you feel He is far away from you. That is because you do not see the resurrected Jesus by faith. If you have faith, you can see Him all the time, everywhere, and in every situation in your life because He is the living One, the resurrected One. He is there with you because He is ever present. All that is required, therefore, is for you to see Him *by faith*. Do you really believe that Jesus is the resurrected One, that He is the all-powerful One? He has overcome every obstacle which stood in His way—even death, the greatest power on the earth. Hence, is there anything which the risen Lord cannot do? Do you really believe that this is He? How you and I need to be assured and reassured that this is the Christ whom we believe!

His Appearings Demonstrate a New Way of Life

The second reason Jesus' post-resurrection appearances are important for us is because by these various appearings of his He demonstrates to us a new way of life. When Jesus was in the flesh, He was with and alongside the disciples, always taking care of them; but when He told them He was leaving, they were sorely grieved because He had been a great comforter to them. So Jesus explained to them that though He was going back to the Father, He would send to them another Comforter—the

Holy Spirit—who would be with them forever because He would be in them (John 14:12b, 16-17a, c).

When Jesus was in the flesh, sometimes He was with the disciples and sometimes He sent them away; at other times, He was alone on a mountain praying; nevertheless, they would come back and seek Him and touch Him to know that He was there. But now during these forty days the risen Lord showed them that this would no longer be the way with Him. Henceforth Jesus by the Spirit was to be with them inwardly all the time; for it was during His first appearing with the locked-in gathered disciples on the evening of His resurrection that He breathed into them and said: "Receive the Holy Spirit" (John 20:19, 22). I personally believe it was on this specific occasion that the risen Lord gave to His disciples—and, by extension, to us—the indwelling Holy Spirit: the "another Comforter" whom He had promised.

Let us recall again Jesus' last and lengthy conversation He had with His disciples on the evening of his arrest, as recorded in John's Gospel, chapters 14 to 16. And among the many things Jesus had said to them was this: "I am going to the Father, but I will ask the Father, and He will give you another Comforter, another of the same kind. He is just as I am, but there is a difference. Right now I am a Comforter *with* you, but He is going to be a Comforter *in* you. The Holy Spirit will come and dwell in you, and He will never leave you nor forsake you. He will be in you to teach you all things. He will glorify Me and reveal to you all that is of Mine" (see 14:12c, 16-17a, 18, 26; 16:7, 13-15). In other words, the Lord was showing them that from then on their life with Him was to be on an entirely different level. It was no longer on the level of the physical, being alongside, but it was on the level of the spiritual; His life was to be in them. They were to live no longer a life in the flesh but in the spirit. They were no longer to seek things according to the flesh, but they were to let the indwelling Holy Spirit teach them and show them Christ; they were to learn Christ inwardly. It was to be a spiritual life.

A Christian life is an inner life and not an outward walk alone. It is an inner life that lives from within by the indwelling Holy Spirit. We live the Christian life by learning to obey the teaching of the Holy Spirit and not by people telling us what to do according to various rules and regulations. Our problem with Christianity today is that we try to live our Christian life outwardly. We are given rules and regulations, and if we keep them, then we are good Christians. What is that kind of life but a living under law and not under grace. But in the appearing of the Lord Jesus on that resurrection night the risen Lord was showing His disciples how He lived in the spirit, and He wanted them to live in the spirit as well by the indwelling Spirit; that is spiritual life.

Even today, when we seek the Lord we too often try to seek Him outwardly. It is just like the disciples who wanted to continue to touch and handle Him and have Him continually with them physically. Why is it that the Catholic Church has images? Although the Catholics say they are not worshiping these images, that these images simply help to arouse within them a devotion to God, what in reality this means is that they need those outward things in order to touch God. That is not the way the resurrected Lord intended for His followers to live their Christian life.

Today in Christianity there is a teaching called visualization which teaches that you must try to visualize Christ: Christ comes and touches you; He embraces you, and by doing so, you are brought near to God. That is not the authentic Christian way of living, for it is not the way which the Lord

Jesus is leading His followers; rather, He is leading them to walk inwardly and not outwardly. It is not trying to visualize; it is not by touch, by taste, by feeling, nor even by smell. Some people today say that they smell Christ. But the Christian life is not to be lived out by these outward means but it is by the indwelling Holy Spirit that you touch Christ. Inwardly, you know Christ is there by His Spirit teaching you, guiding you, leading you. Jesus has never left you; He has never forsaken you; He is ever present with you. Such is the new way of life for the Christian to experience, in that a new relationship is formed: for He said to Mary of Magdala on that resurrection morning, "I go to My Father and your Father, to My God and your God. Go tell this to My brethren" (see John 20:17b). It is indeed a new relationship that is formed inwardly in the saints of God.

When Jesus was in the flesh, He tried to share with His disciples and with the Jews that the Father was in Him and He was in the Father, but they could not believe it (John 10:30, 38; 14:10a). For how could the Father be in Him and He in the Father? It is impossible, they reasoned, for me to be in you and for you to be in me. Yes, we can stand side by side, but how can one be in the other? Impossible! The Jews could not believe it, and even the disciples could not believe it. Yet Jesus tried to tell them again and again: "If you cannot understand it, then at least you can believe the works which I have done, and by those works you will know that the Father is in Me" (see John 10:38, 14:11). But still they could not believe it because this is naturally beyond us to comprehend and believe. That inner relationship of which Jesus spoke is beyond man's human concept. Nevertheless, it is true: the Father is in Christ, and Christ is in the Father, and thus the Father and the Son are one (John 10:30). There is an inward unbroken relationship, but the world cannot understand and even the disciples could not understand; but Jesus held out hope for them, saying: "In that day, you shall know that I am in the Father, you are in Me, and I in you" (see John 14:20).

What did Jesus mean by "that day"? That day was the day of His resurrection. After He was resurrected, they knew that Jesus is in the Father, we are in Him, and He is in us. Yet how do we come to know this? It is through the Holy Spirit dwelling in us. So we learn that our relationship with the risen Lord is an inward one: He is the vine; we are the branches (John 15:5a). There is a oneness there which cannot be broken, and because of this, we need to abide in Him and He in us, and we will bear much fruit (John 15:5b).

So our relationship with the Lord is an inward and not an outward one. Any outward relationship can be broken, but an inward one cannot. We are in Him, and He is in us.

How do we know Christ? It is to be no longer according to the flesh but according to our inner spirit. In this connection, let us recall the words of the apostle Paul, who declared in II Corinthians 5 that "we no longer know Christ in the flesh. If ever we did know Him in the flesh, we are no longer to know Him in that way but we are to know Him now in the spirit" (see v. 16).

If you want to know the Lord Jesus, you have to know Him in the spirit. Or to put it another way, we are to know Him through the revealing of Him by the Holy Spirit to our spirit. Such is the only way to true spiritual knowledge. Apart from that means our knowledge is not truly spiritual. Even our mental knowledge of the word of God is but letter that kills; such knowledge has not been quickened or made living by the spirit in us (II Corinthians 3:6). Now, of course, we need to know the letter of God's word; for if we do not know that, how can we judge the spirit? But knowing the letter of God's word alone is not true knowledge; we cannot by that means really know the Lord. It is only by the Holy Spirit revealing His word to our spirit that we have the true knowledge of Christ.

Our knowing one another as brethren in Christ is no longer to be according to the flesh. In the past, we knew each other in the flesh by the outward appearance and by outward contact; but now we no longer know each other by that means. We henceforth are to know each other in the spirit, that is, in Christ. We see *Christ* in each other, not Adam or Eve. Our relationship is now on a spiritual basis, and that is the reason there is no distinction of race, social status, educational background, or whatever other distinction there may be. We are all one in Christ Jesus because this is a new way of life, and this new way of life was demonstrated by the resurrected Jesus through His appearings to His first disciples and His leading them into that new way of life. This is what His various appearings during those forty significant days did for them and what they can do for us today.

His Appearings Reveal the Spiritual Kingdom

There is a third reason why the risen Lord's appearings are important for us today. And for us to understand this third reason for their significance in relation to us today, we need to know what Jesus actually taught during those forty days of His appearings. We are told in Acts chapter 1 that after Jesus' sufferings He was seen by His disciples, gave many convincing proofs to them that He was alive, and taught them about the kingdom of God; but they still did not understand Him when it came to this matter of the kingdom. We may recall that prior to

Jesus going to the cross, neither the Roman authorities, nor the Jewish, nor even His disciples understood His teaching concerning the kingdom of God. The Roman governor over Israel, Pontius Pilate, asked Jesus: "Are you the king of the Jews?" To which He replied: "My kingdom is not of this world. I was born to be a king. In fact, I came into this world for this very reason that I may bear witness to the truth." Without waiting for an answer to his question to Jesus as to what the truth is, Pilate went away from Him (John 18:33-38b).

The Jews at that time likewise did not understand Him. Whenever He talked about the kingdom their various responses would be: "Where is the kingdom?" or "When is the time that You will end the Roman yoke over us?" "When will you deliver us and revive the nation of Israel?" They could not understand what He taught concerning the kingdom.

Even His disciples could not understand Jesus on this subject. He preached to them; He talked to them; and He taught them regarding the kingdom of God. Said Jesus on one occasion: "Blessed are the poor in spirit, for theirs is the kingdom of the heavens" (Matthew 5:3). His disciples heard and yet they did not hear. Even at the very last, they were still striving against each other as to who might sit on His right hand and on His left. They thought He was going to Jerusalem to be crowned (Matthew 20:17-24). They did not understand because their concept of the kingdom was earthly and materialistic in character and they could not rise above that.

After Jesus was resurrected He continued to preach and to teach His disciples on the kingdom of God. Was it a new teaching? No, it was the same old teaching but now accompanied by a new atmosphere, a new environment. Jesus was no longer teaching them in the flesh but in the spirit. When previously He had taught them in the flesh concerning the kingdom of God, whose nature is heavenly, they could not understand it; but now the risen Lord was teaching them in the spirit. By means of His appearings the resurrected Jesus revealed to them what the kingdom of God truly is. As the apostle Paul made clear in one of his writings, the kingdom of God is not eating and drinking; it is righteousness, peace and joy in the Holy Spirit (Romans 14:17). What, then, is the kingdom of God? It is where God reigns and rules. He reigns and rules in our hearts. The kingdom of God is not to be seen by fleshly eyes; it is spiritual. Where Christ reigns in our hearts, there is the kingdom of God. Now, therefore, living and walking within a totally new environment, hopefully, the disciples understood their Master's old teaching on the kingdom somewhat better.

The apostles took up this theme of the kingdom of God in their preaching. On the day of Pentecost Peter stood up with the Eleven, and having preached a powerful, spirit-filled message, his conclusion was this: "Let the house of Israel know that this Jesus whom you crucified, God has made both Lord and Christ"—meaning that He is Lord of all and He is the King (see Acts 2:36). Those who repented were baptized in the name of the Lord Jesus (vv. 38, 41a). In other words, they submitted themselves under His authority to let Him be Lord over their lives. Now that essentially is the kingdom of God.

Now this which the apostle Peter preached on Pentecost Day is recorded at the beginning of the book of Acts. And when we come to the very end of that same book, we find the apostle Paul many years later is in his rented apartment in Rome, bound in chains but nonetheless for two whole years "welcoming all who came to him" to hear what he had to say, which was the same theme as Peter had spoken at the beginning—for Paul was "preaching the kingdom of God, and teaching the things concerning the Lord Jesus Christ" (28:30-31). Indeed, the preaching of these two apostles was precisely in line with what Jesus had himself declared to His disciples as He sat talking with them on the Mount of Olives shortly before He was arrested and crucified: "This gospel of the kingdom shall be preached in all the world for a witness to all the nations, and then shall the end come" (see Matthew 24:14).

Are we today preaching what Jesus preached both before and after His resurrection? Are we preaching what the apostles preached as told of in the book of Acts? Today we over-emphasize the gospel of grace and under-emphasize the gospel of kingdom truth. We tell people that Jesus is our Savior who died for our sins and who has saved us, but we do not tell them that Jesus is Lord—that He is our Master, Sovereign, and Majesty; and that we all need to surrender our lives to Him. This is the reason Christianity is so weak. This is why our Christian life is so weak. This is why the church of Christ is so weak, because His church can only be built on the basis of the gospel of the kingdom of truth (cf. John 19:36-37). We need to preach the gospel of the kingdom of God. We need to tell people that Jesus is not only Savior, He is also Lord. We need to prepare for His coming kingdom.

We are not talking here about dominion theology or reconstruction theology, which is being taught by various theologians today. They tell us that Christians are to convert the world and bring the world to the feet of Christ. We have not been sent to convert the world; we have been sent out into the world to overcome it. Let us be clear that the world will never be converted; on the contrary, it will only get worse. But if we preach to the world the kingdom of God, the result will be that out of every nation, every people, every tribe, and every tongue, God will call forth a people to himself (Revelation 5:9b), so that under His name and under His authority He may reign and rule as supreme in their lives. And when this is accomplished, then Jesus will return to the earth to judge the world and bring this unconverted world under His feet. It is therefore important for us to understand that we need to preach not only the Saviorhood of God but the kingdom rule of God as well.

The Great Commission

Let us not overlook the fact that it was during this forty-day period of Jesus' appearings, and before He ascended to heaven, that He issued to the church the Great Commission. It is most fitting that in the Scriptures this Commission is recorded at the end of the Gospel of *Matthew*, since this Gospel's emphasis is the presentation of Jesus as *the King*. So what is the resurrected Jesus' Great Commission? Essentially, it is for His disciples—His church, if you will—to bring to the feet of Jesus as their Lord and King as many people in the world who shall believe in Him as Savior. For the risen Lord instructed His disciples as follows, prefacing His instructions by first declaring that all power and authority in heaven and on earth has been given to Him: "Therefore, I command you to go to the world and make disciples of all nations, baptizing them in the name of the Father, Son, and Holy Spirit, teaching them to do all things I have commanded you yourselves, and surely I shall be with you always, even to the very end of the age" (see 28:18-20).

Hence, we see here that the Great Commission given to the church involves more than that of just evangelizing. It is quite true that from Luke 24 we learn that the resurrected Jesus commanded the disciples to go and preach forgiveness, repentance, and remission of sins, but the gospel—even the gospel of the kingdom—is more than that; it is to disciple all the believing peoples of the nations. Let us be clear here that discipling people simply means to bring them to Christ—yet, not only *to* Him as Savior by faith, but to be *under* Him as Lord. For instance, after one believes in the Lord Jesus, why must that one be baptized as the Great Commission calls for? Why, in other words, is believing not enough but one must also be baptized? (Mark 16:16) It is because when a believer is baptized, that one is being baptized into the name of Another. In other words, we give up ourselves to Christ. We allow Him to be our head; we now belong to Him; you and I take Him as our Lord; you and I submit ourselves to Christ; we become His disciples; we allow Him to teach us, to transform us, to mold us, to fashion us according to His image. You and I are being taught all things that He had commanded His first disciples. Now *that* is true discipleship.

Discipleship is therefore not being discipled to any man but a being discipled to Christ, to learn of Him so that you may be like Him. As He is, so shall you be (I John 3:2b). This is the church's Great Commission. Have we as living members of Christ's church fulfilled that Commission? Are we being faithful to what the risen Lord has committed to us?

All these things happened during those forty days of Jesus' appearings. You may never have a personal appearing of the Lord in your life, but at least what you find recorded in the Scriptures of these various appearings of His are yours for your spiritual benefit. In other words, all that He did and said during this forty-day period of appearings is for you. It is for you to see Him as the living One who is ever present and almighty. It is for you to see that you serve a living Christ, for you to see that you live because He lives. It is for you to understand that He has given you an inward life, a spiritual life, by which to live, and that you are to live out that life in an inward way. It is for you to understand that your relationship with the resurrected Jesus is not physical but is spiritual, and that your relationship with your Christian brothers and sisters is likewise spiritual and not physical. It is for you to see that you are to live by faith and not by sight, that you are to live in the spirit and not in the flesh. This is the way of life that by His post-resurrection appearings Jesus has demonstrated to us and has led us into, and this is the way we should live.

We also need to know and experience more of the kingdom of God—how it is a spiritual, heavenly kingdom; how, though it is hidden today among God's people, there will come a day when it will publicly appear on this earth. But before that time it is our responsibility to bring people to and under the authority of Christ and to teach all nations, and then the end will come.

These are the things that we need to receive, to stand on, and by which we shall experience the full salvation of God.

Chapter Seventeen

His Ascension

Acts 1:6-9—They therefore, being come together, asked him [Jesus] saying, Lord, is it at this time that thou restorest the kingdom to Israel? And he said to them, It is not yours to know times or seasons, which the Father has placed in his own authority; but ye will receive power, the Holy Spirit having come upon you, and ye shall be my witnesses both in Jerusalem, and in all Judaea and Samaria, and to the end of the earth. And having said these things he was taken up, they beholding him, and a cloud received him out of their sight.

Revelation 5:6-14—And I saw in the midst of the throne and of the four living creatures, and in the midst of the elders, a Lamb standing, as slain, having seven horns and seven eyes, which are the seven Spirits of God which are sent into all the earth: and it came and took it out of the right hand of him that sat upon the throne. And when it took the book, the four living creatures and the twenty-four elders fell before the Lamb, having each a harp and golden bowls full of incenses, which are the prayers of the saints. And they sing a new song, saying, Thou art worthy to take the book, and to open its seals; because thou hast been slain, and hast redeemed to God, by thy blood, out of every tribe, and tongue, and people, and nation, and made them to our God kings and priests; and they shall reign over the earth.

And I saw, and I heard the voice of many angels around the throne and the living creatures and the elders; and their number was ten thousands of ten thousands and thousands of thousands; saying with a loud voice, Worthy is the Lamb that has been slain, to receive power, and riches, and wisdom, and strength, and honour, and glory, and blessing. And every creature which is in the heaven and upon the earth and under the earth, and those that are upon the sea, and all things in them, heard I saying, To him that sits upon the throne, and to the Lamb, blessing, and honour, and glory, and might, to the ages of ages. And the four living creatures said, Amen; and the elders fell down and did homage.

The days of Jesus in the flesh on earth were days of humiliation. He emptied himself and took up the form of a slave. Being in the fashion of a man, He humbled himself and was obedient to the Father even to the death on a cross. So Jesus' life on earth was one of humility. He refused the glory which Satan offered Him at the time of His wilderness temptation. He refused to be crowned king by those thousands of people who had been miraculously fed by Him. He lived a life of humiliation, for He was rejected and was crucified. The cross is a sign of the Son of man; it is a sign of humiliation; nevertheless, for Jesus the cross was the beginning of His glorification. It was the hour for which He had come.

After Jesus was crucified He lay buried for three days, but on the third day He was raised from the dead. Let us understand that resurrection is glory. Whereas death is always shameful, resurrection is always glorious. So, in resurrection Jesus took upon himself a glorious spiritual body, and in that body He appeared to His disciples for forty days. During those forty days He taught them further about the kingdom of God. Jesus was teaching them under a new atmosphere and environment, and I believe that it made it much easier for His disciples to understand the real nature of the kingdom of God, which is spiritual and heavenly. The resurrected Jesus established a new relationship with His own, it no longer being only an external one but an inward relationship—He in us and we in Him. Jesus also gave His disciples a new commandment: "Go into the world and disciple all nations, baptizing them in the name of the Father, the Son, and the Holy Spirit, teaching them to observe all the things which you have been taught, and I promise to be with you to the completion of the ages" (see Matthew 28:18-20).

At the end of the forty days Jesus led His disciples to the Mount of Olives and there He ascended up to heaven (Luke 24:50-51 with Acts 1:9, 12a). It was but right for Him to do that; for He who descended ought to ascend, He who came from heaven ought to return to heaven, He who came from the bosom of the Father ought surely to return to His Father's bosom (see Ephesians 4:10; John 3:13, 1:18). During that last conversation with His disciples in the upper room Jesus had told them: "If ye loved me ye would rejoice that I go to the Father" (John 14:28b). He also said to them: "I came out from the Father and have come into the world; again, I leave the world and go to the Father" (John 16:28). It was therefore but right for Him, who had humbled himself and had accomplished all the work the Father had commanded Him to do, to return to heaven.

In all four Gospels the fact of Jesus' ascension is there, but only two of them give us the scene of His ascension. There are reasons why the other two Gospels do not include this scene. Matthew tells us that He gathered His disciples, gave them a commandment, and then said, "I am with you all the days, until the completion of the age" (Matthew 28:20b). As King, He never leaves us. He is with us as we go forward to disciple all nations. In the Gospel of John there is no ascension scene because, as the Son of God, Jesus is eternal. Time and space do not affect Him.

Only two Gospels actually record Jesus' ascension. In Mark 16 we learn that after He talked with the Eleven He was taken up to heaven and sat down at the right hand of God (vv. 14a, 19). And Luke 24 tells us that as He was blessing His disciples He was separated from them and was carried up into heaven (v. 51).

We then learn from the first chapter of Acts that as the disciples were looking at Jesus He was lifted up and then a cloud carried Him out of their sight (v. 9). They saw that He was ascending, and then, suddenly, a cloud took Him away so that they could not see Him anymore.

How do we know that the resurrected Jesus *reached* heaven? You may recall the story about Elijah and how he was taken up to heaven; yet the sons of the prophets did not believe it. They told Elisha to let them go out and search the mountains and the valleys round about, because the Spirit of the Lord, they said, might have perhaps taken him and set him down somewhere there. They had not believed that he was taken up to heaven (II Kings 2:11-18). So, I think it is but right for us to ask the question I posed a moment ago. The Eleven had seen Jesus going up; and then a cloud took Him, but to where? Did He arrive in heaven? How do we know? Is there any proof? Thank God, there is.

The Proof of His Ascension

The Coming of the Holy Spirit

Ten days later, on the day of Pentecost, 120 of Jesus' disciples were gathered together in that Jerusalem home's upper room and, suddenly, there was a hard breathing. The Holy Spirit came, and they were baptized into one body (Acts 2:1-4). When this news went out and people began to gather outside around the home, Peter stood up and told them what had happened: "Having been exalted to the right hand of God, Jesus of Nazareth has received from the Father the promised Holy Spirit; for the Spirit has come down and poured out what you now see and hear" (see Acts 2:33). Then he said: "Therefore, let the whole house of Israel know that this Jesus whom you crucified, God has made both Lord and Christ" (see Acts 2:36). The coming down of the Holy Spirit was the proof that the ascending Jesus had arrived in heaven because, after He arrived, He received the promise of the Father and the Holy Spirit came down.

The Concluding Scene of Christ's Ascension As Described in Revelation

We read in Revelation 4 and 5 that the apostle John was taken up to heaven in the Spirit, and there he saw the concluding scene of the ascension of the Lord Jesus. Revelation 5 is a detailed description of that scene. He saw a Lamb; and from the original Greek it actually would be translated as reading: "a Lamb newly slain but standing." How can a lamb which has been newly slain be standing? The only explanation is resurrection. The Lamb, even the resurrected Jesus, was standing before the throne of God, surrounded by the four living creatures and the twenty-four elders, and He came forward and took into His hands from the right hand of Him who sat on the throne the book written inside and on the back and sealed with seven seals because He is worthy to open and unseal it, thus causing the whole heaven to burst forth instantly with the praises of thousands and thousands of angels, followed by the whole creation bursting into praise and worship. Such is the concluding scene of Jesus' ascension into heaven. Thank God, the Lord Jesus not only was raised from the dead but He also ascended into heaven and arrived at God the Father's throne.

The Meaning of Ascension for Jesus Himself

He Returned to His Glory with the Father

What did ascension mean for the resurrected Jesus? First, Jesus returned to the glory that He had had with the Father from eternity. In His so-called Great Intercessory Prayer recorded in John 17, Jesus had prayed to the Father this request: "And now glorify me, thou Father, along with thyself, with the glory which I had along with thee before the world was" (v. 5).

That is a reference to the glory of deity. The Lord Jesus is the eternal Son of God. He and His eternal Father and the eternal Spirit share the glory of deity. Even before the world existed—before there was time, before there was matter—Jesus shared with His eternal Father the glory of God. He is therefore worthy to be worshiped and to be honored. He is omnipotent, omnipresent, omniscient—He is very God of very God. Yet one day the Son of God emptied himself of that glory. He could not empty himself of His deity because He, being God, cannot deny himself (II Timothy 2:13b). Even when He came down upon this earth, He was still God. That is what Jesus is. He could not empty himself of that, but He did empty himself of the glory that belongs to the Trinitarian Godhead.

So Jesus came to this earth, becoming a humble man: and as a man He was not omnipresent, for when He was in Jerusalem He could not be in Galilee; He was not omniscient, for He once said to His followers concerning His return: "Nobody knows the day, not even the Son of man; only the Father knows" (see Matthew 24:36, Mark 13:32); He was not omnipotent, for He said He could do nothing by himself (John 5:19). He emptied himself of the worship of the angels; He emptied himself of the worship of creation. He temporarily lay all that glory aside during the days of His flesh. But after Jesus' work in fulfilling the Father's will was done, He returned to His Father and to the glory that He had constantly shared with His Father from eternity: even the glory of the Godhead. And once again He is omnipotent, omnipresent, omniscient, and worthy to receive all the praises and the worship of the angelic forces and of all the creation. So, in Jesus' ascension He returned to the glory that He had had with His Father from eternity as the Son of God.

He Entered into Glory as the Son of Man

Second, Jesus' ascension enabled Him to enter into the glory which the Father has given Him as the Son of man. There is a glory which from Creation God had ordained for man. When God created man, He did so in His own image; and thus, from the beginning of mankind there was a glory connected with that creation: man was to fulfill God's purpose, to subdue all things, to bring all things back to the feet of God, to receive dominion, to rule and reign for God (Genesis 1:26-28). But in the Fall, man forfeited his right; he lost his glory. But there came forth the second Man, Jesus, who came into this world as a perfect man; and as a man He walked humbly before God, being obedient to Him in all things and pleasing Him throughout His entire earthly life. Never once, for a single moment, did Jesus rebel against His Father but submitted himself to Him with complete humility. Moreover, Jesus as the second Man walked on this earth full of grace and truth (John 1:14b, 17b), and obeyed His Father even to a death on a cross in order to accomplish the work of redemption. So as a man, He was glorified by the Father. Hence, Jesus' ascension meant for Him that He could enter into the glory which the Father has bestowed upon Him as the perfect Son of man. And this again is reflected in the Lord's prayer of John 17, wherein Jesus prayed: "Father, as to those whom thou hast given me, I desire that where I am they also may be with me, that they may behold my glory which thou hast given me, for thou lovedst me before the foundation of the world" (v. 24).

Let us see that, on the one hand, there is a glory which belongs to Jesus, as it were, as His birthright: it is not bestowed or given but is a glory which belongs to Him as the Son of God. On the other hand, there is another glory that is indeed bestowed upon Jesus as the Son of man because He fulfilled all which God had originally ordained for man. In other words, Jesus *earned* this second glory. So when Jesus ascended back to heaven, He entered into a double glory. One can therefore say that when Jesus came forth from heaven, He left behind Him one glory but that when He returned to heaven via His ascension, He entered into two glories: as both Son of God and Son of man. And hence, most assuredly He is worthy to be worshiped and adored.

He Received His Inheritance

Third, Jesus' ascension meant for Him that He would receive His inheritance: "Ask of me, and I will give thee nations for an inheritance, and for thy possession the ends of the earth" (Psalm 2:8). In accordance with this prophetic verse, it signified that at His ascension the Lord Jesus asked of the One who sits upon the throne, and there and then He was given that book mentioned in Revelation 5 which is the title deed to the entire universe. In other words, when God created the universe, He created it for His Son who was made heir of all things (Hebrews 1:2). God loves His Son and created all things to give to His Son as His inheritance.

Unfortunately, because of the fall of the first man, that inheritance was challenged by Satan who usurped the earth and hence became the god and prince of this world (II Corinthians 4:4a; John 14:30b, 16:11, 12:31) because he had deceived man and thus robbed him of that inheritance. But Jesus, as the second Man, came to the fight, and through His work of redemption He recovered all things, having reconciled all things to God by the blood of His cross (Colossians 1:19-20); and so, He received from God the title deed to the whole universe.

Satan only usurped the earth; he did not have the title deed. The title deed is forever in the hands of God. God possesses the universe because it belongs to Him by virtue of Creation. But now His Son, because of His victory at Calvary, is worthy to take that book and open its seals. He was found worthy to execute the Father's will and to bring all things back to God that the Son may inherit all things. It is not only a legal right of His, it is His moral right: the ascended Jesus is morally worthy to inherit all things. We see, therefore, that Psalm 2:8 is fulfilled in Revelation 5.

Proof That His Work of Redemption Is Finished

Fourth, Jesus' ascension meant for Him that it proved that His work of redemption was accomplished. On Calvary's cross Jesus had said, "It is finished" (John 19:30). How do we know His redemptive work was finished? How do we know that what Jesus uttered on the cross is true? We know it to be true because He ascended to heaven and was made to sit at the right hand of God, even as the psalmist of old had prophesied: "Jehovah said unto my Lord, Sit at my right hand, until I put thine enemies as footstool of thy feet" (Psalm 110:1). That the ascended Jesus did indeed sit down at God the Father's right hand is made clear in the apostle Paul's writings, for in his Ephesians letter he tells his readers that the Father of glory raised Jesus from the dead and seated Him at His right hand in the heavenlies (1:20).

Now it is obvious that when a person is working, he stands and walks about; but after the work is done the person sits down. So in Psalm 110 we are told that Jehovah God said to the Lord, "Sit at my right hand, until I put thine enemies as footstool of thy feet." Even today, therefore, the Lord Jesus is still seated at the right hand of the Father, His work of redemption having been finished. The Jewish priests of old who served in the temple stood while serving, but after their temple service was done, they could sit down. So Jesus' ascension back to the Father is proof that His work of redemption has been fully accepted by the Father, and thus His work is indeed finished.

He Was Anointed As King and High Priest

Fifth, Jesus' ascension meant for Him that He would be anointed by God as both King of kings and Great High Priest. First as to His Kingship, we read in that same prophetic Psalm

2 this declaration by God: "I have anointed my king upon Zion, the hill of my holiness" (v. 6). Mount Zion in Scripture always speaks of royalty or kingship. So this prophetic verse, too, refers to the ascension of Jesus. When He ascended to heaven, God declared that He had now anointed His king upon Jerusalem's Mount Zion, the hill of His holiness.

As was already mentioned earlier, Peter had declared in his Pentecost sermon that God had made Jesus of Nazareth both Lord and Christ. So the ascended Jesus is now King and has thus been given all power in heaven and on earth and that He is to rule and reign forever (Ephesians 1:21-22). He is the King of kings and Lord of lords, and because of that fact, it is the psalmist's admonition expressed in his same writing that the kings of the earth should kiss the Son (Psalm 2:10-12).

But second, as to Jesus' Priesthood, His ascension meant for Him that not only would He be anointed as the King of all but He would also be anointed as the Great High Priest. That same prophetic Psalm 110 cited earlier has this to say as well: "[God] hath sworn, and will not repent, Thou art priest for ever after the order of Melchisedek" (v. 4).

In Jesus' ascension He was likewise anointed as the Great High Priest who ever lives to make intercession for God's people and to save to the uttermost extent those who approach God through Him (Hebrews 7:24-25). When Jesus was on earth, He was the Apostle (the Sent One) of our confession (Hebrews 3:1b). God the Father sent Him on a mission, and he fulfilled that mission. And hence, now, having ascended to heaven, God has anointed Him as the Great High Priest. The picture of this has been beautifully described for us in David's Psalm 133: "Like the precious oil upon the head, that ran down upon the beard, upon Aaron's beard, that ran down to the hem of his garments; as the dew of Hermon that descendeth on the mountains of Zion; for there hath Jehovah commanded the blessing, life for evermore" (vv. 2-3).

When the resurrected Jesus ascended on high, the Father anointed Him by pouring the oil of the Spirit upon His head. Aaron's head is cited here because Aaron is an Old Testament type of Christ. When Aaron of old was set apart as the high priest of God's people, he was anointed profusely with oil, so much so that the oil flowed down upon his beard, then went down over his garment, until it finally reached the very hem of his garment. We have here, then, in parabolic fashion, the following picture: the Lord Jesus ascended on high, and God poured out the Spirit upon Him profusely. The Spirit flowed down upon the beard. I often imagine the beard here represents those first 120 followers of Jesus gathered together in the upper room on Pentecost day. Then the oil of the Spirit flows down over all the garment covering the whole body, and down to the hem of the garment. In other words, everyone who belongs to the body of Christ is anointed with the oil of God's Spirit. We are all therefore made priests unto God (Revelation 5:10a, I Peter 2:5). Every believer is a priest, for we are born again to serve as priests under our Great High Priest, the Lord Jesus (I Peter 2:9).

The second parabolic depiction of this anointing of the ascended Jesus as Great High Priest is further pictured in Psalm 133 as being like the dew of Hermon that descends on Jerusalem's mount or hill of Zion. In Scripture, Zion, as was explained a few moments earlier, always speaks of royalty and kingship. So when Jesus ascended to heaven and was anointed as King upon Mount Zion, that dew, which symbolizes life, descended upon Mount Zion and filled it with the freshness of life. When He was anointed King, we also were made kings unto God (see again Revelation 5:10a). He is the King of kings and we are made kings—kings to rule the earth for God (Revelation 5:10b), to rule in life, even abundant life.

Hence, in delving deeper into this matter of Jesus' ascension, we come to realize that it held out immense significance for Him. Indeed, all the aforementioned facets to the risen Lord's ascension were but the natural consequences to Jesus' entire life on earth.

The Meaning of Jesus' Ascension for Us

Made Possible the Holy Spirit's Descent

What does Jesus' ascension mean for us? First, His ascension made possible the descent of the Holy Spirit. Said Jesus to His disciples: "I am going back to the Father, and I will ask Him and He will give you His promise to Me of the Holy Spirit. If I do not go away, another Comforter will not come; but if I do go to My Father, then I will send Him—even the Spirit of truth—to you. He will not only be with you just as I have been; but He will also be in you, which I cannot be when I am in the flesh" (see John 14:12c, 16-17, 26a; 16:7). So after Jesus ascended to heaven He sent the Holy Spirit upon the earth. In the Holy Spirit we who are the Lord's people have all been baptized into one body (I Corinthians 12:13a). When Jesus was on earth, He taught and did many things in that body of flesh which He had taken upon himself from Mary's womb; but now He has ascended on high as the Head over all things to the church (Ephesians 1:22b).

So, by the coming of the Holy Spirit and the baptism with the Holy Spirit, the resurrected and ascended Lord Jesus took upon himself a mystical, spiritual body—that which Scripture calls the body of Christ—which is the fullness of Him who fills all and in all (Ephesians 1:23). His ascension means so much for us because with His ascension we are baptized in the Spirit into one body (see again I Corinthians 12:13a). We are Christ's body. And in and through this body the Holy Spirit continues to teach and to do—not only as was recorded in the book of Acts but even today. How glorious it is! If Jesus had not ascended, the Holy Spirit would not have come, and if the Holy Spirit had not come, we would not have become one body. But thank God, we *are* one body, the body of Christ. What a privilege! How glorious it is! Our Head, Christ Jesus, continues by God's Spirit to speak in us and through us and to act in us and through us. Yet what a responsibility we have!

Made Jesus Our High Priest

Second, Jesus' ascension means for us that it made Jesus a great high priest for us in the heavens (Hebrews 4:14a). Because He was the Apostle (or Sent One) of God, we have a confession (Hebrews 3:1b). We have a faith to believe in and profess (4:14b), a salvation to trust in; but because He is now our Great High Priest, we are able to live a Christian life. The entire New Testament book of Hebrews gives us but one message: The Lord Jesus is now our Great High Priest. Without Him we cannot live a Christian life. We are saved because He went to the cross, but after we are saved how can we live a life day by day that is like Christ's? How can we continue and persevere? How can we grow? How can we be transformed and become conformed to the image of Christ (Romans 8:29a) if the ascended Jesus did not become our Great High Priest? Let us not forget that the children of Israel had depended upon the priesthood for their life before God. Without the priesthood, how could they have communed with God? How could they have lived a godly life? But today it is because the ascended Jesus is our Great High Priest that we can live.

Hebrews 7:25 informs us that Jesus ever lives, making intercession for us and is thus able to save to the uttermost—that is, to the very end—those who come to God by Him. The Lord Jesus is living forever (v. 24a), and there at the right hand of God He represents us before God and is interceding unceasingly for us. He knows each and every one of us and sympathizes with us (4:15a). He knows what is going on with each one of us. He loves us and is determined to bring us into conformity to His image. Such is the present ministry of the ascended Jesus in heaven. His ministry on earth as the Apostle is finished and He is now seated at God the Father's right hand; even so, He is not there for leisure; rather, He is there working as our Great High Priest, never ceasing to pray but interceding for us and supporting us before God the Father.

And while the ascended Jesus is doing that, something is happening on earth in you and in me because in tandem with the intercessory ministry of the ascended Jesus the Holy Spirit is working in you and me. We may sometimes think the high priesthood of the Lord Jesus is too vague, too abstract. We may therefore wonder, Are we in the good of His high priesthood today? Perhaps we are, we say to ourselves, but how does that come about? For He is in heaven and we are on earth. Yes, the ascended Jesus is praying for us, but how do we know His prayer is being answered? Yes, He is concerned for us, but how do we know His concern is effective in our daily life? We need to understand and recognize that the Holy Spirit is representing the risen and ascended Jesus in you and in me. As He prays before the Father, the Holy Spirit is at work in us to teach us, to guide, comfort and encourage us, to remind us, warn us, restrain us, constrain us, convict us, and reveal to us (John 14:26, 15:26, 16:8, 12-15).

We often do not know what we truly are, nor do we know what is going to happen in our lives, but Jesus is praying for us in regard to such matters. For instance, Peter thought he loved the Lord; he was confident in himself that if necessary he would be willing to die for his Master. He even boasted that the other disciples may flee, but he would even go to death with the Lord. He was so sure of himself; he was sincerely of such a mindset. Yet, he did not know what was going to happen; Jesus, however, knew that there was a serious flaw in his life. And because of that flaw, God allowed Satan to test Jesus' cocksure disciple, to sift him that he might be purified. Jesus knew that Peter would deny Him three times, so He said to him, "I have prayed for you that your faith may not fail" (see Luke 22:31-32a).

Humanly speaking, his faith would fail. Such faith is certain to fail; for how can a person deny their Master and Lord three times and be at all able to maintain one's faith? So Jesus said to His disciple: "I have prayed for you, and when you are restored, strengthen your brethren" (see v.32b). Peter did not appreciate Jesus' prayer for him. Perhaps he said to himself in his self-confidence, "Pray for the others, but not for me. I do not need such support." Jesus knew His disciple's flaw, however, and it was through His intercession that Peter's faith did not fall completely away. Instead, he turned back and his faith was recovered. This is but one example of our need for the Lord's intercessory prayer support as our Great High Priest.

Day by day your Great High Priest knows you most thoroughly and knows times beyond numbering what is going to happen to you throughout your life. For has He not numbered even the hairs on your head? (Matthew 10:30) Indeed, how much He cares for you! He knows every detail of your life, and He is praying and interceding for you constantly. In fact, you are still here today, not because you are strong or are steady; you are still here today because heaven's Great High Priest has prayed for you. It is the intercessory work of the ascended Jesus which enables us to continue in perseverance even to this day. On the one hand, there are many things which happen to us of which we are not in the least aware; on the other hand, many things happen to us of which we *are* aware; but regardless the circumstances, we know it is He who will get us through or else we cannot get through.

That is the present ministry of our ascended Great High Priest. How we need to come to Him and look to Him daily that He may save us to the furthest extent. The Holy Spirit represents our Great High Priest in you and me to deliver us, encourage us, and to bring us into conformity to the image of God's Son (Romans 8:29a). And this is in part what Jesus' ascension means for us today.

Made Us a Heavenly People

Not only that, but third, Jesus' ascension means for us that His ascension made us a heavenly people. This we learn from what the apostle Paul writes in Ephesians 2: "God, being rich in mercy, because of his great love wherewith he loved us, (we too being dead in offences,) has quickened us [made us alive] with the Christ, (ye are saved by grace,) and has raised us up together, and has made us sit down together in the heavenlies in Christ Jesus, that he might display in the coming ages the surpassing riches of his grace in kindness towards us in Christ Jesus" (vv. 4-7).

God has not only made us spiritually alive, He has also raised us up together with the resurrected Jesus, and has even seated us together with the ascended Jesus in the heavenly realm. In other words, Jesus' death is our death; His resurrection is our resurrection; and even His ascension is our ascension. Have we been made spiritually alive in Christ Jesus? Thank God, we have. Have we been raised with Jesus from the dead? Thank God, we have. Have we been seated with the ascended Jesus in the heavenlies? Have we, indeed? Physically, we are on earth but, spiritually, we are in the heavenlies. We are seated with Him in the heavenly realm. There is a realm called the heavenlies, and we are seated with the ascended Jesus there. Hence, what Jesus' ascension means for us is that it made us a heavenly people: and thus, we are no longer an earthly people, for our citizenship is now in heaven (Philippians 3:20a ASV) and our life is hid with Christ in God (Colossians 3:3).

Therefore, nothing can touch us: there is nothing in heaven or on earth now and forever which can separate us from the love of God that is in Christ Jesus (Romans 8:38-39). We are now seated with the ascended Jesus in the heavenlies. If that be true, and it certainly is, then we need to ask ourselves, Are we living in the heavenlies?—Do we mind the things above?—Or are we still minding the things here on earth below? We need to take to heart these additional words of Paul's: "Blessed be the God and Father of our Lord Jesus Christ, who has blessed us with every spiritual blessing in the heavenlies in Christ" (Ephesians 1:3).

We are in the heavenlies, and God has blessed us with every spiritual blessing there in Christ Jesus. What an inheritance we have! The riches of Christ are all ours, and we are seated there with Him; which is to say that we enjoy all that

Jesus has done for us. All the spiritual blessings in the heavenlies are ours, and thus there is nothing lacking. What an inheritance we have, indeed! Even so, let us realize that the heavenlies are not only the place where we live spiritually and enjoy all the spiritual blessings in Christ Jesus, but there is another aspect to this: which is, that our really true ministry actually begins in the heavenlies.

There is a spiritual warfare into which we have been called, for in Ephesians 6 we are told that our warfare is not against flesh and blood; rather, our warfare is against the principalities, authorities, powers of darkness, and spiritual forces of wickedness in the heavenlies. What happens on earth is merely a shadow. In fact, people are shadow-boxing on earth. Nothing is real. The real battle is occurring in the heavenlies, and the heavenlies decide what is going to happen on earth.

Permit me to use an illustration here from the history of the Israelites. The very first battle which the children of Israel fought in the wilderness after they came out of Egypt was with the Amalekites. Moses had selected Joshua to lead the people to fight against the Amalekites, but let us notice how this battle was conducted by the Israelites. Moses went to the top of a hill which overlooked the battlefield, and whenever his lifted hands remained up, Joshua overcame the Amalekites; but whenever his hands grew tired and dropped down to his sides, Joshua was defeated by the Amalekites. So finally, they had Moses sit on a stone and had Aaron and Hur hold up Moses' hands until the Amalekites were completely defeated (Exodus 17:10-13). That was how the battle was fought.

In the same way, all the battles on earth are fought in the heavenlies overlooking the earth, and the real issue is whether God's purpose will prevail. Can and will God's will be opposed? That is decided in the heavenlies, not on earth. So far as the ascended Jesus is concerned, He has overcome all opposition and every obstacle to His Father’s will. On Calvary’s cross He inflicted upon the enemy a fatal blow, winning a decisive victory over him. We therefore read in Colossians 2 that Jesus captured and disarmed all the powers and authorities of darkness and made a public spectacle of them by means of His cross (v. 15). Yes, the serpent-enemy of God suffered a fatal blow at the hands of the Son of man by His having crushed the head of that Old Serpent, the devil. Nevertheless, though the serpent’s head has been crushed (Genesis 3:15), his tail is still quite active and slashing about; and that is where we believers and followers of Jesus enter the scene.

As the body of Christ, as those who are in the heavenlies, we are to apply the victory of Christ against all opposition to the Father’s will until all things are brought under the feet of the Lord Jesus (I Corinthians 15:25-28, quoting Psalm 8:6). What a responsibility! There is the privilege, quite true, because in the heavenlies we are blessed with every spiritual blessing in Christ Jesus. But with the privilege comes also the responsibility. As God’s servant Paul made clear in his Ephesian letter, we are responsible to stand, to withstand, and to stand: “Put on the panoply [whole armor] of God, that ye may be able to stand against the wiles of the devil. ... Take to you the panoply [whole armor] of God, that ye may be able to withstand in the evil day, and, having accomplished all things, to stand. Stand therefore ...” (6:11, 13, 14a).

In his Bible translation J. N. Darby has a footnote accompanying the phrase, to accomplish all things. He writes that in the Greek original the phrase is meant to convey the following thought: “to carry through and put in execution all that is purposed and called for in spite of opposition.” There is opposition, no doubt, but the will of God must be carried through and be fully implemented. All that is purposed and called for must and will be done, and that is the ministry of the church. The church has a ministry of completing that for which the crucified, resurrected, and ascended Jesus has laid the foundation. We are to declare His victory over every item, every notion, every issue, and everything else in our lives which would oppose God's will. There is definitely opposition to the will of God in the world, but there can be, and often is, such opposition in us as well; and we are therefore to claim the victory of Christ over every opposing issue or area in our life until the victory in Christ is carried through and executed. Basically, this has to be accomplished through prayer. Hence, prayer is the ministry of the church. But what a ministry that is!

This, then, is what we have received through Jesus' ascension back to the Father. And all I can say in conclusion is: Glory! Glory!!

Chapter Eighteen

His Return

Acts 1:10-11—And as they [the disciples] were gazing into heaven, as he [Jesus] was going, behold, also two men stood by them in white clothing, who also said, Men of Galilee, why do ye stand looking into heaven? This Jesus who has been taken up from you into heaven, shall thus come in the manner in which ye have beheld him going into heaven.

Acts 3:19-21—Repent therefore and be converted, for the blotting out of your sins, so that times of refreshing may come from the presence of the Lord, and he may send Jesus Christ, who was foreordained for you, whom heaven indeed must receive till the times of the restoring of all things, of which God has spoken by the mouth of his holy prophets since time began.

Matthew 24:32-44—But learn the parable from the fig-tree: When already its branch becomes tender and produces leaves, ye know that the summer is near. Thus also ye, when ye see all these things, know that it is near, at the doors. Verily I say to you, This generation will not have passed away until all these things shall have taken place. The heaven and the earth shall pass away, but my words shall in no wise pass away. But of that day and hour no one knows, not even the angels of the heavens, but my Father alone. But as the days of Noe, so also shall be the coming of the Son of man. For as they were in the days which were before the flood, eating and drinking, marrying and giving in marriage, until the day on which Noe entered into the ark, and they knew not till the flood came and took all away; thus also shall be the coming of the Son of man. Then two shall be in the field, one is taken and one is left; two women grinding at the mill, one is taken and one is left. Watch therefore, for ye know not in what hour your Lord comes. But know this, that if the master of the house had known in what watch the thief was coming, he would have watched and not have suffered his house to be dug through into. Wherefore ye also, be ye ready, for in that hour that ye think not the Son of man comes.

Jesus came 2,000 years ago to this earth and accomplished the work of redemption, but if He should not come the second time to the earth, do we realize that His work would be unfinished? When Jesus died on the cross He said, "It is finished." So far as the work of redemption is concerned, it is finished. But Peter preached that heaven must receive Jesus until the times of the restoring of all things (Acts 3:21). In other words, during the years of His first coming on earth He laid the foundation for the restoring of all things, and this restoring will continue on till it be finished at His second coming. Hence, Jesus will come again; and this is the blessed hope of the church (Titus 2:13). We are here waiting for His return.

So we find in the Bible that there are two comings of the Lord Jesus to the earth. Two thousand years ago He first came as the Lamb of God. Though He was born King, He came incognito. In obscurity was He born in a manger, and in obscurity was He reared in Nazareth, a hilly backwater village of Israel. When Jesus was about thirty He began to preach, and

He was rejected. He lived His whole life in humility. Finally, He was crucified on the cross. As the Lamb of God He shed His blood for the remission of our sins. He gave His body to be our life, to be our food. That was His first coming.

The Bible also tells us that He will come again; but this time He will come as the Lion of Judah. He will come to judge the world; He will come to claim the earth; He will come to establish His kingdom upon this earth. It is very clear, therefore, that there are two comings of the Lord Jesus, not just one.

Old Testament Prophecies: the Messiah Comes Twice

During the Old Testament era the Jewish prophets prophesied much concerning the coming Messiah, and in their prophecies they on the one hand described the Messiah as a glorious, reigning figure, but on the other hand they described Him as a lowly, suffering Messiah. To the Jews this was a puzzle: how could the Messiah be the glorious, reigning One and at the same time the humble, suffering One? It so happened that these prophets, in prophesying about those two aspects of the Messiah, had no knowledge that He would come twice. And between these two comings of Jesus there was to be a period shrouded in mystery. Indeed, Paul speaks in his Ephesian epistle of a mystery hidden throughout the generations and which had not been made known to the prophets and apostles of God until God revealed it by the Spirit to His holy apostles and prophets in Paul's day (3:4-5). So as we look back into Biblical history in our day we today know that in between Jesus' two comings there is the church period—the mystery that had been hidden throughout many centuries. Thank God, it has been revealed!

The Old Testament is full of prophecies concerning the coming of the Lord. And to those prophecies of old the apostle Peter made reference. This he did in his second epistle, 1:19. But Peter first spoke about "the power and [second] coming" of the Lord Jesus and said he was an eyewitness "of his majesty." He was obviously referring to the event which had occurred on the Mount of Transfiguration, because there he had seen Jesus appear in glory in His kingdom. It was, in fact, a preview of the kingdom to come. Hence Peter could testify that he was a personal witness *in advance* to the second coming of the Lord Jesus. But he then declared that the prophetic words of old concerning Jesus' (second) coming were made more sure (or were guaranteed to be true) by what he had witnessed on the sacred Mount, and to which words God's people would do well to pay attention until, added Peter, "the day dawn and the morning star arise in [our] hearts" (1:16-19).

It is very important, indeed, that we pay attention to the prophetic words in the Old Testament, but there are so many that we shall not be able to cover them during today's message. It would require months, perhaps even years, to cover all such prophecies; nevertheless, we do very much need to take heed to them: we need to study them and understand them. In fact, we would do well to take heed to them throughout our life so that we may be awake, waiting, and prepared for Jesus' return—that is to say, for when the day dawns and the morning star—even the Lord Jesus himself—arises in our hearts.

As examples of Old Testament prophecies regarding Jesus' coming to the earth, I would simply mention two here. The first one concerns the utterance of the Gentile prophet, Balaam, which can be found in the book of Numbers: "I shall see him, but not now; I shall behold him, but not nigh: There cometh a Star out of Jacob, and a Sceptre shall rise out of Israel, and he shall cut in pieces the corners of Moab, and destroy all the sons of tumult" (24:17).

Balaam prophesied during the time after the exodus from Egypt of the children of Israel but before they entered the Promised Land. In his prophecy he said, "I shall see him, but not now; I shall behold him, but not nigh." In other words, there is Someone coming in the future, and that Someone is referred to as a Star out of Jacob. I believe when we hear mentioned the word star, immediately, we remember that there was a star which appeared when Jesus was born, and that wise men in the East saw it and somehow discerned that a King—a very important King—had been born. That was the so-called Star of Bethlehem—"a Star out of Jacob."

Balaam continued by prophetically declaring: "and a Sceptre shall rise out of Israel." We can accurately say that in Biblical history there has appeared to mankind on earth a Star—the Star of Bethlehem; but there has yet to appear on earth a Sceptre. When Balaam prophesied, Star and Sceptre were mentioned together, but today we know that the Star has reference to Jesus' first coming and the Sceptre, to His second coming. And the rest of Balaam's words here—"and he shall cut in pieces the corners of Moab, and destroy all the sons of tumult"—have reference to the fact that when Jesus appears on earth the second time, He shall come with kingly power and authority and, wielding His scepter, shall bring judgment upon the world.

A second example is found in Isaiah 9: "For unto us a child is born, unto us a son is given; and the government shall be upon his shoulder; and his name is called Wonderful, Counsellor, Mighty God, Father of Eternity, Prince of Peace. Of the increase of his government and of peace there shall be no end, upon the throne of David and over his kingdom, to establish it, and to uphold it with judgment and with righteousness, from henceforth even for ever. The zeal of Jehovah of hosts will perform this" (vv. 6-7).

"Unto us a child is born." We know that that event occurred 2,000 years ago; but what about "a son is given"? The child who was born is the son who was given—the Son of God. "And the government shall be upon his shoulder." This Son shall sit on the throne of His father David and He shall rule with righteousness and with judgment. Let us observe again that like Balaam with the Star and Scepter, when Isaiah was prophesying, he put child and son together as though one because he had no idea that there would be two comings of the Messiah. To him there was only one coming but we today know that the One who was born is the One upon whose shoulder the government will be, and He will come one day to sit upon the throne of His father David.

Jesus Prophesied His Second Coming

With respect to the New Testament and its prophetic utterances regarding Jesus' return, someone has calculated that of every one hundred verses there are twenty-five which speak of the rapture of the church and of the coming of Jesus into His kingdom.

Now when Jesus was on earth, He talked about His coming once more, especially did He do so on the Mount of Olives; His words in this regard are a part of the so-called Olivet Discourse. In the following fashion He told them that He would be coming: "As the days of Noah, so shall be the coming of the Son of man." He testified before the Sanhedrin council that they would see the Son of man coming on the clouds of heaven (Matthew 26:64b).

On the day of Jesus' ascension His disciples were looking at Him and then seeing Him rising up, and as they continued looking up they beheld a cloud taking Him away out of their sight. They could no longer see Him, but they were still gazing towards heaven when two men in white appeared. We do not know who those two men were. There are different interpretations. The Scriptures say two men, not two angels. Who were those two men? I will leave it with you to guess. Those two men said, "Men of Galilee, why are you standing here and looking up? This Jesus who is being taken up from you into heaven will come back in the same manner" (see Acts 1:11).

Ever since that time the church throughout the ages has been preaching about and waiting for the coming back of the Lord Jesus. In every generation those who love the Lord have waited for His return coming. And we who are approaching the end of the twentieth century are also waiting for His coming back.

Jesus acknowledged that no one knows the time, the season, the hour of His coming back—yes, not even the angels know. Now the angels are more intelligent than we human beings, and yet they themselves do not know. So if they do not know and if they are more intelligent than we humans are, why are we always trying to figure out the time of Jesus' return? Even while Jesus was on earth as the Son of man, He confessed that He himself was ignorant of His return's timing, He declaring that only the Father knows the time of His return. But He did say this: "When you see these [end-time crises, troubles and trials of all kinds] coming to pass, you will know My coming back is near, at the doors."

Throughout the centuries the church has been waiting for Jesus' return, but we believers do not know when; nevertheless,

He has given us some clues, some signs. He has said, "When you see all these terrible end-time events coming to pass, you know the time of My return is near." How near? At the doors. When reading the Bible we need to be very careful. This scripture does not say, "at the door"; it says, "at the doors." People need to live in the Orient to understand this use of the plural number because here in America, if a visitor is at the door of one's house, when that door is opened to the visitor, he is already, as it were, in the house; but not in the Orient. There, when a visitor is at the *doors* (plural), he is at the outer gate of the courtyard, and if it is a very wealthy family or a royal family, a visitor may need to pass through *several* courtyards before he arrives at and gains entrance into the actual residence. So this is the figure of speech being used here—"at the doors"—in reference to the timing of Jesus' return to the earth. Perhaps He is at the front gate of the *first* courtyard or at that of the *second* because there are several doors to cross before a person arrives at the actual entrance of the residence. But if Jesus is merely at the doors, His arrival is nonetheless near enough to be concerned if one has not been watchful; for He cannot be miles away.

Signs of Jesus' Coming Again

Moral Condition of the World

In the Bible there are many signs or clues given as to His coming, but I will mention only a few. The first one is what the moral condition of the world will be like at the return of Jesus to the earth. Here is one clue which Jesus gave: "As in the days of Noah, so shall be the coming of the Son of man." What were the characteristics of the days of Noah? These can be found in

Genesis chapters 4-6. On the one hand, civilization had advanced quite rapidly; at the same time, however, there was an explosion of population (6:1a); and whenever there is an increase in fallen mankind's population, there is bound to be an increase in wickedness, corruption, and violence.

There was even spiritism present at this time, for we are told that the sons of God came and married the daughters of men (6:2). One interpretation of "the sons of God" is that this has reference to the angels since in the Old Testament book of Job, which was the first book in the Bible to be written, reference is made to "the sons of God," and this book makes clear that they are angels. So on that basis it is thought by many Bible scholars that the sons of God refer to the angels. Now we know from the New Testament (Matthew 22:30) that angels do not marry; yet at this time some of them obviously did not keep their proper place. They came down from heaven and mingled with the daughters of men, and the result of such carnal unions was giants upon the earth; and this was an abomination in the sight of God.

Indeed, immediately after the telling of this development the Bible narrative records God's reaction: "My Spirit will not strive with mankind forever, for he is flesh—carnal" (see 6:3a). Now these are the things which happened during the days of Noah. The imagination of men's minds was all evil and wickedness (6:5).

Does this sound very much like our time? Strangely, when Jesus said, "As the days of Noah, so shall be the coming of the Son of man," He did not emphasize these wicked, evil things; instead, He stressed a different matter that had marked the days of Noah: people were eating and drinking, marrying and giving in marriage. Now these are legitimate actions and activities; these are ordinary things of life. Nevertheless, Jesus was critical of the people in Noah's day for their eating and drinking, marrying and giving in marriage. The people back then had become obsessed with eating and drinking, marrying and giving in marriage; they had become fully occupied with the pursuit of so-called happiness, they having made these activities the very purpose of their life on earth. Now *that* was what Jesus had found to be quite wrong with those people back then.

It is quite true that it is the will of God for us to eat and drink. He had himself prepared food (manna) and water (out of the rock) for us. And it is also the will of God for man to be married; for He himself had declared that it is not good for man to be alone (Genesis 2:18). Yet these things are not the purpose of life. When you make these things your life's very purpose, when you are obsessed by these things, you end up neglecting your spiritual life, so that, like the people in Noah's day, you are unaware of the approaching overwhelming crisis in your life and you end up being swept away. Hence, the days of Noah were the days when the world of that time made the pursuit of pleasure and happiness the very meaning of life. Are we in our day also in such a state?

Besides this, Jesus issued another and similar warning, as is recorded in Luke 17:28-30, which began: "As in the days of Lot." Now what were the days of Lot like? We are told in Genesis 19 that Lot lived in Sodom, and Sodom and Gomorrah were so wicked that God finally destroyed them by raining down fire and sulphur from heaven. What was the specific sin of Sodom? Because of what had occurred in that city back then, we today have in the English language the word sodomy whose act constitutes one form of homosexual practice. And in the Scriptures the term sodomites is used to describe those committing this sin (e.g. Deut 23:17, I Timothy 1:10). And hence, the specific sin of Sodom was that of homosexuality, of which the world is becoming increasingly aware today. Such were the days of Lot.

Strangely enough, however, Jesus again emphasized otherwise. He said this: "In the days of Lot they ate, they drank, they bought, sold, planted and built." Once more it can be said that these are very natural activities in the life of man: We eat, drink, buy, sell, plant and build. How very normal they are; so why did Jesus warn about "the days of Lot"? Then we recall what Jesus added in His warning: "Remember Lot's wife!" In other words, Jesus was wanting to draw His audience's attention to but one fact: that in the days of Lot many people pursued after the world and the things of this world, conduct that is in conflict with God's word: "Love not the world, nor the things of the world, because if you love the world, the love of the Father is not in you" (see I John 2:15).

As we live on this earth we can legitimately enjoy everything which God has given to us. It is not His mind at all that we should be monks or nuns. In fact, many monks and nuns do not live like monks or nuns. Indeed, surprisingly, you may find the world to a greater degree in the monastery and nunnery than what you may find even in the world. Yes, God has given us all these things to enjoy richly (I Timothy 6:17b), and He wants us to enjoy them; but if we make the world and its pleasures the very goal of our life, if we seek after them and love them and allow them to occupy us completely so that we forget to love God, then something is seriously wrong. And that, noted Jesus, was what the days of Lot were like.

Therefore, the sign which Jesus gave regarding the moral condition of the people of the world was the pursuit of pleasure and love of the world to the extent of neglecting their spiritual welfare. How similar in lifestyle to that of the people in Noah's and Lot's day are many who today are living at near the end of the twentieth century!

The Sign of the Geopolitical World

What is the sign or clue provided in Scripture which reveals what the world's geopolitical situation will be like at the time of Jesus' return? For this, we must consult the prophetic book of Daniel chapter 2. Therein is described the huge image representing the successive kingdoms of this world; and the final stage is marked by the two feet and their ten toes. At some point the little toe comes in and destroys three toes and becomes the leader of that final phase of the kingdom rule (cf. Daniel 7:7-8). In other words, during the final stage in the world's geopolitical situation there will be a polarizing of the earth's nations, and out of that development will emerge a confederacy headed up by the beast—the Antichrist—and he will rule this earth. But when this happens, wrote the prophet Daniel, a stone that is not cut out of a mountain by human hands will come forth and strike the image and the image will disappear; but the stone will grow into a huge mountain and fill the whole earth. That stone refers to the unending kingdom of our God and of His Christ. So such is the sign concerning the political world and its situation at the time of Jesus' second coming.

The Sign of the Church

What is the sign concerning the condition of the church at the time of Jesus' coming again? This is reflected in what the risen and ascended Jesus had to say about the condition of the church in Laodicea as revealed in Revelation 3:14-22. Now I believe that the seven churches of Asia Minor that are discussed in Revelation chapters 2 and 3 refer prophetically to the history of the church on earth throughout the generations and centuries; and, therefore, when the end of the church period arrives, it will be like the condition described by the Lord Jesus as that of the last church mentioned—that of the Laodicean church.

What are the special features of that Laodicean church, all of which are negative in nature? Something is revealed by this church's very name, for Laodicea in Greek means "the opinions of man." We understand that the church is the body of Christ and that if there is any opinion to be expressed, it has to be the opinion of the Head—Christ. To put it another way, the church does not have its own opinion; rather, the church's opinion is none other than that of Christ the Head. Unfortunately, when the church arrives at its final historical stage, instead of holding fast to Christ her Head (Colossians 2:19a), she will have become a democracy instead of remaining a theocracy: she has come to be ruled by the opinion of the many, and thus the majority rules. The church will have come to be governed by the opinion of man rather than she having the mind of Christ in all things. That, then, will be one of the special features which will characterize the condition of the church in the last days just prior to Jesus' return.

Other negative features were noted by the Head of the church: Laodicean believers were lukewarm, they being neither hot nor cold; and so, they were advised by the Lord Jesus to buy gold refined by fire. Gold refined by fire is a reference to faith, living faith (I Peter 1:7). Brethren in the Laodicean church had all the truth, doctrines, dogmas; they also held tenaciously to the Christian creed of that day, but there was no living faith. And because they lacked that living faith, it was no wonder they were lukewarm. There was no fire burning within the hearts of these Laodiceans, and yet they boasted of their riches, for they claimed they lacked nothing but had everything they needed.

Little did they realize, the risen Christ remarked, that they were naked. In other words, they did not have Christ as their righteousness (I Corinthians 1:30). Moreover, they did not have the righteousnesses of the saints (Revelation 19:8), that is to say, Christ not having been formed in their lives. They were totally naked before God and, furthermore, noted the Lord Jesus, they were also poor, blind, wretched and miserable.

At the time of Jesus' return there will not only be heresies but also apostasies. This we learn from reading II Thessalonians chapter 2, in which we are told that before the son of perdition—the man of sin and lawlessness—appears, there will be a general falling away from the faith, that is to say, there will occur a general apostasy among the people of God (vv. 1-4). That is a further clue which Scripture provides. And it is obvious to any discerning observer that insofar as what the condition of the church is like today, we are living in that very period of apostasy.

The Sign of Israel

Jesus provided another clue or sign of His coming again when speaking of the fig tree. For among the many things He talked about with His disciples in His Olivet Discourse, He said this: "Learn the parable from observing the fig tree. When you see it begin to bud and produce leaves, you know that the summer is near." It so happened that not long before this Discourse with His disciples Jesus had been making His way to Jerusalem during His last week on earth. And one day Jesus came upon a fig tree that was full of leaves. And being hungry He looked for some fruit on this tree, but there was none. So Jesus cursed that fig tree and it dried up immediately.

Now the fig tree in Scripture represents the people and nation of Israel. God had planted the Israelites as a chosen nation in the earth. And Jesus had later come and worked on them for some three years, yet—like the fig tree—they only produced leaves but no fruit for God. So the nation of Israel came under a curse: God set them aside, and throughout the centuries since then they have been scattered all over the world—no land, no definable nation, no government. But the Lord said, "When you see the fig tree begin to grow and to leaf, you know the summer is near." Meaning that the situation with Israel will change, and that her restoration will be a further sign that the time of Jesus' return will be near—even at the doors.

Only in recent decades has the world witnessed the restoration of the nation of Israel, and it most surely is a miracle. No politician, no statesman, no historian could foresee her restoration; nevertheless, on 14 May 1948 Israel was revived as a nation on the earth. And some twenty years later, on 6 June 1967, which was during the Six Days War, Jerusalem was captured by Israel and, for the first time, the city came under her rule. From history we know that in 70 A. D. Jerusalem was destroyed and, as was foretold by Jesus (Luke 21:24a), the people were scattered among the nations. Only once since that time and only, for a short period, in the year 135 A. D. was Jerusalem ever controlled by Israel; so that aside from that brief period, it had always been under the control of the Gentiles until 1967. In this connection, it is interesting what Jesus had to say about Jerusalem. Said Jesus: "Jerusalem will be trampled under foot by the Gentiles until the times of the Gentiles be fulfilled" (see Luke 21:24b). And in 1967 Jerusalem finally reverted back to Israel's total control. As a consequence, people have been wondering whether that event constituted the end of the times of the Gentiles. Even so, we realize that this has only been a *political* restoration, not a full one.

Having reviewed all these various clues and signs, it becomes clear to us that the coming of the Lord Jesus is very near. He is even at the doors—and that is the parable to be learned from the fig tree.

Two Characteristics of His Coming

How will Jesus come? I am afraid the reason we are so confused about His second coming and how He shall come back to the earth is because we do not pay close and careful attention to the text of the word of God. For instance, the two men in white mentioned in Acts 1 said, "He who was taken up to heaven shall come back in the same manner as you saw Him go." We need to pay attention to the words, "in the same manner."

So, how did Jesus go up? As we learned from Scripture, Jesus had gathered His disciples to the Mount of Olives; and as He was talking with them there, He began to be taken up from their midst. He left the Mount of Olives and went up. They saw Jesus going up. Then, a short while later a cloud appeared and took Him away. They could not see Him anymore, but we know He was still going up. So they were still gazing and gazing, and then those two men in white said to the Eleven, "Why do you continue to gaze? This Jesus will come back in the same way." So what was the way He went up? He went up first from the Mount of Olives to the cloud—a visible phase; He then went up to the throne of God, having been received in a cloud which carried Him out of sight—an invisible phase. Nevertheless, we know He arrived at God's throne because there are many proofs, which we have already mentioned. In His coming back, therefore, Jesus will do so in like manner, but in reverse order; which is to say, His coming back will be first from the throne to the cloud—the invisible phase; and then from the cloud to the Mount of Olives—the visible phase.

In the Bible there are different Greek words employed for our English word coming, but there is one particular Greek word used repeatedly here in Matthew 24 which translates into English as: the coming. For example: "As the days of Noah, so shall be *the coming* of the Son of man." The Greek word for this phrase is *parousia*, which means "presence." Today Jesus is absent, but one day He will be present. How does He "presence" himself with us? Jesus' *parousia*—His coming—does not refer to a single moment in time or to just one event. His *parousia*, His coming, comprises a period of time and will include more than one event. In short, Jesus will "presence" himself from the throne to the air and from the air to the earth. That, in general terms, will define Jesus' *parousia.* It begins from the throne, it ends on the Mount of Olives, and it shall cover a series of events within each of those two phases.

Now Jesus employed two teaching methods to illustrate the characteristics of His coming again: the use of a simile was one, and the other was to explain and correct false declarations as to where He could be found and seen on earth at His coming. Jesus said He would come like a thief (Matthew 24:42-44). Now when a thief comes to your house, does he blow a trumpet announcing his coming? Does he tell you when he is coming? Certainly not! He comes, as it were, almost invisibly. When the thief comes, does he come into your house to steal your garbage? Not at all! He seems to know where your treasure box is. He will pick out and take your best jewelry. Moreover, when the thief comes, most people do not know he has come. He comes and then goes. Only a few who are actually on the alert and watching will see him. Jesus said that if you knew when the thief was coming, you would watch and not let your house be broken into. Therefore, concluded Jesus, you must be ready, because I will come at an hour when you do not expect Me.

Jesus also warned not to be taken in by false claims about where He could be seen at His coming. He said, "At the end time, when people will say, 'Christ is here' or 'Christ is there,' don't believe it" (see Matthew 24:23-26). Why? Because His coming will be like lightning that flashes from the east to the west, and hence, everybody will see Him. It is therefore quite different from the illustration of the thief, whose appearing only a few will know of and see. So the thief's coming and appearing can represent the hidden phase of Jesus' *parousia*—the *invisible* period of His presence covering His movement from the throne to the air; whereas the lightning phase of Jesus' *parousia* can represent the *visible* period of His presence that will cover His movement from the air to the hill of Olivet on the earth.

The Beginning of Jesus' *Parousia*

When will Jesus' *parousia* begin? How is it started? Jesus explained it this way: "Then two shall be in bed; one is taken, one is left" (see Luke 17:34); "Two will be working in the field; one is taken, one is left. Two women will be grinding at the mill; one is taken, one is left" (see Matthew 24:40-41). What does all that signify? Two in the Scripture is the number of witness, and the "two" here refers to the Christians who are still living at the time of *parousia*. Many saints have passed on throughout the generations and centuries of human history. They can be likened to the ten virgins who went to sleep because the bridegroom—in this case, the Lord Jesus—delayed

His coming (Matthew 25:5), but there are two still living; and twelve (ten plus two), Bible scholars believe, is the number of the church in Scripture. The two in each of these three scenarios refer to those who are still living, and the people in each set of two are exactly the same, in that Jesus did not differentiate between them. For instance in the first scenario both people are sleeping; so let us not be afraid to go to sleep tonight; we need sleep, and hence, let us all go to bed.

Let us not think that because Jesus is coming, therefore, we will not do anything but wait for His coming. No, go to sleep; grind at the mill; go to the field and work; let us all be engaged in our duties and responsibilities. For Jesus knows where the treasure is (cf. II Corinthians 4:7-12). Outwardly, believers are the same; in these three scenarios they are all engaged in the same activities, and their lives continue on as usual; nevertheless, the Lord Jesus knows who is prepared and waiting for Him and who is not, for He knows the heart of each believer. Do not therefore be deceived by outward appearance: Jesus knows the heart, and this one or that one who is a peculiar treasure to Him will be taken as He himself was taken.

Revelation 12 mentions a woman in travail, and she betokens the church in the last stage. Out of that woman comes forth a manchild, and as soon as that manchild is born he is taken right up to the heavenly throne (v.5). It is believed by many that that manchild represents those who will be raptured to begin, as it were, the *parousia* of the Lord Jesus. They will be taken up to the throne to bring back upon the earth the One who sits on the throne. May the Lord have mercy on us.

These who make up the manchild are the firstfruits, for they have ripened earliest (see Revelation 14:4, 15). Then there will be the harvest to follow. So the first stage of Jesus' *parousia* is triggered, so to speak, by one day, suddenly, all over this earth, some Christians disappear; they are taken. Why is it that in His teaching Jesus cites those three different activities that are being engaged in by the believers; for some shall be sleeping, some shall be grinding, and some, working in the field? Well, people sleep in the night, people usually grind meal in the morning, and people work in the daytime at noon out in the field. Now we know that the earth is round; so given the fact that the earth rotates on its axis around the sun, there will simultaneously be—at any given moment—some places on earth where it is night, other places where it is dawn, and still other places where it is noonday.

And hence, from the whole earth there shall be some who—being first fruits—are ready and prepared for the Lord Jesus. They will be raptured to the throne to welcome the King of kings and Lord of lords and then follow Him back to the earth. Glorious!

Watch and Be Ready

The return of the Lord is so imminent; it can happen at any moment. All the prophecies which needed to be fulfilled *prior* to *parousia* have been fulfilled. There are many others waiting to be fulfilled, but such are to occur either after *parousia* or during *parousia*. We know His return is very, very imminent, very close to happening. It could even happen today.

What, then, should be our attitude? The Scriptures use a few words to describe what the Lord Jesus desires us to be doing. One word He says is, "Watch." That means we are to be on the alert; we are not to be sleeping when we should be awake; we are not to be ignorant of what is going on—what is happening in the world. We are to be watching, and noticing things and events, and when we see any change, we should turn it into prayer.

Watch and pray, that you will not allow the love of pleasure and the things of this life to so occupy your heart that when the Lord comes, you are not ready to be taken. Pray that you may be delivered from such preoccupation. Pray that He will come soon, very soon. Then wait for His coming. Do not say that the Lord delays His return as did the wicked servant in Jesus' parable (Matthew 24:45-51); so he began to beat his fellow servants and became drunk with the drunkards. And when the Lord shall come in a day and at an hour that he knows not of, then the Lord will come and cut him in two and assign him a place with the hypocrites. We need to watch, pray, and wait—wait patiently, wait with expectancy, just like the farmers do after they plant and wait for the time of harvest. Let us wait with the blessed hope of the coming of the glory of the Lord Jesus into His kingdom. Let us wait, let us be ready, let us be prepared.

Yet how do we ready ourselves? We should be like the five wise virgins who, besides having oil in their lamps, had oil also in their jars (Matthew 25:1-13). In other words, we need to be filled with the Spirit of God and not filled with the things of the world. Let us be ready for Him in such a way that we may hasten His return (II Peter 3:12a).

Why has the Lord not come back yet? It is not because He is not ready or that He is not anxious and eager; rather, it is because we are not ready. If we ready ourselves for Him, that is to say, ready ourselves to be like Him by allowing the Holy Spirit by means of the cross to work in our lives until Christ is formed in us, then Jesus will come and claim us as His bride, as

His like, His counterpart. It is because the church is not ready that He delays His return. Let us be those who, by the grace of God, watch and pray, wait and prepare for—and even hasten—His return.

Chapter Nineteen

HIS REIGNING

I Corinthians 15:20-28—(But now Christ is raised from among the dead, first-fruits of those fallen asleep. For since by man came death, by man also resurrection of those that are dead. For as in the Adam all die, thus also in the Christ all shall be made alive. But each in his own rank: the first-fruits, Christ; then those that are the Christ's at his coming. Then the end, when he gives up the kingdom to him who is God and Father; when he shall have annulled all rule and all authority and power. For he must reign until he put all enemies under his feet. The last enemy that is annulled is death. For he has put all things in subjection under his feet. But when he says that all things are put in subjection, it is evident that it is except him who put all things in subjection to him. But when all things shall have been brought into subjection to him, then the Son also himself shall be placed in subjection to him who put all things in subjection to him, that God may be all in all.)

We have been considering together for some time the life of Jesus. We firmly believe that it is the Father's will that we should behold His Son. He is the gospel that we believe in, and it ought to be our passion to know Him and to know Him more fully. That is the reason we have spent such a long time in considering together Jesus' life.

We began with His incarnation—"The Word became flesh" (John 1:14a). He came into this world, walked on this earth for some thirty-three years, and died on the cross for us. He was buried, was raised, and ascended; and during our last time together in continuing to consider the life of Jesus, we spoke of His second coming, His return to earth.

Reconciling All Things to the Fullness of God

At first, I thought His return should be the concluding discussion in this series of messages on the life of the Lord Jesus; however, one day, as I was considering I Corinthians 15, I realized that our study together on His life would be incomplete if we did not consider His reigning as well, since this chapter very clearly states in verse 24: "Then [comes] the end." When, therefore, does the end of the life story of Jesus reach its conclusion? That same passage continues and gives the answer: when He gives up the kingdom to Him who is God and Father; when, further, He will have put down all rule, authority and power, He reigning until all His enemies have been put under His feet and abolishing death as the last enemy: when all of that will have happened, then Christ will place himself in subjection to God the Father, so that God may be all in all. Only then will the story of Jesus have arrived at its end.

We mentioned last time Acts 3:21a: "Heaven must receive [Jesus] till the times of the restoring of all things." Furthermore, Colossians 1 tells us that by the blood of His cross Jesus shall reconcile all things to *itself*, whether things in heaven or things on the earth (v. 20). Some translations read, "to himself," but actually the Greek original has "to itself." That word "itself" simply refers to "the fullness of God" that is alluded to in the preceding verse 19. In other words, the work of Jesus was to reconcile all things to the fullness of God; or to put it another way, that all things are to be brought into subjection to God by His Son so that God's glory may be manifested in all things.

By the shedding of His blood on Calvary's cross Jesus laid the foundation for such reconciliation. After that foundation was laid, God raised Jesus up and set Him at His right hand on the throne, thus placing Him above every principality, authority, power and dominion, and has put all things under His feet, and made Him to be Head over all things to the church, which is His body, the fullness of Him who fills all in all (Ephesians 1:20-23).

After that foundation of reconciling all things to the fullness of God was laid on Calvary's cross, Jesus, in His ascended position, has ever since been executing and carrying through by himself and also through His church, the bringing of all things into subjection to God. With regard to Jesus, it is His right that all things be in subjection to Him; and with regard to the church, it is by grace that all things shall be brought into subjection to Him. And hence, the Bible makes clear that God has made Jesus the Head over all things to the church.

We therefore need to understand that the reconciling of all things to the fullness of God—indeed, the restoring of all things to God's original purpose—must first be realized in the church; and then, through the church, all things in the entire universe will eventually be brought into subjection to Christ. And thus, it can be said that we are in the days when this work is going on, and that it shall continue until, finally, it is fully realized.

The Second Coming of Christ Brings Judgment

We mentioned before that in the first coming of Jesus He came as the Lamb of God. He came to accomplish the work of redemption. He himself said that He did not come to judge the world but to save it (John 12:47b). So in the first coming of Jesus He came to save the world by accomplishing the work of redemption. That was the purpose of His first coming. But at His second coming Jesus shall come as the Lion of Judah, and thus He is coming to judge the world. Indeed, the work of God will not be completed until judgment also comes upon the earth.

Now with regard to Jesus' return, we would probably have the following questions: What happens when Jesus returns? What will He do after the period of His second coming is over? And what will happen upon the earth? These are the things which we would like to answer as we consider the conclusion to the life story of Jesus.

The Church

The letter of I Peter states that judgment shall begin with the house of God (4:17a). After the work of redemption is accomplished, the work of judgment follows. Redemption is offered to the world, but if redemption is rejected or is neglected, then judgment will come upon the world to finish the work of God. Thank God, we have believed in the Lord Jesus, and because we belong to Him, therefore, judgment must begin with God's house. Christ has offered himself fully to us, and whether or not the church as the body of Christ is to become the fullness of Christ is something that needs to be considered most seriously. God's will is that the body of Christ may be the fullness of Him who fills all in all. In other words, Jesus has given himself fully to the church and He wants her to be the expression of His fullness. This is the will of God, that everything in the church is to be brought into subjection to Christ. Everything in the church is to express Him and nothing else. It is to be Christ who fills all in all. This is the eternal will of God concerning His church. But whether or not His church comes into that fullness is a matter which will be judged by the Head, even Christ.

As a matter of fact, judgment has already begun upon the house of God. For the apostle John has reported to us in Revelation chapters 2 and 3 that he witnessed seeing the risen Lord, as the Priest-King, walking in the midst of the seven churches of Asia Minor and judging each one of them. Yet He was judging not for the sake of punishment; He was judging for the sake of restoration, of recovery. There among those seven churches the risen Christ was trying to find himself in His fullness in His church; instead, He found that there were many things that were not of Him, and also that many things that are of Him were not there. He was judging in order that He might bring His church back to repentance and to recovery and full restoration. So even in the Early Church the judgment of God's house had already begun. And it may be added that in a very real sense the church has been continuously under His judgment throughout the twenty centuries ever since. Whether individually or corporately the church has been under God's discipline.

Even today the Holy Spirit has been bringing the light of God to us believers, both personally and corporately. "If we walk in the light as God is in the light, we have fellowship one with another, and the blood of Jesus Christ, God's Son, cleanses us from all our sin" (see I John 1:7). When the light of God comes upon us, it judges all darkness so that we may be cleansed from all sins by the blood of Jesus and have fellowship with God and with one another. That is the reason we need to walk daily in the light of the judgment seat of Christ. Thank God, the judgment as to eternal life or death has passed for us because we who believe in the Lord Jesus have passed out of death into life. But one day, as part of the house of God, the family of God, the household of God, we will all appear before the judgment seat of Christ (II Corinthians 5:10a).

At the Lord's coming we will all be gathered before the Lord Jesus as His household, and there we will be judged according to all our works, for the issue will be that after we believed in Jesus how did we live? What did we do with our Christian life?—Did we glorify Him or did we bring shame to Him?—Did we allow the Holy Spirit to discipline us?—Were we obedient to the discipline of the Holy Spirit so that Christ might be formed in us or did we continue to live according to the flesh?—Were we building with gold, silver and precious stones or were we building with wood, hay and stubble (I Corinthians 3:12)? On that day, as God's children, as the family of God, as the household of God, we shall all appear before the judgment seat of Christ and there we will be judged (II Corinthians 5:10). We will either receive reward or suffer loss. Such loss has nothing to do with eternal death, but we may nonetheless suffer loss.

With this judgment in view, how we need to live daily in the light of that coming judgment seat. If we live today under that light and allow the blood of Jesus to cleanse us from all our sins and shortcomings, then on that day when He shall return and judge His household, we will not be put to shame. This day and event is what Paul often mentioned in his epistles—that he was looking forward to the day of Christ when he should be counted worthy and not be put to shame.

We need to encourage one another to walk in the light of God. We should always have the judgment seat of Christ in view and walk in the light as He is in the light; then we will be cleansed, and when we shall see Him we shall not be put to shame (I John 2:28). So, when the Lord Jesus comes back, He will judge the church.

Israel

Judgment does not end with only the church being judged, because in the world there are three classes of people (I Corinthians 10:32) with whom God through Christ must deal—the church, the Jews, and the nations. At Jesus' coming, the Jewish people will also be judged. As a matter of fact, that judgment is already in progress. When Jesus first came into this world He went initially to the house of Israel. He even told His early disciples: "Do not go to the Gentiles, but go to the house of Israel" (Matthew 10:5-6). So He offered himself as the Redeemer Messiah first to His own people Israel. Unfortunately, they rejected Him as their Messiah. Not only did they reject Him but they also put Him away and arrogantly declared: "Let his blood be upon us and upon our children" (see Matthew 27:25). So judgment began on Israel. Upon those who fall and refuse to repent, God is severe (Romans 11:22).

Now after the children of Israel rejected and crucified Jesus they over time were dispersed throughout the world and were scattered into many nations. And from within the prophetic passage in Ezekiel 20:33-44 we learn that God will judge them in "the wilderness of the peoples" (v. 35). What is meant by that phrase, the wilderness of the peoples? Providing some background here will help in understanding those words. Let us recall that after the children of Israel were delivered out of Egypt but before they entered the Promised Land they wandered about in the Sinai wilderness for forty years. There, God judged them. He uncovered and exposed what was in their hearts by such judgment; for He tested them and showed them how disobedient and rebellious they were so that they might learn the lesson and be brought, eventually, into the Promised Land.

That earlier wilderness judgment, however, cannot be compared with the severe judgment which God has been meting out upon Israel ever since she and her people had rejected their Redeemer Messiah. For God's judgment "in the wilderness of the peoples (or, nations)" has been far greater in severity. This is because throughout these many centuries the Jewish people have been scattered abroad into the nations of the world; and for the people of Israel it has been like an unending wilderness—even desert-like—experience. And the reason? God has been extremely severe in judging them by exposing and showing them their wicked hearts. He has been disciplining them in order that, one day, His mercy may return to them. In fact, God's mercy began to be shown to them at the mid-point of our current twentieth century.

It is quite true that in the mercy of God the nation of Israel was restored in 1948, but we must acknowledge the fact that it has only been a political restoration and not a spiritual restoration as well. What God has always had in mind for His chosen people is a spiritual restoration—to recover them to the covenant promises of God. What God promised Abraham, Isaac and Jacob will all be fulfilled to them eventually because God is faithful, and in order to accomplish that, He is working in their midst: through judgment God is bringing them into that restoration. So the children of Israel have been returning to their Promised Land, but it is only a prelude.

Their greatest problem is security. The Jewish people never feel secure as a nation. They will employ every means apart from God to have that security instead of trusting and waiting upon Him and returning to Christ. They will try their own ways and one day, for the sake of security, they will even make a pact with death—that is to say, with the Antichrist—because he will promise to give them security. According to Daniel 9 Israel will make a pact with the Antichrist for the sake of security, but in the middle of this seven-year pact or agreement the Antichrist will break his peace pact and show his true colors (v. 27). Then the time of Jacob's trouble will come upon Israel, as was prophesied in verse 7 of Jeremiah 30. The people of Israel will go through great trouble and tribulation because, as the chosen people of God, they will refuse to bow to the image of the beast.

Such sufferings are part of the judgment of God. God will use judgment to bring them, finally, to their senses. Then, when they are at their lowest point, Jesus will return and deliver them. God is judging them in order to purify them, to bring them back to what He had ordained for them as His chosen people. We will recall that Jesus once told His twelve apostles that one day they would sit upon twelve thrones and judge the twelve tribes of Israel (Matthew 19:27-28). All the wicked in Israel will be judged and purged. Then Israel will weep and repent (see Zechariah chapters 12-14). And so, according to Romans 11:26 all Israel shall be saved. God's work began with redemption and it will be completed with judgment. Indeed, these two actions of God work together and not against each other.

The Nations

Then there will be the judgment of the nations (Matthew 25:31-46). When Jesus returns to the earth He will sit on the throne of glory with His angels and all the nations on earth will be gathered before His throne. He will divide them into two classes—the sheep nations and the goat nations. The sheep ones will be on the right side of His throne and the goat ones will be on the left. He will tell the sheep nations: "You are blessed; you shall enter into the kingdom that My Father has prepared for you, because when I was hungry, you fed Me; when I was thirsty, you gave Me drink; when I was naked, you clothed Me; when I was sick, you visited Me; and when I was in prison, you came to Me." These nations will say, "Lord, when did we do these things?" And He will say, "If you did it to one of the least of these My brethren, you did it to Me."

We do not know for sure who are the least of Jesus' brethren to whom He refers here. It may be the Jews or it may be the Christians or it may be both; we do not know. Those nations which have been kind to the least of Jesus' brethren will one day receive the blessing of being moved into the millennial kingdom as part of the nations on earth under His rule, but those nations which have been cruel to the least of Jesus' brethren in this present age will in future be cast into eternal punishment. So we see that the nations will also be judged.

The Events of Jesus' Coming

Next to be considered briefly will be the prophetic, chronological coming of Jesus and what will take place thereafter. As was mentioned in the previous message, His coming back will be like His going away. Let us recall Acts chapter 1 where we are told by those two men in white: "Men of Galilee, why do you stand here gazing upward? This Jesus who has been taken away from you shall come back in like manner" or, in the same way. Let us recall further that when Jesus ascended back to the Father, the first phase of His ascension was visible because from the Mount of Olives He went upward and the disciples were able to see Him. Then a cloud took Him further upward but they could no longer see

Him, yet we know He was still ascending up. So Jesus' going away from His disciples was effected in two stages—a visible one and an invisible one. From the Olivet Mount to the cloud was the visible phase; and from the cloud to God's throne was the invisible phase. When He returns He will do so in the same manner but in *reverse* order. From the throne to the cloud will be invisible; hence, said Jesus, He will come like a thief. And from the cloud to the Mount of Olives will be visible; and so, added Jesus, He will come like lightning, for when lightning strikes from the east to the west, everybody shall be able to see it.

Rapture of the Manchild

Chronologically speaking, as far as I can understand, the events surrounding Jesus' return will probably happen in the following order. First will be the rapture of the newly-born manchild that is spoken of in Revelation 12. A woman is also mentioned there who is in travail to bring forth the manchild (vv. 2, 5a). That woman represents the church in the last age or end time; and so, out of the travail of the church comes forth a manchild. That manchild represents the overcomers at the end time—those who are still living and have overcome (v. 11). They shall be changed and taken upward alive through the air right to the throne where the Lord Jesus is (v. 5b). Is it not exciting that we are on the verge of this event occurring! Those of us, whoever they may be, who are totally devoted to the Lord, are not waiting for death but are waiting to be raptured alive. If Jesus should delay His return, we may, of course, go through death; but if He should come today or at any time very soon, it is possible that we could be raptured alive straight to Jesus' throne, depending on our spiritual condition before God. What a blessing that would be!

This manchild will be raptured to the throne to welcome the King of kings and Lord of lords and to bring Him to the earth (Revelation 19:14). When this happens, there will be war in the air (v. 7a). Michael and his angels will war with Satan and his fallen angels, and as a consequence there will no longer be a place for Satan and his angels in the air (v. 8b), which until this moment has been the headquarters of the evil kingdom (Ephesians 2:2). So Satan with his evil angels will be cast down to the earth (v. 9), thus clearing the air of all opposition and enabling Jesus and the manchild to descend in the cloud—the invisible phase of Jesus' return. When that happens, Satan and his angels will be on the earth and, according to Revelation, the entire trio of evil—Satan, the beast (who is the Antichrist), and the false prophet—will be together on the earth (cf. Revelation 12:7-9, 19:20, 20:2). So when the trio of evil is on earth, what can you expect but great tribulation? For the Jews it will be the time of Jacob's trouble (Jeremiah 30:7); for those Christians who are not matured and who are therefore not prepared it will unfortunately be the Great Tribulation, though it will serve as a second opportunity to be matured through sufferings (Revelation 20:4).

Christ Descends to the Mount of Olives

Now as we learn from Zechariah the prophet, towards the end of the second three-and-one-half-years period of the Great Tribulation the armies of the whole world will be gathered along the plain of Megiddo in Israel. Jerusalem will be broken into and surrounded, many will be killed and, at that time, Jesus will descend with His chosen army, the overcomers (14:5c).

They will descend, and Jesus' feet will touch the Mount of Olives once again, and the Mount will be split into two—the result of an earthquake (14:3-5). Archeologists have already discovered the fault line there; so that if there is ever an earthquake, they know that the Olivet hill will suffer cleavage into two halves (14:4b-c). Those Jews that remain in Jerusalem will flee through the opening in Olivet, and the Lord will come to deliver them (14:5a-b). There will be the last battle, the battle of Armageddon in the Megiddo Plain, and those armies which oppose the Lord Jesus will be destroyed (see Revelation 19:11-21). The false prophet will be thrown into the lake of fire (Revelation 19:20, 20:10a), and Satan will be bound and cast into the bottomless pit for a thousand years (20:2-3a). Then the millennial kingdom shall begin. And thus this present age shall pass away and the age to come shall finally arrive, and Christ shall reign for a thousand years (20:4c, 5b).

The Millennial Kingdom

What will Jesus do when He returns? After He clears up everything with judgment, His kingdom shall then come upon the earth. This will be the public manifestation of the kingdom of the heavens. It will be the time when the heavens shall rule upon the earth. As I best understand it, the time-length for the kingdom will be a thousand years, and there will actually be two governing aspects to it. First will be the heavenly aspect, which is called the kingdom of the heavens. This aspect will be characterized by Christ Jesus reigning from heaven with His overcomers during this thousand-year period. This will also be the time when the overcomers of the church shall be rewarded. As Jesus once declared: "One will rule over five cities; another will rule over ten cities" (see Luke 19:16-19). These cities, of course, will be on earth, but *heaven* will rule over the earth.

But there is another governing aspect to the millennial kingdom, and that aspect will be centered on the earth. It is called the Messianic kingdom, and it will be the occasion when Israel shall become a nation of priests as God had originally ordained for them to be (Exodus 19:6a, Isaiah 61:6a); and whatever God has ordained must come to pass. During all these past thousands of years Israel had forfeited what God had ordained for them; yet God has not forgotten His promise. So the day will indeed come when Israel shall be a nation of priests. Zechariah chapter 14 tells us that at this time every vessel in Jerusalem will be a holy vessel (vv. 20-21). As a nation of priests the inhabitants will go out and teach the nations (see Zechariah 8:20-23). All those peoples upon the earth who comprise the sheep nations will gladly come to worship the Lord during the Feast of Tabernacles (Zechariah 14:16), but if any nation refuses to come, judgment will be quick (vv. 17-19).

Today is the age of grace; therefore, punishment meted out in judgment seems to come very slowly. However, during the kingdom age, Jesus will sit upon the throne of David, and He will maintain His kingdom with righteousness and with judgment (Isaiah 9:7). The kingdom age is the age of righteousness. Righteousness shall rule over the earth. We know, of course, that during Jesus' first coming He did not solve social, political, economic, and other problems of this world. He did, however, heal the sick, feed the hungry, and preached the gospel to the poor (Isaiah 61:1); but He did not come to the earth at that time to resolve the many problems of the world but came exclusively for accomplishing the salvation of souls; He came for our spiritual and soulical well-being.

That does not mean, though, that the Lord Jesus was never concerned about the problems of the world. For during His second coming He will resolve all the world's problems. Whatever is not of God will be done away with. In fact, during this governing aspect of the millennial kingdom that will be centered on the earth, it will almost seem like a return to the days of Adam before the Fall. Creation shall be liberated from corruption and vanity (Romans 8:19-21). The lion will eat grass with the ox (Isaiah 11:7b, 65:15a). Nothing on earth will hurt or harm (Isaiah 11:9a). The knowledge of the Lord shall fill this earth as the waters fill the sea (Isaiah 11:9b, Habakkuk 2:14). There will be peace and righteousness ruling over this earth (Isaiah 9:7). Jesus will rule the earth with an iron rod or scepter during this aspect of millennial-kingdom rule (Revelation 19:15a; cf. Psalm 2:9). What does all this signify? It indicates that He will rule this earth with righteousness and that punishment will be meted out quickly. A man one hundred years old who dies will be accursed (Isaiah 65:20). (If today a person reaches the age of one hundred, that one is blessed!) How glorious it will be to find the Lord Jesus on the throne, ruling over the world. The millennial period will be a glorious one.

With respect to the heavenly-ruling aspect of the millennium, the overcomers who will reign with Christ from heaven will already have spiritual bodies and will no longer be in their mortal bodies. In their rule from heaven upon the earth, therefore, they will not need airplanes or any such other vehicles for travel because if they wish to come to the earth, they will already be here. It will be just like after the resurrection of Jesus; for Him it was simply a matter of appearing and disappearing and no longer a matter of coming and going. So will it be with the overcomers. Which means that ruling five cities or ten cities on earth can be done very easily without any problem. But the inhabitants of the earth will still be in their mortal, physical bodies.

Yet, let us be aware that even with such a perfect environment, many people's hearts will still be hard, stiff-necked and rebellious; for though living under the righteous rule of Christ—when everything will be so peaceful and so wonderful—many people will nonetheless continue to remain unconverted. Critics of redemptive faith continue to claim today that the reason people are imperfect on earth is due to the environment and not to so-called original sin: change or improve the environment and citizens of the earth will be perfect. But as will be evident during the millennial kingdom, a perfect environment cannot and will not produce a perfect person. Thus, there will still be sinful, rebellious people on earth who will need to be dealt with.

The Last Rebellion

After the millennium there will occur the last rebellion (Revelation 20). Satan will be released from the bottomless pit (v. 7) to be used by God. Satan will go everywhere on the earth deceiving the nations, resulting in great multitudes who will follow him into the last rebellion (vv. 7-8). They will come up to surround Jerusalem and the camp of the saints (v. 9). Whereas Jerusalem represents the governing center of Jesus' Messianic kingdom on earth, the camp of the saints represents the center of the governing aspect of the kingdom of the heavens. This I find to be most interesting!

Why will Satan surround Jerusalem? It is because it is the place of the throne of David. And why will he also surround the camp of the saints? What exactly is meant by this phrase, the camp of the saints? I can only paint for you a word picture from olden times. I think it will be something like back in the days of the feudal age. There was an emperor, and then there were lords, earls, counts, viscounts, dukes. All these princes would have their own domains or estates over which they ruled, but they were all subordinate to the emperor. Back then, these princes used to reside in the city where the emperor had his palace; but now and then the emperor with his princes would visit the estates of his subordinates. When he did so, there would be a camp set up, and there would be feasting and festivals and other activities like those which you may have read about in history.

That is the word picture which may help to explain this camp phrase. And in applying it to our present discussion, we can perhaps say that the Lord will reign in the air over the earth with His princes (the overcomers), but He and they will now and then come down and visit, and that will be the camp of the saints. So in the last rebellion, Satan and his forces will try to attack Jerusalem and the camp of the saints, but they will all be destroyed except for Satan, who will be thrown into the lake of fire to suffer eternal death—the place God has prepared for him (vv. 9b-10).

The Great White Throne

After the last rebellion comes the final judgment, that of the Great White Throne. All the dead will be raised and they will be judged according to the works they did on earth. Anyone whose name is not in the book of life will be judged at that time and will be thrown into the lake of fire (Revelation 20:11-15).

The Bible then states that "death and Hades [will be] cast into the lake of fire" (v. 14a). That is the time when death—the last enemy—shall be destroyed.

Everything Is in Subjection to Christ

The apostle Paul states in I Corinthians 15 that the Lord Jesus will annul all powers, principalities, authorities, and rulers who as enemies of God have opposed Him, and that the last enemy that shall be destroyed is death (vv. 24-26). So at that time the work of Jesus will be fully accomplished. Everything then will be in subjection to Christ. There will be no more opposition. His redemptive work will be completed, accepted, and realized; and at that moment the Son of God, the Christ of God, will place himself in subjection to God the Father in order that "God may be all in all" (v. 28). That is the glorious end of the story of Jesus Christ.

What is the principal lesson which we need to learn through having reviewed in some detail together the life of the Lord Jesus? I think we need to see first that Jesus, the Son of God who is equal with God, thought it not something to be grasped at or held on to; and that, in obedience to the Father, He emptied himself by laying aside the glory of His place in the Godhead. But, then, He took upon himself the form of a bondslave; that is, He subjected himself as a bondslave of love to His Father. He also came in the likeness of a man, becoming the last Adam but the second Man. Next, throughout His life Jesus was obedient to God in all things, always denying himself, always subjecting all things under the feet of God His Father. And towards the very end of His life Jesus was obedient even unto death, and that, the death of the cross. What a work of redemption He has accomplished! Even after that, having been exalted to the right hand of God, Jesus is still executing His Father's will. He will bring everything into subjection to God. Everything will reflect the glory of God.

What a price our Savior and Lord has paid! How faithful He has been! What a Christ He is to us! To me, I feel the greatest lesson to be learned from this entire review is to see the Christ we have, that we may truly worship Him with all our heart and love Him with all our heart, mind, will, and strength. He alone is worthy.

TITLES AVAILABLE
From Christian Fellowship Publishers

By Stephen Kaung

"But We See Jesus"
Discipled to Christ
God's Purpose for the Family
The Gymnasium of Christ
In the Footsteps of Christ
New Covenant Living & Ministry
Shepherding
The Songs of Degrees–*Meditations on Fifteen Psalms*
The Splendor of His Ways–*Seeing the Lord's End in Job*

The "God Has Spoken" Series
Seeing Christ in the Old Testament, Part One
Seeing Christ in the Old Testament, Part Two
Seeing Christ in the New Testament

